The World of the Italian Renaissance

E. R. CHAMBERLIN

T0204317

London
GEORGE ALLEN & UNWIN
Boston   Sydney

George Allen & Unwin (Publishers) Ltd,
40 Museum Street, London WC1A 1LU, UK

George Allen & Unwin (Publishers) Ltd,
Park Lane, Hemel Hempstead, Herts HP2 4TE, UK

Allen & Unwin Inc.,
9 Winchester Terrace, Winchester, Mass 01890, USA

George Allen & Unwin Australia Pty Ltd,
8 Napier Street, North Sydney, NSW 2060, Australia

First published in 1982
Second edition 1983

British Library Cataloguing in Publication Data

Chamberlin, E.R.
The world of the Italian Renaissance.
1. Italy—Civilization—1268–1559
I. Title
945'.05   DG445
ISBN 0–04–900036–5

Picture research by Anne-Marie Ehrlich

Set in 11 on 12½ point Sabon by
Computape (Pickering) Ltd
and printed in Great Britain
Short Run Press Ltd, Exeter

Contents

The World of the
Italian Renaissance

Books on related subjects by the same author

The Count of Virtue: Giangaleazzo Visconti, Duke of Milan
Everyday life in Renaissance times
Life in Medieval France
Cesare Borgia
The Fall of the House of Borgia
The Bad Popes
Marguerite of Navarre
Antichrist and the Millennium
Rome
The Sack of Rome
Florence at the time of the Medici

Illustrations

Introduction

What was the Renaissance?

'"Renaissance" is the most glamorous piece of shorthand in historical language,'[1] J. R. Hale remarks in his history of Renaissance Europe. Certainly it is one of the most overworked. As a generally used adjective it is vaguely, but now indelibly, infused with the idea of something brilliant but corrupt: Hermann Goering can be described as a 'Renaissance figure' along with Cesare Borgia. As an historical label it is, in E. M. W. Tillyard's words, 'connected generally and principally with Italy and carries with it specific if little formulated associations with Florence and Amalfi, carnivals, poisonings, orange trees and red wine, the Brownings, honeymoons on Lake Como and churches full of highly coloured paintings'.[2]

The term is protean and all embracing, taking whatever shape, absorbing whatever content, the historian chooses. At one extreme it is regarded as the ultimate in human achievement. Thus nineteenth-century historians could confidently dismiss all that came before the Italian fifteenth century as a long preparation. 'The arts and inventions, the knowledge and the books which suddenly became vital at the time of the Renaissance had long since lain neglected on the shores of that Dead Sea we call the Middle Ages,'[3] J. A. Symonds declared. To describe as a Dead Sea those long centuries which, among other things produced the cathedrals, the logical system of Aquinas, the literature of Dante and Chaucer, the illuminators of the Très Riches Heures and the empire of Charlemagne is, to put it mildly, short-sighted. But, in our own time, we have seen the pendulum swing to the other extreme with a denial that there was ever such a thing as 'the' Renaissance, that the Italian phenomenon was simply one of a series of steps by which western civilisation moved forward or, alternatively, that it is irrelevant even if it existed. 'It is a great misfortune that the idea of a Renaissance has been attached to a period of history that is presumed to mark the transition from the Middle Ages to modernity ... The epithet is so imprecise, has so many subjective meanings, is open to so much controversy, that it can communicate little to the reader,[4] a modern scholar, Peter Laven, notes – but the book in which he makes this dismissal is itself entitled *Renaissance Italy*, testimony to the potency of the word.

It is one of the ironies of history that the English language has adopted a French word to describe an Italian phenomenon when there is an equivalent Italian word for it, a word coined, moreover, while the phenomenon was in process. The coiner was Giorgio Vasari, first of the art historians who, in his *Lives of the most excellent Italian architects, painters and sculptors*, remarks that the reader 'will now be able to recognise more easily the progress of (art's) rebirth (il progresso della sua rinascita) and of that very perfection whereto she had risen again in our times'. Three centuries after Vasari, the French historian Jules Michelet used the word, but translated into French, as a useful portmanteau description for the appropriate period of French history, and such was his influence that it passed into international use.

Historical labels are usually created long after the period they describe: nobody in the twelfth century was aware of living in the 'Middle Ages', the 'Industrial Revolution' has significance only for posterity. In this, 'the Renaissance' is different from all other periods. Giorgio Vasari not only gave a name to the phenomenon: unequivocally, he demonstrated the fact that those who were experiencing it were perfectly aware that they were living through a period of climacteric change.

Nearly two centuries before Vasari, at the very dawn of that period, the scholar and poet Francesco Petrarch declared, 'I stand as a man between two worlds, looking both forward and backward.' In the *Decameron*, Petrarch's friend and contemporary Giovanni Boccaccio, says of the painter Giotto, 'He brought back to life that art which for many centuries had been buried under the errors of those who in painting had sought to give pleasure to the eyes of the ignorant rather than the eyes of the wise.' There might be uncertainty as to what was rediscovered or reborn, or when it happened: but there is no doubting the conviction of those who experienced it that something had changed direction.

Until the nineteenth century, the idea of 'the Renaissance' was, on the whole, limited to Vasari's vision of a rebirth of the arts. The idea could be extended to include the humanities generally, and there was a growing awareness that an outward change must also signify an inward change. But it was left to Jules Michelet simultaneously to extent the concept, and give it a lapidary – an imperishable – form that would transcend cultural and political frontiers. The seventh volume of his *History of France*, published in 1855, was entitled simply *La Renaissance* and in it he inquired rhetorically if 'that beautiful word Renaissance' should be limited to 'the coming of a new art ... the renovation of the study of antiquities'. Those who did so overlooked two minor details 'which distinguish that age from all its predecessors – the discovery of the world and the discovery of man'.[5]

'La découverte du monde, la découverte de l'homme.' Rarely can a scholar have created a phrase that would have so many repercussions. Those nine words gave an impress to the period, summing up an almost incomprehensible richness in an elegant formula. Five years later the Swiss historian Jacob Burckhardt elaborated the formula in his distinguished work *The Civilisation of the Renaissance in Italy*, published in 1860. There was no indication at the time that one of the seminal books of history had been launched. Burckhardt, a 42-year-old professor of history at Basle University, received no payment for the thousand copies of the first edition. Eight years later, many were still unsold and the publisher did not even trouble to tell the author that rights in the work had been sold to another publisher. But thereafter the book swiftly gained its dominant position in the field of Renaissance history. It has great and evident limitations of subject which has brought it under increasing attack from academic historians. It is courtly history, with the barest of glances at the ordinary man. It is cultural history, largely ignoring the humdrum subjects of trade and economics and, as a result of this, shows the Renaissance as coming almost magically into being. But apart from its glamorous subject matter *The Civilisation of the Renaissance in Italy* owed – and owes – its immense popularity to the fact that this cool, restrained Swiss attempted, and in very large part succeeded, one of the most difficult and dangerous of historical exercises: the attempt not simply to illustrate by documents but to explain by intuition – by entering into the very spirit and mentality of a departed age. In the hands of lesser men, such intuitive attempts may lead to embarrassment. Burckhardt's solid learning ensured that imagination illuminated, but did not create, the details in his book. 'Its unique place in the history of Renaissance historiography is attested by the virulence of its opponents, no less than by the moderate defence of those who still find in it an essential verity,' was the judgement of Wallace Ferguson, doyen of Renaissance historians[6] when, in 1948, he surveyed the controversy raised over some years by his colleagues regarding the value of Burckhardt's work.

By developing that magical formula 'the discovery of man' with its emphasis on the uniqueness and individuality of 'Renaissance man', Burckhardt unwittingly did a disfavour to his thesis and let a species of djinn out of the bottle. Over the next century, that djinn took ever more variegated and lusher forms, the characters of the Italian Renaissance developing into virtually superhuman figures whose vices were more beastly, spiritualities more holy, aesthetics more brilliant than those born in any other time and place. An example of the preposterous development is that of Victor Hugo's play, *Lucretia Borgia*, where the passive, essentially tragic, daughter of Alexander Borgia is transformed into a poison-brewing maenad, a monster, from whom her son backs in horror. Her palace, as seen by her son, is the archetypal Renaissance palace that would figure in endless novels, plays and near-biographies, 'Voilà donc son exécrable palais! Palais de la luxure, palais de la trahison, palais de l'assassinat, palais de l'adultère, palais de l'inceste, palais de tous les crimes, palais de Lucrèce Borgia!'

For English-speaking readers, the idea of the Renaissance was to pass through one more dyeing operation before it took on its final colours. In 1875, John Addington Symonds published the first volume of his seven-volume work, *Renaissance in Italy*. Specifically and explicitly he rejected the charge that it was based on Burckhardt's work, a not unreasonable assumption, so closely did his plan of work resemble Burckhardt's. But while it could be said that, wittingly or unwittingly, Symonds placed the flesh on the skeleton provided by Burckhardt, their approaches could hardly have been more different. Burckhardt was the scholar seeking to vivify his material: Symonds was the imaginative writer seeking a shape for his vision. A semi-invalid: a homosexual in a rigidly heterosexual society: an aesthete with a sensitivity sufficient to torture, but not quite sufficient to allow original creation, 'the Renaissance' allowed him an escape into a fuller life. What it meant to him as a land of Cockaigne, and through him, to at least three generations of English readers is summed up in that first volume of his enormous work, 'No ages of enervating luxury, or intellectual endeavour, or life artificially preserved or ingeniously prolonged, had sapped the fibre of the men who were about to inaugurate the modern world. Severely nurtured, unused to delicate living, these giants of the Renaissance were like boys in their capacity for endurance, their inordinate appetite for enjoyment. No generations hungry, sickly, effete, critical, disillusioned trod them down. Ennui and the fatigue that springs from scepticism, the despair of thwarted effort were unknown ... They yearned for magnificence, and instinctively comprehended splendour. Everything seemed possible to their young energy nor had a single pleasure palled upon their appetite. Born, as it were, at the moment when desires and faculties are evenly balanced, opening their eyes for the first time on a world of wonder, these men of the Renaissance enjoyed what we may term the first transcendent springtide of the modern world.'[7]

But when was it that the Renaissance came into being? Until the twentieth century it was assumed, quite simply, that it came into being as an act of God or, if the writer were not religious, by Man pulling himself up by his own bootstraps. 'It started from nothingness. It was the heroic outburst of a general will,' was Michelet's opinion, echoing Voltaire who had said as firmly, 'We owe all these fine innovations to the Tuscans. They caused everything to be reborn by their sole genius, before the small amount of science which remained in Constantinople had flowed into Italy with the Greek language ... It is not to the fugitives from Constantinople that the renaissance of the arts is due. These Greeks could teach the Italians nothing but Greek.'[8]

Voltaire's passing reference to the fugitives of Constantinople was to develop into a firm scenario, becoming one of the great myths of history. In its final form, this event is set in the year 1453. As the walls of the Greek-speaking Byzantine capital fall to the Turks, scholars escaped, clutching their precious codices, to Italy. There, the codices become a species of magical seed, taking root, growing and bearing fruit almost instantaneously to produce 'the Renaissance'. This scenario excludes, however, the roles played by Petrarch and Giotto a century earlier: it ignores the fact that Greek was by no means unknown in Italy long before 1453 (there was even a colony in Basilicata speaking a bastardised but still recognisable form of Greek) and that most of the impetus for the Renaissance came from the Latin. But the scenario had all the attraction of the dramatic and, as such, for long did duty for an explanation – and indeed, continues to do so in many a potted account.

And even as the controversy over the origins and nature of the Renaissance swung from one extreme to the other, so does the controversy regarding its dating. Its origins are now pushed back well into the twelfth century to encompass the undoubted 'renaissance' that took place then, now pushed forward well into the fifteenth century to try and account for the surviving 'medieval' traces. Petrarch, who died in 1374, is now regarded as a founding father, now dismissed as an offshoot, even as Dante, who died half a century earlier, is dragged into, and thrust out of, the opening scenes depending upon which of his works in Latin and Italian emphasis is laid. Dubiously assessing, hesitantly weighing, all that posterity can say with certainty is that a change in European history became evident around 1350. And that that change was first detected, or made, in the Italian peninsula.

'Italy is the land where best grows the plant, Man'

Of all geographical shapes, Italy is the most familiar: a peninsula in shape of a boot some 600 miles long and about 80 miles wide at the widest point, its top lying in the snows of Europe's major mountains while its foot stretches towards Africa so that it acts as a bridge from north to south, from east to west. Going south, a small craft can island-hop to the African coast. From its eastern coast a similar vessel can safely make landfall among the Balkan countries, or work its way down into the tangle of islands off the coast of Asia Minor. From its western coast, a sea-road leads into the heart of western Europe so that the traveller can, if he wishes, skirt the Alps which are themselves pierced by great passes. Over the millennia, travellers moving inward along these routes bring in new ideas, new fashions: travellers moving outwards take these ideas, modified and enriched, into the peripheral lands. Geography itself has made of Italy one vast, natural Exchange.

Generations of travellers from the north have built up a picture of the land as of something from a fairy tale – rich, gentle, sensuous. In certain favoured places this is true enough. In Lombardy and Tuscany and along the volcanic coast below Naples, the soil has an astonishing fertility, producing a range of crops that includes potatoes and lemons, rice and grapes. Elsewhere the peasant – and the visitor who strays off the beaten path – encounters another aspect, a hard hostile land tamed only by centuries of unremitting toil. The city of Urbino in the north-eastern Marches is as good an example as any of the contrasts between the works of man and nature. The city sits in a landscape which, from a distance, seems infinitely inviting, a rich tapestry of fields and terraces, vines and cypresses, the 'classical landscape with figures' of countless paintings. Close to, the picture alters: the lion-coloured fields are seen to consist of great clods of earth that are baked like a brick in summer and become glue-like in winter: the inviting meadows are, in fact, heavily laced with brambles, mocking that distant promise of coolness and greenness: the fields themselves cling to the steep hills only through dogged tenacity.

Apart from the great plain of Lombardy, there seems scarcely a square yard of ground that is not, in its natural condition, steeply tilted. Much of the peninsula is above the 500-metre contour line so that the cities are separated into natural blocs or clusters. The Lombard plain produces the richest of urban harvests – Milan and Pavia, Verona, Piacenza, Ferrara, Modena and a dozen more between the wall of the Alps to the north and the lesser but still formidable barrier of the Appennines to the south, a spinal column which twists its way down the peninsula. South of

Lombardy, the next major enclave lies in Tuscany where, beyond the first high ridge of the Appennines, Florence, Pisa, Lucca, Siena and Arezzo share a relatively level area. South again, and Rome dominates the Campagna, sharing it with a ring of lesser cities while to the east and north-east Orvieto, Perugia, Urbino and Aquila cling to the less precipitous hills. Beyond Rome, the interior becomes harsher so that civilisation develops along the supremely beautiful coastline. Here was probably the biggest of all pre-industrial European cities, Naples, and a string of small urban communities that, in their time, were independent states – Amalfi, Sorrento, Salerno. And finally there are the cities of Sicily, not merely Italy's but Europe's outpost, cities which have absorbed invader after invader so that their culture is a palimpsest of half a dozen civilisations.

Historically, the neighbours in these clusters were by no means automatically friends and allies: on the contrary, the tendency was to go to war with the immediate neighbour while making alliances with the more distant: thus Florence's most bitter enemies were her neighbours Pisa and Siena who traditionally allied themselves with Milan, safely distant, against her. But the members of each cluster did share certain basic similarities which separated them from the rest: Lombards were as different from Tuscans as Scots were from English: Romagnols and Neapolitans might have belonged to different races. Nevertheless, though the groups might differ profoundly from each other in temperament, customs and appearance all – north or south, mountain or plain – shared one great common good, the same Italian language. Dante once calculated that there were a thousand dialects of Italian: but Sienese could still communicate with Venetian, Milanese with Neapolitan, Pisan with Roman. And, together with that common language was the consciousness of belonging to a common stock. That consciousness did not remotely resemble nationalism; rather was it simply an awareness of an Italian and a non-Italian world, an 'us', and a 'not us'. Italy was, in effect, a universe composed of island universes that were in communication with each other, cultural and geographic accident combining to create a species of forcing house in which cross-fertilisation could take place under the most auspicious circumstances. Each of the individual cities, itself composed of

The walled city: detail from The Deposition by Beato Angelico

The Pincio Gate, Rome

brilliant individuals, was able at once to develop its particular potentiality to the full and yet to affect, and be affected by, its neighbours through the medium of a common language and a common blood.

The city and its functions is the pre-eminent expression of Italian genius. Nothing more clearly symbolises this than the survival into the late twentieth century of most of the cities' walls. Elsewhere in Europe such survivals are rarities, the attention of the visitor to York or Carcassone being drawn with pride to the intact circumvallation. In Italy, they are the rule rather than the exception. Verona's walls still confidently climb their steep hill: it is still possible to make the circuit of Rome, to get the 'feel' of both the ancient and the medieval city, by following the walls of Aurelian. Even Milan, intent on carving itself an industrial future, in piety has preserved large sections of its giant walls. The walls of some of the cities played at least a rudimentary defence role until surprisingly late in history. The army of the new-born Kingdom of Italy had to batter down a section of Rome's wall in September 1870 in order to effect entry into Rome, territory of the papal monarch.

The survival of the city walls was rooted as much in psychology as in military defence: the wall was, in a very real sense, the skin and carapace of the city. For the city was, essentially, one: an organic compound of brick and wood and human beings. Any study of Italian history at virtually any period encounters at the outset a profound paradox: a race composed of some of the most fiercely independent, individualistic people on earth found its supreme expression in an almost ant-like corporate action. The cities are the true heroes, and the true villains, of Italian history, their most brilliant sons being simply their means of expression. 'Man is born first to God and then to the commune and he who hurts the commune angers God,' said the fourteenth-century chronicler of Lucca, Giovanni Sercambi. Given the pre-eminent cultural role of the cities, Italy's political fragmentation, cause of so much bloodshed and tragedy over the centuries, was also the precondition for the Renaissance. Francesco Guicciardini, the sixteenth-century Florentine historian who was the first Italian to rise above the fragmentation and see Italy as one, was quite explicit about that. As far as Italian culture was concerned, 'a monarchy would have been more unfortunate than fortunate'.

But that diversity of cities which was a prerequisite for the Renaissance in Italy itself creates an almost insuperable barrier to understanding it as a whole. Discussing the Florentine contribution, Vincent Cronin sums up: 'Like singers in a polyphonic composition, each (city-)state had its own distinctive note to add to the whole, and as one voice slackened or fell silent, so another struck up.'[9] This is the especial problem that faces any historian of the Italian Renaissance: the voice that falls silent now may well take up the refrain again – but in a different key. The new voice may add only a few bars – but these could be vital to the whole composition. If the development of the Renaissance is followed chronologically, then it is necessary to interweave confusingly between the cities. But if the development is followed spatially – in terms of one city's development – then a totally false impression of cultural isolation can be given, as though that one city provided the dynamism for the rest.

There is a further problem involving the time-span. Assuming that the movement began in the mid-fourteenth century – that is, coinciding with the maturity of Francesco Petrarch – its closure can be placed at the sack of Rome of 1527. It would be a crudely mechanistic view of history to argue that the sack 'ended the Renaissance', but it would be a remarkably insensitive view that failed to note that the Roman trauma marked another point of change. Certainly, art historians use it to mark their distinction between the 'early' and the 'high' Renaissance. The changes that took place during those 175 years are, admittedly, as nothing, compared with the changes that have taken place during, say, the eighty years since 1900. But, compared with the static society that had existed before, they are great indeed. What is true of Florence in 1350 is by no manner of means necessarily true for Florence of 1500: Rome in 1370 was a decrepit country town while Rome in 1500 was enjoying its Golden Age. Cities like Siena and Genoa which were independent at the beginning of the period, were vassal cities at the end.

Nevertheless, while one has to admit the dangers that necessarily attend any attempt at simplification, it is possible to reduce the chaotic richness to a pattern and out of all the cities which contributed directly to the Renaissance, choose perhaps half a dozen to stand as representative for the rest. Florence, Milan, Venice and Rome are virtually self-selecting. At first sight, Naples, too, should be in this company. It was not only the biggest city in Italy but, as a state, it occupied nearly half of the entire peninsula. The Kingdom of Naples (known simply as *Il Regno* without further qualification) stretched from the toe of Italy almost up to the gates of Rome. It was an hereditary monarchy, and had been for centuries, unlike most of the other Italian states which were endlessly tinkering with their constitution. But since 1266 the French house of Anjou, and the Spanish house of Aragon, and their descendants, had been chasing each other on and off the throne, rarely becoming assimilated while the native Neapolitans blandly accepted the changes of dynasty. There were cultured kings of Naples and the city itself was a byword for luxury, as the young Giovanni Boccaccio found to his delight. But it contributed little to the common pool of culture. In his book *The Italian Renaissance in its historical background* Denys Hay draws attention to the triumphal arch of Alfonso V built into the Castle Nuovo. The elegant marble arch crushed between the two gloomy brick towers – the subordination of the Renaissance to 'the grim realities of feudal power'[10] seems to encapsulate the Neapolitan Renaissance.

Florence presents a problem exactly opposite to that of Naples on account of its predominance in Italian affairs. Again and again, attempts have been made to analyse the springs of the Florentine effervescence, postulating causes ranging from the poverty of the soil, to the quality of the light. But in the last analysis it is no more possible to explain than any other mystery of the human psyche. Does one need to discuss Renaissance statecraft? Then it is impossible to do so without reference to the Florentine, Machiavelli. Is material needed to describe family life? Then the best source is undoubtedly *The Book of the Family*, written by the Florentine, Alberti. Commerce? The book written by the Florentine, Pegolotti. Contemporary art history? The Florentine, Vasari. The new approach to architecture? The Florentine, Brunelleschi. The arts? The Florentine, Giotto – not to mention the Florentines, Botticelli, Michelangelo and Leonardo. 'You Florentines are the fifth element' Pope Boniface

VIII burst out – whether in irritation or admiration it is hard to say – when he found that yet another inter-city deputation waiting upon him was composed largely of Florentines.

And after the giants – after Milan, Rome, Venice, Florence – there is a host of lesser cities. But lesser only in the Italian context, for each would be a rare jewel elsewhere. Siena, Orvieto, Perugia, Verona, Cremona, Amalfi – the list could be lengthened until it included virtually every city in the country. Three have been chosen to round out the picture here – Urbino, Mantua and Ferrara. To a certain extent, the choice is arbitrary, and can scarcely be otherwise but they have been chosen, too, to stand as representative of a certain type, the smaller urban community, ruled unequivocally by a single family, each linked dynastically with the others, but somehow maintaining its independence in an embattled society, contributing its unique gift to the general treasury.

Map of Renaissance Italy

1
The geographical expression

The four powers

There had been no fall of the Roman Empire in the sense of an abrupt and cataclysmic ending as there was for the end of the Byzantine empire in 1453. Looking back down the long perspective of their history, Italian historians were hard put to say just when the Empire had come to an end. Some, the idealists, tended to link the ending of the Empire with the coming of the Caesars. Others, more logically, chose the sack of Rome of AD 410 as the dividing point between the ancient and the modern worlds. Few paid much attention to the date AD 476 when the last Roman Emperor of the west, the ironically named Romulus Augustulus, abdicated and brought the western Empire legally to a close.

There was no dramatic break, nothing clearcut, simply a redirecting of energy as men became aware there was no longer a central authority, that every man must shift for himself and that power henceforth would go to him who could grasp it. It was a common experience throughout the western world but where, with most other peoples, the struggle fairly rapidly polarised itself into a two-way tussle between a monarch, who stood for a restoration of central authority, and barons, who had a vested interest in anarchy, in Italy historic accident made the struggle four-cornered. There was a so-called Holy Roman Emperor, who was always a foreigner, who claimed sweeping rights over the land but who, in fact, had only his title with which to back up those claims: there was a pope who was usually Italian, who originally had only spiritual powers but who developed into one of the major despots of the peninsula. And there were the cities, each supposedly owning allegiance to one or other of these two powers but whose total freedom was, in fact, limited only by their immediate neighbours and rivals. In the fourteenth century, this triangular tussle between imperial, papal and civic authorities received another dimension with the emergence of the companies of mercenary soldiers, whose only interest lay in short-term financial gain, but whose internal discipline turned them, in effect, into nomadic republics exerting unpredictable strains on the already creaking social fabric.

Emperor and Pope

When, in AD 330, the Emperor Constantine transferred the administrative capital of the Roman Empire to his new city of Constantinople, he divided the empire in effect, if not in law, and created a vacuum of power in the western half. Gradually the Bishops of Rome – who also boasted the title of Universal Pope – grew in stature to fill that vacuum, inheriting many of the styles and attributes, as well as the titular city, of the Caesars. But while they possessed immense prestige, these early popes had little power and, hard pressed by the successive waves of barbarians, they looked for a champion. Early in the ninth century the reigning pope, Leo III, found that champion in the most powerful barbarian ruler in the west, the Frankish monarch Charlemagne. He was invited to Rome and, in exchange for his protecting sword, Leo crowned him emperor on Christmas Day 800. Technically, it was an entirely illegal act. There could be only one ruler of the Roman Empire and he still ruled in Constantinople, even though he now spoke Greek and his court was termed Byzantine, from the older name of the city. But Charlemagne's coronation simply recognised reality.

'The Holy Roman Empire of the German nation' as the hybrid came to be known, was doubtless a fantasy. 'Neither holy, nor Roman, nor an empire' is the standard gibe against the rams-hackle structure and it is true enough. Nevertheless, for a thousand years most Europeans, and Italians in particular, acted as though there were such a thing, or as though there should be. At a time when the northern nations were grappling with the realities of monarchical rule, those Italians who hungered for a centralised authority put their faith in the fantasy. There was, for them, no break between the modern Germans and the Caesars of the ancient city. Annalists had only one chronological sequence from Augustus down to the most obscure Teutonic princeling who could claim the title. During their visits to Rome, emperor and empress were lodged in chambers called Livia and Augustus. Their processions were still adorned with the wolf, eagle and dragon standards. But even this awesome tradition was raised to greater heights by the Christian infusion which saw the emperor as successor to St Paul, Christ's Warrior, even as the pope was the successor to St Peter, Christ's Priest.

So the theory. It found its most able expression in the treatise *De monarchia*, written in the early fourteenth century by Dante Alighieri. Dante was in exile from his city of Florence and his appeal to the Emperor Henry VII to come into Italy and restore order among the battling cities was as much rooted in self interest as in a genuine, noble desire to see the establishment of a Christian Roman Empire. Henry's expedition in 1310–13, the last true attempt of a Roman emperor to rule his titular land, was a disastrous failure, the ideal collapsing before the reality of inter-city strife. How far and how swiftly the ideal fell was demonstrated in 1354 when a Germanic king was again summoned to Italy to take the crown and bring peace to a land that seemed intent upon destroying itself. But where Henry VII had come in majesty the progress of his son, Charles IV, 'was more as a merchant going to mass than an emperor going to his throne', the Florentine merchant, Villani, observed sardonically. Charles's journey through Italy was undertaken simply to obtain the crown so that, through it, he could peddle his honours and privileges for solid golden florins. At Rome itself he was allowed to stay only the few hours necessary to receive his consecration, and from there he was hurried out to return north 'with the crown which he had obtained without a sword-thrust, with a full purse which he had taken empty to Italy, with little glory for manly deeds and with great disgrace for the humiliated majesty of empire'. Thus Villani sadly concluded his account, and his sadness is all the more poignant in that he was a staunch republican and a Guelf, a member of a party traditionally opposed to the emperor. Francesco Petrarch, who had inherited Dante's splendid, hopeless dream of empire, was considerably more forthright. Addressing Charles rhetorically he asked, 'If thy father and grandfather were to meet thee in the passes of the Alps, what do you think they would say? Emperor of the Romans but in name, in truth you are nothing but the king of Bohemia.'

Nevertheless, side by side with the Italians' contempt for the emperor himself, was the unquenchable belief in his office as the source of all legality, the true Lord of Italy. Again posterity, particularly non-Italian posterity, encounters a paradox at the very heart of Italian affairs. Burckhardt could say confidently of the appointments made by this Germanic emperor, 'The imperial approval or disapproval made no difference, since the people attached little weight to the fact that the despot had bought a piece of parchment somewhere in foreign countries, or from some stranger passing through his territory.' Burckhardt is, moreover, able to cite a fifteenth-century writer, Francesco Vettori, to support his case: 'The investiture at the hands of a man who lives in Germany, and has nothing of the Roman emperor about him but the name, cannot turn a scoundrel into the real lord of a city.' And a modern historian, Ephraim Emerton, emphatically makes the point that, 'What was called the empire, was really a national kingdom, the kingdom of the Germans, imposing itself on less forceful peoples to the north and south and then decorating itself with the borrowed symbols of a sham imperialism.'

It seems unlikely, to say the least, that Italian merchants would assent – as they did – to the disbursing of several millions of gold florins over the years for the purchase of rights from a Germanic sham. And Francesco Vettori was indulging rather more in propaganda than providing description. He was a Florentine republican and, as such, was seeking to impugn the title-deeds of Florence's major enemy, Milan, whose principal citizen, Gian Galeazzo Visconti, purchased the title of duke from the Emperor Wenceslas in 1394 – and paid 100,000 florins for it. The sale of that title was one of the weapons used to depose the drunken Wenceslas five years later, the indictment accusing him of corruption because he turned an official into a ruler. Nevertheless, though Wenceslas could be deposed, his Act would not be annulled. That Act had created the first duke in Italy, and over the following two centuries more and more ambitious Italians

The coronation of Gian Galeazzo Visconti by a representative of the Emperor Wenceslas: detail from an illumination by Imbonate

would purchase the glittering titles of duke from the same 'Germanic sham' – testimony to the power of an idea over reality.

The theory of the Holy Roman Emperor saw in emperor and pope not the conflicting authorities they became, but a duality appointed by God himself, the one to rule over the souls of all men, the other over their bodies. Rarely was this harmony attained. With an occasional setback, papal power increased at the expense of its divinely ordained protector until that day in 1300 when Pope Boniface VIII could disclose himself to the pilgrims thronging into Rome, throned and crowned, shouting, 'Ego, ego sum imperator.' Boniface could challenge an imperial puppet with safety, but made the mistake of assuming that he could do the same with a real territorial monarch, Philip IV of France. Ostensibly, the cause of their quarrel was the humdrum subject of taxes: in reality it was to decide where power lay. 'It is necessary for the salvation of all human beings to be subject to the Roman pontiff' was the burden of Boniface's most famous Bull, *Unam Sanctam*. He lost the battle, lost it not metaphorically in a debating chamber but actually, physically. Even those who hated the man – and there were many – professed themselves ashamed and appalled at the treatment meted out to him by a commando of Frenchmen and Italian renegades who, in the little city of Anagni in 1303, seized his sacred person, the ultimate humiliation of the Papacy, as reaction to its ultimate claim to dominance.

Boniface died in Rome. His successor died after a brief reign and Clement V, a Frenchman elected in France in 1303, saw no pressing reason to enter that violent, undisciplined city, nor indeed to enter a land where the person of even the High Priest of Christendom was not safe. Hindsight makes it appear that the so-called 'Avignonese Papacy' was a deliberate creation. More likely, it came about simply as a result of human procrastination. That first Avignonese pope, Clement V, made no clearcut declaration of his intention to stay: rather, one can imagine him postponing the unpleasant necessity of returning first day by day, then week by week and finally month by month. It was not until 1336 that the great Palace of the Popes was begun in Avignon by his successor, John XXII, and another sixty years were to pass before it was completed. But whether the 'Babylonian captivity' in Avignon, as Petrarch termed it, was deliberate or not, the result was the same. The Papacy became divorced from the land of its origins, but still claimed those revenues and privileges which it had enjoyed as an Italian institution. To enforce those claims, the Avignonese popes sent legates into Italy who could not have been better chosen to enrage Italians. 'Demoni incarnati', St Catherine of Siena called them in her vehement Tuscan fashion. 'Evil pastors and rectors who poison and putrefy this garden.' Bitter though it was to witness the pope as a French 'captive', infinitely more bitter was it for Italians to submit to the demands of foreign legates and watch Italian wealth pass into French hands. One by one the cities broke away from their allegiance, acknowledging still their filial obedience to the Vicar of Christ but rejecting, vigorously, the claims of the papal monarch.

For the Papacy was not simply a spiritual or even an administrative organisation, but a very powerful territorial sovereignty. In addition to the city of Rome itself, the popes ruled, as sovereign, a wide swathe of land that stretched across the entire width of the peninsula, the so-called States of the Church. Supposedly, it had been granted to the popes by Constantine (see Chapter 3) and was an endless source of bitterness and dispute. 'It is now more than a thousand years since these territories and cities have been given to the priests, and ever since then the most violent wars have been waged on their account and yet the priests do not now possess them in peace, nor ever will be able to possess them. It were in truth better before the eyes of God and the world that these pastors should entirely renounce the temporal *dominium* ... Truly, we cannot serve God and Mammon, cannot stand with one foot in heaven and the other on earth.' So wrote the chronicler of Piacenza, Giovanni de' Mussi, in the early fourteenth century. His protest was to be echoed again and again over the centuries, until, in 1870, the Papacy was forcibly deprived of that temporal *dominium*.

The Papacy returned to Rome in 1377 – but even this return merely precipitated the far worse evil of the Schism, with an Italian pope in Rome and a French pope in Avignon mutually excommunicating each other. The Schism healed, finally, in

The Donation of Constantine: mural from the Church of Santi Quattri Coronati, Rome

1417 when an Italian pope, Martin V, established himself in Rome. But by then the cities of Italy had become accustomed to treating their Holy Father as another temporal rival to be outfought, outwitted or simply cheated like any other.

The cities

By no means all Italians regarded the fall of the Roman Empire, and the consequent ending of central control, as a disaster. Leonardo Bruni, who wrote the first true history of Florence in the 1440s, and his contemporary, the papal secretary, Flavio Biondo, who attempted to make a survey of Italy from AD 412 to

1414, both believed that the demise of the empire allowed the cities to develop their true natures. In his study of the early Italian republics, Daniel Waley calculates that, at the end of the twelfth century, 'some two or three hundred units existed which deserve to be described as city-states'.[11] The story of Italy over the next three centuries is a story of political cannibalism as these city-states absorbed each other, the hundreds becoming scores, then dozens and finally a handful. And an integral part of the story is the transformation of the communes, the 'free cities', into states ruled by one man, or controlled by one family, the 'despotisms'. Republican propagandists distorted history by dramatising that transformation, turning it into a black and white story where an unscrupulous, bloodthirsty 'tyrant' imposed his will upon a freedom-loving, but disorganised 'people'. The reality was seldom as satisfyingly clearcut as that.

The communes, the 'free cities', had begun to emerge as identifiable entities from the tenth century onwards. Even contemporaries seemed uncertain as to what they meant by 'commune': the word could be verb or noun, sometimes referring to an action being taken 'in common', sometimes as a formal community, lending itself to that punning in which Italian writers delighted. Thus a Dominican preacher in Florence informed his congregation that, 'You should promote the good of the commune because that which is done *in commune* should be for the common good (*pro bono communis*).' Perhaps the best definition of a commune was one made by a Jewish traveller in Italy who noted that in these cities 'they possess neither king nor prince to govern them, but only judges appointed by themselves'.

It was these 'judges' or elected officials of the city who turned the commune into a despotism. Allowing for his emotive use of the word 'corrupt' Machiavelli's theory for this is admirably succinct. 'Cities that are once corrupt and used to the rule of princes can never again be free. One prince is needed to extinguish another and the city can never know peace, save by the creation of a new lord.'

The evolution of the Milanese 'despotism' illustrates this dictum perfectly. In 1262 Pope Urban IV appointed Ottone Visconti as his own nominee to the archbishopric of Milan in an attempt to counterbalance the power of the then dominant

family, the della Torre. Sheltered under the wide, legal powers of
the archbishop the lay branch of the Visconti family rooted itself
deep in the state, obtained the Imperial Vicarship of Milan from
the emperor and, with his help, made a final end of the della
Torres, their only rivals. Now rapidly the family outgrew the
need for protection. The archbishopric virtually became a
Visconti appanage – but the family were still careful to observe
the proprieties. Thus, when the ruling archbishop, Giovanni
Visconti, died in 1351, sovereign power theoretically returned to
the sovereign people. They lost no time in returning it, the Great
Council delegating one of their number to offer their freedom
back to the dead man's three heirs, three Visconti brothers. The
ceremony took place in a public square – in theory again, the
sovereign people meeting to make their free choice and the
delegate, at an astrologically propitious moment, handed over
three batons of white wood which were the outward sign of
power. Little by little over the next half century the effective
independence of the people was whittled away, but the family
still observed the forms of democratic government until that day
in 1394 when Gian Galeazzo Visconti purchased the dukedom
from the emperor and thereby instantaneously transformed his
erstwhile fellow-citizens into subjects.

Although there are endless local variations in the transformation of the communes, Milan and Florence can stand as models
for the two main classes, the two choices that presented
themselves to the majority of Italians. Both cities had known the
earlier ideals of the commune: both had known the clangour of
partisan violence within the walls. Milan sought peace and
stability by creating the 'despot' or, more accurately, by allowing
him to create himself. Florence cut down her dominant figures
when they became too strong, distributing power as far as
humanly possible among all citizens. But the reforms introduced
by the Medici heralded the eventual transformation of even this
bastion of 'liberty' into another dukedom.

Each Italian city not under the rule of an hereditary monarch
called itself a republic even though, as in Florence's case, less than
5,000 of its pre-Black Death population of 95,000 enjoyed full
rights, or, like Venice, the city was ruled by an immovable
aristocracy. Or, like Siena where citizenship was either heredi-

tary in a caste, or conferred as a reward for merit. A republic could perhaps best be defined as a society in which most of the leaders were chosen by at least some of the led. But a despotism was by no means a totalitarian dictatorship. 'What means your bells and your trumpets but come hangman, come vultures?' Dante apostrophised the tyrant and certainly it is easy enough to collect grisly examples whether it is Bernabo Visconti burying victims alive, or Esselino da Romano walling up an entire family. But as the major city-states engulfed their smaller neighbours, the results more closely resembled a federation even in the states of the 'tyrants', for no one family could possibly have maintained absolute rule over half a dozen cities. And the citizens of those subject cities were only too often glad to exchange the chimera of 'liberty' for the safety of a strong prince's rule. The citizens of Como actually petitioned the Visconti family to be allowed to become part of the Milanese state 'because of the frequent murders, rapines and tumults within the city, and people are without hope of health save under a lord', a phrase which Machiavelli could have taken as a text.

The case for the 'tyrant' – or the Signore as he was commonly and less pejoratively known – is graphically illustrated on the tomb of Guido Tarlati, Bishop and Lord of the little Tuscan city of Arezzo. Two of the marble bas-reliefs on the tomb are entitled, simply, 'the plucked commune' and 'the commune under the Signore'. In the first the commune, represented as a defenceless, ailing old man, is being mercilessly plundered by a group of seven greedy men – a satire on the republic where all seek to enrich themselves from the public purse. The second relief shows the commune as a vigorous old man, flanked and supported by the Signore portrayed as a bearded Justice. Significantly, even this favourable portrait of the Signore shows him, essentially, as executioner: the men on their knees before him, presumably criminals, are about to be beheaded while three richly dressed citizens look on with approval. These onlookers, indeed, sum up the case for the Signore: they are the men, in whatever community, who have come to believe that 'liberty' is only too often an excuse for licence and larceny, men who prefer the rule of one strong man who will help them protect their goods. The argument will go on for a century and more until the genuine

The Plucked Commune

The Commune under the protection of the Signore

republic is extinguished throughout Italy, until even Florence has its lord, enlightened Medici though he be. The path which Italy was to follow is vividly illustrated by two large murals, one painted in Siena's Palazzo Pubblico in 1340, the other in a private palace in Florence in about 1459. In Siena, Ambrogio Lorenzetti's elaborate allegory of *Good Government* enshrines the city itself as the source of all good: in Florence, Benozzo Gozzoli's fresco supposedly commemorating the procession of the Magi is, in fact, the adulation of a single family, the Medici.

The mercenaries

The condition of virtually permanent warfare between the city-states destroyed the last true guarantee of the free city – the armed citizen soldier, the cobbler or baker or banker who, summoned by the great bell of the commune's palace, rushed out to defend his city from its internal or external enemies. It became impossible for a man to follow his own trade and yet render adequate service to his own state as it expanded its frontiers at the expense of its neighbours, or was obliged to protect those frontiers from the expansion of others. The obligation to serve in the militia had included all able-bodied males between the ages of fifteen and seventy – indeed, so deep-rooted was this custom that it was the universal habit to compute population sizes by calculating the number of men able to bear arms in any one community.

This extended age group ensured the suspension of normal life within the city when war broke out, and resulted in an appalling effect upon the city's economy. In each city, therefore, the wealthier citizens began to compound for a cash settlement, turning their defence over to professionals who were discharged at the end of each war. The system worked well enough until the discharged soldiers began to form themselves into mercenary companies, known as Compagnie di Ventura, and inaugurated a new political pattern in Italy.

The Companies were, in effect, nomadic states of 15,000 men or more with an internal discipline that many a small, faction torn city might have envied. Discipline, though strict, could be enforced for every soldier knew that nowhere else could he find such a combination of profit and security. They were, in fact, far

Mercenary captains receiving their pay, 1468

truer democracies than the so-called republics, for each soldier had an equal vote. A company came into being only through the personality of its commander – its 'condottiere', but his decisions away from the battlefield were subject to the approval of the soldiers in council. No longer could a city treat with half a dozen small groups, playing one against the other, but was obliged to enter into a formal contract ('condotta') with a company of men equal to the fighting strength of a city.

The companies which dominated Italy in the mid-fourteenth century were mostly foreign. Hungarians, Germans and, in particular, English moving south from the endless wars in France, formed their own national bodies. 'In truth, their military success was more owing to the cowardice of our men than to their valour and military virtue', was the judgement of the Florentine chronicler, Giovanni Villani, in the 1340s, but in this he was less than fair to his compatriots. The foreign mercenary had no stake in the land: fighting neither for survival, nor honour, nor territory but simply for cash, he could be employed by a state without fearing his political ambition. In order to ensure this, most contracting cities inserted in the condotta a clause stipulating that no citizen – and certainly no exiled citizen – should be a member of the contracting company.

Outstanding among these foreigners was the Englishman John Hawkwood, whose career was a textbook example of the

IOANNES·ACVTVS·EQVES·BRITANNICVS·DVX·AETATIS·S
VAE·CAVTISSIMVS·ET·REI·MILITARIS·PERITISSIMVS·HABITVS·EST

·PAVLI·VCCELLI·OPVS·

The Signore and the Condottieri (I) John Hawkwood: fresco by Paolo Uccello

forces which made a mercenary. He was fighting in France, probably as a bowman, when the Treaty of Bretigny in 1360 brought a temporary halt to the long war between France and England. English soldiers, Hawkwood among them, drifted south, attracted to the rich, disturbed land of Italy. They formed themselves into a group known as the 'White Company' – from its high standard of 'spit and polish' – and, with Hawkwood at its head it was destined to become the most efficient of all the Compagnie di Ventura. Hawkwood, having fought both at Crécy and Poitiers, was among the first to realise that war was no longer an affair of banners and honour and personal chivalry but essentially an exercise in logic from which a canny man could make money. But it was not only his military skill that brought him to the height of his profession: he was a rarity among mercenaries in that he could not be bribed, once he had accepted a contract. After some twenty years soldiering for various employers, he ended his career as Captain-General of the Florentine State. In his hands lay the totality of Florence's defence and, after his death, in recognition of that signal service, the Signoria commissioned Paolo Uccello to paint his portrait on the walls of their cathedral – an unprecedented honour but one which other states were to follow with statues to their con-dottieri. A dour, hard, but just man, Francesco Sachetti's anecdote about Hawkwood neatly sums up not only the man himself, but that of all his profession. Saluted by a pair of wandering friars with the customary 'God give you peace', Hawkwood snarled back, 'God take away your alms'. Astounded, the friars protested that they only wished him well. 'How so? Is not begging your profession? And is not war mine? If you wish me peace, how shall I live? So I say – God take away your alms.' The anecdote has the ring of truth about it, echoing the pawky humour of the East Anglian.

The wars conducted by the foreigners were usually inconclusive and relatively bloodless. Blood and decisiveness came back into Italian wars only when native Italian soldiers began to form their own companies. The first of these was that formed by the Romagnol, Alberico da Barbiano, during the Schism when his Italian troops, fighting in defence of the Roman pope, defeated the Breton mercenaries fighting on behalf of the Avignonese

The Signore and the Condottieri (II) Bernabo Visconti, Lord of Milan

pope. Thereafter, native mercenaries shouldered aside the foreigners so that by the end of the fourteenth century the totality of military power was in their hands. Fears that they would have political ambitions proved largely unfounded. Some of them gave trouble and at least one, Francesco Carmagnola, was executed by his employer, Venice, on suspicion of disloyalty. But of all the hundreds of young men who hopefully took their own sword on tour, only one was to be the founder of a dynasty, and that was Francesco Sforza of Milan.

Trade and traders

In their massive compendium of original documents entitled *Medieval Trade in the Mediterranean World* the editors remark on the fact that documents from Italian sources outnumber all others. 'We have no apologies to offer. All investigations of medieval commerce must have as their focus the leading towns of Italy, even as all research on the origins of the Industrial Revolution must centre on England.' The editors conclude their comments with the pertinent observation that while posterity is now well aware of its cultural debt to the Italian Renaissance, 'the man in the street is led to forget another gift of that gifted nation to the modern world – the creation of the prototype of modern economy.'[12] And that prototype was, in turn, to provide the fuel for the cultural revolution.

Between the tenth and thirteenth centuries Europe as a whole enjoyed a steady economic expansion which, in certain places, and at certain times, became a boom. Italy knew such a boom. In this context, its geography was of immense economic as well as cultural significance. Water transport was by far safer, quicker, cheaper than any form of land transport and few places on the peninsula were very far from a deep-water port. Even the plain of Lombardy was bisected by the great river Po, navigable far inland so that a sea captain could, in theory, sail his ship from Alexandria in Egypt to Pavia in the heart of Italy. In addition to the personal knowledge gained of all the major ports, captains could fall back on portolan charts with their excellent descriptions such as this of the port of Falmouth in England. 'It is a good harbour for all weathers – but look out for the shoal in the middle of the channel during high tide. You can recognise the town by the high mountain behind it, and the flat, misshapen headland below it.'

Italian merchants had access to a steadily growing collection of travel guides: for them, Marco Polo's *Travels* had a very practical value. In the 1340s the Florentine, Francesco di Balduccio Pegolotti, brought the Polos' work up to date, giving modern advice on how to get to Cathay, and what to do on arriving there. 'It is advisable to let the beard grow long. The road is quite safe, but should the merchant die en route, his goods will be escheated to the local lord.' Pegolotti warns his readers not to be surprised to find paper money circulating in Cathay, 'All the people of the country are bound to accept it, and yet people do not pay more for merchandise although it is paper money.' The entire journey, he calculates, should cost the merchant about five florins the packload.

Pegolotti is in favour of the merchant financing himself, but in this he is unusual. The enormous expansion in trade was made possible only by men combining with each other in the 'commenda', a virtually untranslatable word which implies that one or more of the associates was a sleeping partner. Little people, as well as big, took their share of the risks and the profits. Men like the Medici or the Peruzzi might be thinking in terms of thousands of florins: others were thinking in terms of a few lira. In Genoa, a group of would-be merchants included a tanner and a hemp-seller who between them raised a total of 142 florins, the largest share being 12 florins.

The factor, or agent, was a vital figure. He could be representing his principal in the neighbouring town – or thousands of miles away. In the former case he was probably an employee, paid a salary and without responsibility for his employer's debts. And, as an employee, the contract he signed was usually rigorous. Ugo Gigone, a Sienese factor, actually promised in his contract that not only would he avoid all gambling – a reasonable prohibition – but he would also abstain from sexual relations with women of whatever degree. It is presumed that he was a bachelor.

The more distant agent was likely to be an associate or partner, like Giovanni Maringhi who, from 1497 until his death ten years later, was resident agent in Constantinople for a group of Florentine wool merchants. He seems to have received no salary, but frequently refers to profits and evidently enjoyed a considerable degree of autonomy, controlling a veritable web of sub-agents. His custom was to write to each of his principals every six weeks or so. On 14 May 1501 his messenger was a young man, Bernardo Risaliti, to whom he had entrusted letters and goods. Risaliti's journey back to Florence took him six weeks for he had to call in at a number of places en route, delivering letters of instructions to sub-agents, picking up some goods, leaving others.

The diversity of goods is remarkable. Woollen cloth predominates: it made the fortunes of numberless Italian towns, Florence in particular. After wool, silk and leather are major bulk cargoes. But in the list of commodities that Pegolotti gives, he names over 280 items which he terms, generically, 'spices'. These include goods not usually recognised as spices – fresh oranges, starch, cotton, bitumen, tin, indigo – but he recognises the distinction between these and such items as cinnamon, balsam, camphor, cloves and the like, calling these latter 'minute spices'.

The expanding economy stimulated the search for raw materials, putting money in the pockets of local labourers and craftsmen as well as merchants. In 1445 the Jew, Vitale of Imola and his Christian partner, Stefano of Ragusa ask permission of the government of Siena to mine metals in the Sienese district. They ask for a monopoly but promise, in return, to have all metals smelted and refined by Sienese craftsmen and agree to pay one twelfth of all proceeds to the Sienese government.

One of the most dramatic discoveries of raw material took place in the mid-fifteenth century with the opening up of the alum mines at Tolfa. To the uninitiated, there was no obvious reason why the discovery of a source for this unglamorous mineral should cause the stir it did in European banking circles. But alum probably made more fortunes than the more obviously precious minerals for it was indispensable in both clothing and tanning, Europe's major industries. Few people could afford ornaments of precious metals: everybody had to have shoes and clothing and the demand for alum to produce them had long since exhausted supplies in Europe. Manufacturers were compelled to import it from Asia Minor, paying heavy tolls in the process as well as running the permanent risk of having their supplies curtailed through war. Long before the fall of Constantinople, Europeans had been looking for another, less vulnerable course, and, in 1462, Giovanni di Castro found it

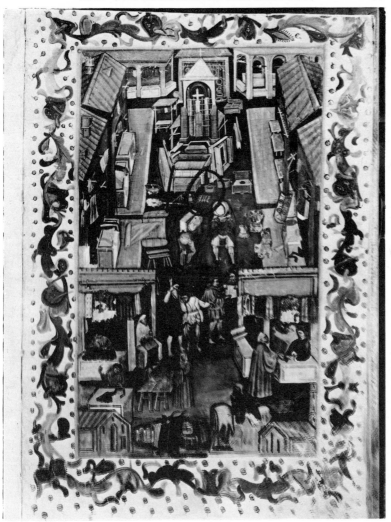

*Cloth market: detail from Statuti della Società dei Drappieri e
Bracciaioli, Bologna*

through a combination of luck and good observation. Exploring
in the hills behind Civita Vecchia, he noticed a locality where the
vegetation grew similar to that near the alum mines of Asia
Minor. Tolfa was papal property and, in a jubilant letter to Pope

Pius II describing his find, di Castro gives a vivid picture of the interlocking worlds of trade, finance, religion and war. 'Holy Father, today I bring you victory over the Turk. Every year the Turks extort from the Christians more than 300,000 ducats, because Ischia produces but little and the alum mines of Lipari have been worked out since the times of the Romans. Today I have found seven mountains so rich in alum that they could furnish seven worlds. You will be able to supply alum enough to dye the cloth of the whole of Europe and thus snatch away the profits from the infidel. The raw materials, wood and water to boil the rocks, are in abundant supply, and the port of Civita Vecchia is near by. From this moment you may start to prepare your crusade against the Turk – the Tolfa mines will finance it.' The crusade never took place but di Castro's prophecy regarding the value of the mines was amply fulfilled. The Papacy used its spiritual authority to enforce the sale of Tolfa alum throughout Europe, the Medici initially handling the business side and paying some 50,000 ducats a year into the papal coffers. Later, the business passed into the hands of Pius's fellow-Sienese, the Chigi, to their very considerable profit.

Money itself became a commodity, an item whose fluctuating value was not only of interest to banks and money-lenders like the Peruzzi and Bardi and Medici but to every merchant. In his manual of commerce a certain Giovanni da Uzzano gives a list of exchange rates which, incidentally, throws light on social and industrial patterns. 'In Genoa, money is dear in September, January and April on account of the sailing of the ships. In Rome, or wherever the pope is, money is dear according to the number of vacant benefices. In Naples and Gaeta it is dear from the kalends of August to mid-September because of the fair of St Michael...'

And as trade expanded, becoming ever more complicated, so the tools of commerce had to be invented and developed. Italians would long have had access to Fibonacci's arithmetic manual, *Book of the Abacus*, written in Pisa in 1202 but still invaluable with its timeless advice on how to translate one currency into another, or the theoretical problems of three partners in a commenda. But from the early fourteenth century onwards there began to be developed the technique of double-entry

Money changers

Page of a ledger with illustration showing merchants bartering wheat for wool

book-keeping, first making its appearance in Genoa. Except to cognoscenti, treatises on double-entry book-keeping must rank among the dullest reading matter known to man. However, it is arguable that the glamorous world of the Renaissance was founded upon this unglamorous skill. Ahead of all their competitors, Italian merchants could get a clearcut picture of their financial standing, their strengths and weaknesses, and much of the profits they made through this skill helped to nourish the cultural world.

The growth of trade stimulated the awareness of the very practical value of book-learning. In 1458 the Neapolitan merchant, Benedetto Cotrugli, stressed the debt that commerce owed to art. Good writing, he insisted, was not simply an ornament but a vital tool for a merchant, and he goes on to identify three kinds of book – the ledger, the journal and the memorandum – which were essential for the conduct of any business, giving clear and succinct instructions how to use them. Unselfconsciously, one of the seedbeds of the new learning was being laid down in counting houses when practical merchants were being convinced of the value of penmanship.

The economic boom came to an end in the 1340s. Although the roots of the cultural Renaissance were fed by trade wealth, it flowered in a period of relative economic stagnation or decline – certainly the Medici, those Maecenaes of Florence, had less capital than their predecessors, the Bardi and Peruzzi bankers who went bankrupt in the 1340s. Altogether the fourteenth century was a period of anticlimax and disillusion and mounting stress – factors which should have extinguished any nascent culture rather than actually accompany its birth. Apart from the economic recession there were three major famines, the mercenaries exercised much power and the epidemic known to history as the Black Death struck the country. Italy suffered no worse than any other country where bubonic plague assumed epidemic proportions, but Italians brought their customary lively observation to bear upon it, recording the cataclysm in detail.

A Franciscan friar, Michael of Piazza, described the circumstances of the plague first appearing in Europe. 'At the beginning of October, in the year of the incarnation of the Son of God 1347, twelve Genoese galleys were fleeing from the vengeance which

Our Lord was taking on account of their nefarious deeds, and entered the harbour of Messina. In their bones they [the sailors] bore so virulent a disease that anyone who spoke to them was seized by a mortal illness.' The Genoese had contracted the plague in Asia Minor, and the friar described the symptoms which were to be all too familiar throughout Europe: the enormous, painful boils that developed within hours, the vomiting and shivering that followed and the death that took place within three days. The plague was brought to the mainland by ships travelling from Messina to Pisa. It arrived there early in 1348 where the Lucchese chronicler, Giovanni Sercambi, took up the tale: 'And thereupon there began a great dying in Pisa, and from there spread over the whole of Tuscany. And it raged most fearfully at Lucca where there died of each hundred more than eighty and the air was so infested that death overtook men everywhere wherever they might flee. And when they saw everybody dying they no longer heeded death and believed that the end of the world was at hand.'

It provided the background for one of Europe's first collections of stories, the *Decameron*. In his introduction to the series of stories, Boccaccio gives a picture of the social disintegration in Florence caused by that first onslaught in 1348, an onslaught which the characters in the book sought to escape by fleeing the city, isolating themselves in a villa and there wiling away the time with stories to each other. Isolation was the only sure remedy. In Milan, the ruling Signore, Bernabo Visconti, retired to a country castle around which a cordon sanitaire was drawn: anybody who crossed that invisible barrier was shot down. In Venice, the technique of isolating newcomers for a set period gave a new word to European languages – quarantine: the period chosen was forty days, 'qaranta', on the analogy of Christ's sojourn in the wilderness. Sercambi's estimate of 80 per cent mortality in Lucca was probably exaggerated; Florence's population dropped by about a third, from 90,000 to under 60,000. In Siena there remains three-dimensional evidence in the form of the immense cathedral which was begun before the beginning of the plague: when normality returned, the available work-force was too small to continue building on the same scale and work was confined to the old cathedral.

'Oh, happy posterity who will not experience such abysmal woe and will look upon our testimony as a fable,' Petrarch concluded his letter in which he describes the same devastation in Florence that Boccaccio experiences. The first epidemic of 1348 was overwhelming in its unexpectedness, the speed of its advance, the statistics of its dead and its universality. But it was not unique. Again and again over the following centuries the plague would strike now this locality, now at that, providing a macabre counterpoint to the rising new culture.

2

Florence:
the search for the past

The citizens and their city

'The city stands in the centre of the State like a guardian and a master. Towns surround her, just as the moon is surrounded by stars. The Florentine State might be compared to a round shield, with a series of knobs surrounding a central knob. This central knob is the City itself, dominated by the Palazzo Vecchio – a mighty castle, the centre of the whole shield. The rings around it are formed first by the walls and suburbs, then by a belt of country houses and estates, finally by a distant circle of towns. Between the towns are castles and towers reaching to the sky.'

So the adopted Florentine, Leonardo Bruni, describes the city and state of Florence in the first decades of the fifteenth century. It is an excellent example of the literary form known as 'laude', that praise of the writer's 'patria' which was a direct expression of the local patriotism that always transcended the national. It is impressionist – Florence is as beautiful as the moon and as strong as a shield – but also descriptive so that the reader can get a clear idea of the city-state's topography. Working inwards, as would a traveller bound for the city, one would pass through that 'distant circle of towns', most of them unwilling subject-cities, which composed the State. The traveller would then pass through the 'contado' proper, the mixture of peasant holdings, farms and villas of wealthy urbanites that made up the rural setting of the city. Unlike most European peasants, the Italian countryman is by no means regarded as an inferior. In his treatise on the running of a family, Leon Battista Alberti strongly recommends his readers to get hold of a farm: not only will it provide the household with first-class produce at the cheapest prices but it will give the family a healthy means of escape from the city. And the sensible citizen, too, will learn how to run the farm himself and not leave it all to a manager: Cosimo de' Medici, the richest man in the city, did not disdain to spread dung and prune vines with his own hands.

After passing through the contado, the city's larder, the traveller will come to the great circuit of the walls. At the time that Bruni was writing, there had been three successive expansions of the circumvallation, for all the world like a crab expanding beyond its shell, but containing the original embedded still within its body. First there had been the ancient Roman circuit, then a major expansion in the twelfth century and finally, during the boom period of the thirteenth century, a greatly extended circuit intended to accommodate a population in excess of 100,000. But that expansion of population had not come about: on the contrary, there had been a steady decline since the peak of 105,000 at the end of the thirteenth century. By the mid-fourteenth century, after the Black Death and two subsequent visitations, the population was little more than 50,000 and those city walls, built in such confident expectation of growth, must have looked like giant's robes upon a dwarf. In order to stimulate building, the Signoria decreed in 1417 that citizenship would be granted only to those who undertook to build a house worth not less than 100 florins and even as late as 1489, a law exempting new houses from taxation was enacted. By then the stimulus was barely needed: Luca Landucci remarked, 'The men at this time were so overworked with building walls that there was a shortage of masons and materials.'

The Catena Map of 1470 shows a cityscape that is immediately recognisable to twentieth-century eyes. Indeed, to compare this map (which resembles a panorama rather than a town plan) with a modern photograph taken from approximately the same position is to be astonished by how little the city has changed over five centuries. The colour-range is the same with warm reds and browns predominating. Today, as in the fifteenth century,

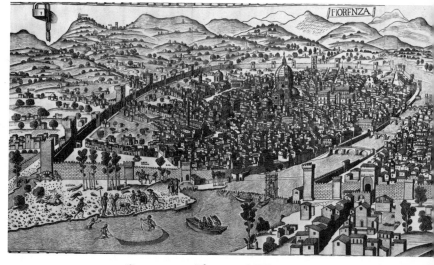

Catena map, Florence 1470

Florence: a modern view from similar viewpoint as the Catena map

the biggest single building is still the Cathedral, towering above the private houses like a liner among tugs. The eye still goes next to the 'mighty castle', the Palazzo Vecchio which, as the municipal building, is the outward symbol of the integrated community. And drawing the whole into one, transforming the myriad individual roofs and spires so that they seem to belong to one vast building, is the circuit of the city walls.

These massive walls are pierced by eleven gates. Some, like the Porta Romana, are named after the city which lies at the other end of the road they guard. Others take their name from some local feature: the Gate of Justice is so-called because it is there that criminals are executed. The gates are more than a fortified means of exit and entrance: each is a small castle in its own right, provided with a permanent garrison and with customs officials. There is a tax on most things that enter the city, whether it is silk from China or eggs from a farm down the road. The road leading to the Porta Romana crosses the Ponte Vecchio, as it does today, and brings the traveller immediately into the heart of the city –

Piazza della Signoria, Florence: showing the execution of Savonarola.
Unknown artist

the Piazza della Signoria. Again, this has changed relatively little over the centuries. The clearest indication of this is the painting by an unknown hand of the execution of Girolamo Savonarola in 1498, a detailed illustration of the piazza where the actual execution is shown almost as an afterthought. Here is truly the heart of the city where the people met on feastdays to enjoy, or on days of crisis to direct, their city. Here the business of government was carried out, partly in the square, and partly in the fortified palace and only too often to the accompaniment of bloodshed.

Between the mid-fourteenth and the mid-sixteenth centuries – the period most commonly recognised as constituting 'the Renaissance' – the population of metropolitan Florence varied between 38,000 and 70,000. It would have been possible for an able-bodied citizen to walk across the widest point of the city, from the Porta Romana in the south to the Porta San Gallo in the north, in three quarters of an hour or less. That same citizen would have known a very high proportion of his fellow inhabitants by sight, and would probably have known most of his peer-group by name. In terms of twentieth-century Europe, Renaissance Florence would rank as a moderate-sized country town. It is to be doubted, though, if any other equal area on the planet, or any other equal group of people, has been subject to such intense and prolonged scrutiny. The Florentines themselves began it, indulging an almost narcissistic self-awareness with an endless stream of literary or graphic records which, by the alchemy of art, have gained immortality.

Subsequent generations of scholars have examined and re-examined those records, commentators commenting upon commentators, heaping up an additional alpine range of material. In Italy, the sheer mass of such material is equalled, if at all, only by that on Venice, exceeded only by that on Rome so that posterity is quite swamped by information. Here, indeed, the trees hide the wood.

There exists, however, a body of material produced between 1427–80 which, in theory, should allow posterity to receive an emotionally neutral, accurate and richly cross-sectional view of Florentine society. The material is provided by the 'catasto', the combined census and tax system introduced in 1427. Until recently, the sheer mass of material has, again, almost defeated the would-be user. It has been used on an ad hoc basis but only since the introduction of computerisation to the catasto returns in the 1970s, has the material presented a coherent picture. Like any other computer output, it provides no more that what is put in, but in a meaningful form that provides a background or scaffolding for a picture of Florentine life in the two climacteric centuries.

The catasto was created for tax purposes but it also discharged the role of census. And, being Florentine, it is impossible to exclude humanity even from a tax return. Thus the sons of Caterina Rucellai give information that their mother is living with them but Caterina adds a note to the effect that 'because we are extremely cramped in the house, I am buying another one for myself'. The head of each household had to make a return, called a 'portate', in which he listed the number of people in his household (providing a census coverage as a priceless by-product for posterity), as well as providing minute information about his financial situation. The assessment of Giovanni's son, Cosimo, shows that the system worked in a very similar way to the modern British income tax system with an allowance for business and for dependants, and the actual amount liable for taxation being that which remained after allowances deducted from the gross. Thus, in 1427, Cosimo de' Medici declared that he possessed some 60,000 florins in real estate, four slaves worth 120 florins, had business investments to a total of 54,000 florins and public stock to the value of 9,000 florins. He claimed 5 per cent administrative expenses and allowances for fourteen 'mouths' – presumably of his personal household – at 200 florins each. A capital of 200 florins would produce an income of 14 florins and, even allowing for the fact that a taxpayer is going to regard expenses as being of an elastic quality, that estimate of living expenses is an invaluable indication of the cost of living in Florence in the 1420s.

The catasto was applied to the state as a whole and not simply to metropolitan Florence, covering a total of 60,000 households with a combined population of a quarter of a million people. Thus, although the catasto returns reflect living conditions only in Tuscany, they do transcend the usual parochialism. They show a society that is certainly comfortably off but that is, equally certainly, not outstandingly wealthy as a group. In the 1427 catasto only eleven families paid more than fifty florins in tax, that is, had a taxable income in excess of 10,000 florins. In general, an income of 3,000 florins placed a family firmly among the ranks of the wealthy, a fact substantiated by another set of statistics showing the imbalance of wealth. The richest 1 per cent of the population owned 25 per cent of all wealth while at the other end of the scale 31 per cent were so poor that they escaped taxation altogether.

The catasto returns show that Florentine society was not only somewhat unbalanced in terms of wealth, but decidedly unbalanced in terms of age. It was, predominantly, a young man's society, the average Florentine male being some twenty-six years old: half the male population fell between the ages of fourteen and thirty-five and most of these were unmarried. In Alberti's book on the management of a family, he places in the mouth of one of the speakers a remark which illustrates that fact, 'I counted the other day no less than twenty-two young Alberti males, living alone without a mate, not having taken a wife, none of them younger than sixteen and none older than thirty-six years.' The late marriage was almost certainly a result of the economic recession – it took a man longer to amass the necessary capital on which to launch a family. In social terms, it meant that his wife was likely to be widowed by the time she was fifty, and his children fatherless while still in their teens. David Herlihy, who analysed the catasto in a paper significantly entitled *Roots of violence in Tuscan cities*, sums up the overall effect of such a social pattern. 'Well before their sons reached adulthood, death was ruthlessly weeding out the generation of the fathers, muting the counsel and weakening the moral guidance they might have offered their children.'[13] And, at the other end of the life cycle, hundreds of young men who would normally have been subjected to the enforced disciplines and restraints of husbandhood and fatherhood, were free to roam the streets of the city in quest of excitement.

The unglamorous evidence of the catasto supplies both justification and depth to the traditional picture of Florence as a restless, effervescent society. 'Like a sick person upon a bed, tossing and turning in a hopeless attempt to find relief and comfort' was Dante's scathing description of his native city.

It is true enough that unrest was probably the most obvious characteristic of Florentine society. As in all other Italian cities, the antagonisms inherent in urban society had polarised into 'Guelph' versus 'Ghibelline'. In theory, Guelphs were for the Church and democracy, Ghibellines for the Empire and aristocracy: in practice, the labels now had little significance except as occasions for brawling. Guelphs cut their fruit horizontally, Ghibellines vertically; Guelphs drank from plain goblets, Ghibellines from decorated; there were prescribed party methods for sneezing, talking and walking, the infringement of which were pretexts for quarrelling among the young and hot-headed. In due course the Guelphs triumphed totally in Florence – the headquarters of the Parte Guelfa was to be one of the first buildings in the city to benefit from the new architecture – but the triumphing party itself merely split into two sections, Black Guelphs and White Guelphs, giving some substance to Dante's contemptuous view of the Florentines as a people incapable of working together.

The basic unit of Florentine political society was the guild. Originally, this was a truly democratic organisation with master and man passing through exactly the same apprenticeship, working side by side at the same bench, praying together at the guild church and, when necessary, fighting under the guild banner. By the end of the fifteenth century, the guilds were falling more and more under the control of the masters. And even though, in theory, all members of a guild were equal, the guilds themselves were far from equal. At one extreme they were composed of such people as fishmongers, cobblers or butchers: a master in these guilds was usually just an ordinary workman or shopkeeper, earning his living as best he could. There were fourteen of these Minor Arts, compared with the seven Major Arts which included that of the lawyers, the all-important cloth, silk and wool guilds, the bankers, the apothecaries and the furriers. The city was run largely by, and for, the Major Arts – seven of the nine members of the supreme governing body, the Signoria, were drawn from these seven guilds. The 'Thin People' and the 'Fat People' so the Florentines, with their fondness for nicknames, christened the Arte Minore and the Arte Maggiore; and most of the troubles in the city stemmed from the struggles between 'Thin' and 'Fat'.

'Nothing in this state is ill proportioned, nothing left vague. Everything occupies its proper place which is not only clearly defined but also in the right relation to all others,' so Leonardo Bruni boasted of his city's constitution and although his picture of an orderly, quiet progression owes more to piety than reality, certainly the provisions of government were drawn up in minute detail. But the actual act of choosing that government was left to pure chance. In the sacristy of the church of Santa Croce reposed eight leather bags: in those bags were the names of all citizens eligible for office – in other words, members of the guilds who were over thirty, were not in debt, had not served recently and were not related to anyone in office. In a public ceremony which took place every two months, nine of these names were drawn out, six representing the Major Arts, two the Minor Arts and the ninth taking office as Gonfaloniere di Giustizia, Standard-bearer of Justice. These nine priors, as they were known, formed the Signoria, the Lordship, for they were, in their corporate personality, the Lord of the City – for two months. For those eight weeks they lived like lords in the great Palazzo Vecchio or Palazzo della Signoria. They received no pay, but lived at public expense – and lived very well indeed in one of the most prosperous cities of Europe. For them was reserved the pink lucco, the dignified gown dyed in a rare and most beautiful colour. They ate off gold or silver plate from the choicest of food and wine while being entertained by the foremost musicians and singers. Each had his servant and each, for those few weeks, could feel himself a person of the utmost consequence before going back to his trade of cobbler or goldsmith or weaver.

Supporting the Priors were two other elected groups: the twelve Buonomini – three from each of the four quarters into which the city was divided for administrative purposes, and sixteen Standard-bearers, four from each of the quarters. The Florentines were passionately addicted to committees; one of their most devastating wars went down in history as the War of the Eight Saints, named after the eight-man war committee who directed it. Committees, or 'balie', were created as and when needed for various terms of office. Power was still vested, both legally and ritually, in the people. In times of difficulty or danger the great bell of the Palazzo Signoria – known as la Vacca because of its deep, lowing note – boomed out its warning and, at that summons, all citizens were supposed to gather in each of the sixteen wards of the city behind their Standard and march to the Piazza della Signoria where, by the very fact of their presence, they formed the Parlamento, in theory the ultimate authority. In the past, such summons were usually the preliminary to war, either with the city's external enemies or to suppress rebels within the walls. More and more, however, they were summoned to give their approval to a fait accompli on the part of the party managers. For this elaborate procedure, with all its checks and balances, could be manipulated at source by juggling with the names of those who went into the bags, a fact which the Medici were to use to their great advantage.

Nevertheless, the system worked. For nearly 200 years it worked, groaning and creaking, subjected to abuse, every so often requiring drastic reform, yet still working. No modern western democracy would have recognised it as a fellow republic: the two extremes of society, the aristocrats and the great mass of men without guilds, remained disfranchised. Citizenship belonged to a male minority and the city was run by a handful of rich men. But it was a rarity in its day, a community where most of the leaders were elected by some of the led and where all were engaged in an endless debate about the nature of man in society. It was in that fertile soil that the seed of humanism took root during the early fifteenth century.

The Florentine humanists

'Humanism' as a definition is as amorphous, as protean as 'Renaissance', and its current twentieth-century use, applied to a vaguely defined atheism and individualism, obscures its meaning even further. The first humanists were anything but atheists. The term itself did not come into general use until the late fifteenth century, nearly a century after the founders of the movement, when it came to be applied to those engaged in the teaching of the humanities – specifically, grammar, rhetoric, history and moral

DOMINVS FRANCISCHVS PETRARCHA

Francesco Petrarch by Andrea Castagno

philosophy. But this definition errs in the opposite direction, turning the 'humanist' into something little different from a grammar school master, transforming what was essentially an explorer into a pedant.

However the term is defined, the inescapable point of departure for the study of humanism is the life and career of Francesco Petrarch. Despite the crowded stage, despite the sheer numbers of his brilliant followers, it is worth looking at that career in some detail for it is literally archetypal, containing in itself the seeds of all that followed. Born in 1304 and dying in 1374, his life acts as a chronological bridge between the old and new worlds. He was seventeen years old when his great precursor, Dante, died and Giotto, his innovating equal in the world of art, died when he was thirty-three. At the end of his life, those of his disciples who were to influence the thinking of his next generation were already established in positions of authority. Indeed, the historian rash enough to assign an exact date of birth to the Renaissance could do worse than choose 6 April 1341, the day upon which Petrarch was crowned Poet Laureate upon the Capitol in Rome. Doubtless the ceremony was a fusty antiquarian revival; doubtless he owed the honour to his ceaselessly canvassing for it; doubtless his major work still lay ahead of him. Nevertheless, the ceremony on the Capitoline Hill marks a moment of vital change in Europe's intellectual climate: secular scholarship was again respectable.

Petrarch was only technically Florentine. He was born, in 1302, in exile in Arezzo; he spent most of his youth in Avignon and in his maturity had the choice of hospitality of virtually every princely house or republican city in Italy. His father, a successful notary at the Avignonese court, had wanted him to be a lawyer. Francesco wanted to be a poet, 'At an age when others are gaping over Prosper and Aesop I buckled to the books of Cicero. I could not understand what I read but the sweetness of the language and the majesty of the cadences enchanted me so that whatever else I read or heard sounded harsh in my ears and discordant.' It was a classic contest between father and son, resolved when the father's untimely death put an end to the son's legal studies. Petrarch and his brothers were fleeced by dishonest executors – or so Petrarch later claimed – although there seems to have been money enough to enable the brothers to cut a wide swathe through Avignonese society over the following five or six years. How Petrarch's social life was financed is obscure – he always tended to be somewhat reticent about his sources of income. But after some years of free-spending in Avignon he took minor orders as the first necessary step to secure an income through benefices.

Shortly after he obtained, through Bishop Giacomo Colonna, a scion of the great Roman family, the first of those patrons which made of his ecclesiastical income a useful addition instead of a vital necessity. In the summer of 1330 he met, in Colonna's palace, two other young men – a German musician and an Italian gentleman – whom he, according to his habit, christened with classical names. As Socrates and Laelius they were to receive, and figure in, his voluminous correspondence. But at the same time, when he was basking in the double warmth of aristocratic patronage and masculine friendship 'in the year 1327, exactly at the hour of prime on the sixth of April I entered the labyrinth of love' – he met Laura.

Carlyle, who condemned Petrarch's sonnets, might not be the best judge of lyric poetry but his opinion that Laura's main function was to spark off a sonnet sequence bears a ring of truth. Certainly her death in 1348 coincided with the exhaustion of Petrarch's lyrical vein. Thereafter follows the relentless work of the experimental scholar, curiously blind to visual art but acutely conscious of all other manifestations of existence, more truly the Complete Man than some of the lauded figures of the High Renaissance, aware of change when change was inchoate and so guiding the new impulses at a vital stage.

Petrarch's very originality serves to obscure the immense extent of his contribution to the new world. The poet endures, but much of the scholar was fated to be overshadowed by men who used, with the greater skill born of familiarity, techniques that he laboriously fashioned. As Latinist, for example – the skill upon which he prided himself most – he was surpassed by his followers, but their Ciceronian elegancies owed everything not merely to his written work but to his actual, physical discovery and transmission of the lost classical texts which were now beginning to serve as models – tasks which absorbed an immense part of his time and money.

The failure of his epic poem *Africa* is index at once to his originality and to his goal, pointing the contrast between his own 'modern' approach and that of the medieval world, barely a generation away. Infused with classicism, he attempted to recreate it, actually challenging Virgil on the Roman's own ground with an epic poem, in Latin, on a great Roman hero, Scipio Africanus. Dante, still immersed in the medieval tradition which was untroubled by anachronism, merely forced Virgil to copy Dante.

Again, the endless flow of quotations from the classics that made of Petrarch's works priceless anthologies for his contemporaries became an irritant for generations granted direct access to the quoted works themselves. So, too, his *Lives of Illustrious Men* became a museum piece as other writers first plundered it, then followed up and improved on its once novel approach.

But his letters retain all their immediacy of impact. Consciously, he intended them for posterity but the bulk of them were written to friends such as Laelius and Socrates and so bear – not spontaneity certainly, for each was a literary exercise – an undying freshness born of the knowledge that each was intended for a unique, living mind. Through them posterity gains a priceless view, at once wide and detailed, into a vanished world. Unlike most of his contemporaries he had a lively eye for nature: indicative of his approach is the fact that he climbed a mountain out of sheer curiosity to see what was at the top when his contemporaries regarded it merely as a larger lump of rock. Unlike so many of his followers, he avoided literary conceits, writing vividly, directly of what he saw and felt. He shared with Chaucer the dawning awareness that the humdrum and humble were as legitimate literary subjects as the noble and extraordinary. Unlike Chaucer, he did not process the material into poetry or fiction so that the peasant and the fisherman, the prelate and the pilgrim remain in reality, but in a single paragraph he can better portray the result of endless warfare in Italy than do pages of polemics from other men, for he writes of what he sees.

And it was as much through his letters, as through his formal work, that the 'new learning' was disseminated. Their fortunate recipients copied them out to send on to distant friends, or formed clubs to read them aloud to each other, acting as informal publishers. 'I stand as a man between two worlds, looking both forward and backwards,' he once wrote. He had little love for the new world; light lay only in the classic past. Nevertheless, he was most vividly aware of living at a climacteric and it was this awareness that paradoxically made of him, supreme recreator of the past as he was, an authentic voice of the future.

Petrarch's scholarship, though bold in so many of its innovations – its techniques of observing the real world instead of taking it for granted – was still medieval in the sense that it was a private affair, something to be conducted in study or cloisters or between friends for their delectation. But like a leaven in the lump, it began to work when some of those friends and disciples took up public appointments. One of those disciples was Coluccio Salutati. Born in 1331, he studied law and was appointed Chancellor of Florence at the age of forty-four in 1375.

Salutati held that office until his death in 1406. The holding of such an appointment for thirty-two years in a city where hatred of the single ruler was elevated into a political principle speaks much for his skill and probity as a civil servant. But the Florentine merchants who approved his appointment, together with its comfortable salary of 100 florins per annum tax free, were less interested in his honesty and his commonplace qualifications as a notary than in the power of his pen. In his hands, the Latin prose he had absorbed direct from the great masters of Latin became a superb instrument of propaganda. During Florence's long drawn out war with Milan, the Milanese lord, Gian Galeazzo Visconti, ruefully admitted that a single letter of Salutati's did him more damage than a thousand Florentine horsemen.

Salutati ran the Florentine Chancery loyally and efficiently, but it was the world of scholarship that fully claimed him and whose cause he was enabled to advance through his high official position. He would have emphatically rejected any claims to being a 'leader': he disliked even the formal style of *dominus* with which it was customary to address a person of his standing in correspondence. But if it was any one person who shaped the pattern of intellectual events in Florence in those vital early years it was Salutati. One of the rare portraits of him shows him, in late

Coluccio Salutati

middle age, as a heavy, stooping man with a somewhat coarse face and heavy mouth. In his correspondence, however, there emerges an attractive human being – religious but not fanatically so, deeply loyal to his friends with a gentle, somewhat ponderous sense of humour, an endless curiosity and a total, steely dedication to scholastic truth. On one occasion he, the Chancellor of Republican Florence, found himself intellectually obliged to defend the Duke of Milan, the 'tyrant' of Lombardy. It was during the course of one of the endless debates on the meaning of the *Divine Comedy* in which the Florentines delighted. Dante had placed the patriots Brutus and Cassius in Hell itself, while merely placing the 'tyrant' Caesar in Limbo – tacitly giving approval to the concept of kingship. Salutati's somewhat reluctant defence of that concept had more than an academic significance. Florence was free and would remain so for another century but, as early as 1400 her principal republican was unwittingly preparing the ground for the Medici, first as unofficial leaders and ultimately as signori, as lords.

Hindsight tends to formalise the relationship between these early humanists, turning them into 'schools' and 'movements'. Later, indeed, such formalisation did take place but in the early, heady days of discovery, the relationship was essentially the casual one of friends pursuing absorbing common interests either through informal discussions in gardens and villas (to be recorded afterwards by one of them) or through the medium of letters. The freemasonry of scholarship transcended even politics and wars. During the war with Milan, Salutati kept up a lively private correspondence with his scholarly opposite numbers in the Milanese Chancery. Members of these groups would introduce outsiders to their friends; the newcomers in turn would introduce others and so on in a chain reaction, a commonplace in human intercourse but given an unusual potency because of the intellectual calibre of the groups.

Among the members of the informal group around Salutati was a certain rich man, Niccolò Niccoli. Born in 1364, he was not only some thirty years younger than Salutati – becoming in effect a transmitter from one generation to another – but, unlike Salutati, he was freed from the necessity of earning a living. His father was one of the men who had made a fortune during the boom years of the Florentine woollen industry and had insisted that his son should at least learn the rudiments of the trade. As soon as the old man died, however, Niccoli promptly abandoned the business to his four brothers and devoted himself entirely to scholarship. So total was that devotion that, by the end of his life, Niccoli was dependent upon the Medici for the necessities of life, having spent his all on acquiring manuscripts and encouraging young scholars.

Vespasiano da Bisticci, the gossiping bookseller, left a vivid portrait of Niccoli. 'He was of handsome presence, lively, with a smile usually on his face and pleasant manner in conversation. His clothes were always of fine red cloth down to the ground; he never took a wife so as not to be hindered in his studies, and was accustomed to have his meals served to him in beautiful old dishes. His table would be covered with vases of porcelain, and he drank from a cup of crystal or of some other fine stone. It was a pleasure to see him at table, old as he was. All the linen that he used was of the finest.' A fastidious hedonist who delighted in the civilised pleasures of life, unlike most of his circle he opted out of active life even to the extent of allowing interference in his own domestic life. He had a beautiful but arrogant mistress, a young woman called Benvenuta, who so enraged his brothers with her high-handed attitude that one of them dragged her into the street and spanked her in public while Niccoli looked on, wringing his hands.

Niccoli's fastidiousness extended to his own attempts at literature: nothing he wrote pleased him and therefore he wrote little or nothing – certainly only two or three minor pieces can be attributed to him. The real reason for his restraint is probably the fact that his grasp of Latin, the only possible medium for a scholar, was something less than ideal. Despite, or because, of this limitation, he emerged as the foremost critic of his day. On one occasion, when an author demanded Niccoli's opinion of his newly finished work, Niccoli replied crushingly, 'I already have to deal with several hundred volumes of authors of repute before I shall be able to consider yours.' No visitor of any standing who came to Florence failed to call in upon him with the result that this stay-at-home, according to Bisticci 'had a great knowledge of all parts of the world, so that if anyone who had been in any particular region, and asked him about it, Niccoli would know it better than the man who had been there, and he gave many instances of this'.

But all Niccoli's activities were of decidedly lesser importance compared with his one abiding passion, the desire to possess books. At one stage, he directly employed more than forty copiers, and was accustomed to spend a certain amount of time each day in pursuing the craft himself, evolving a beautiful script which eventually provided the model for the modern italic script. Before the invention of printing, the survival of a book depended in large part on the accident of a scholar desiring a copy, and arranging for it to be made. It was only too easy for a book first to go out of fashion, and then to disappear altogether. Niccoli's contribution to that mysterious phenomenon known as the revival of learning was the location, copying and circulation of such lost texts. However, before they could be copied, they had to be found, tracked down like deposits of some rare mineral. Nobody in his senses travelled for pleasure and there was neither professional nor personal reason for the sedentary Niccoli to stir out of the comforts of Florence. He needed an agent, and found one in the person of Poggio Bracciolini.

Born in Terranova near Florence in 1380, Poggio Bracciolini was an excellent example of the new race of humanists who were bringing scholarship into the market-place – a man who had a deep and genuine love of learning, but was fully prepared to make money out of it. And Poggio's career was to show that there was quite a lot of money to be made. It was said that he arrived in Florence as a young man with just five soldi in his pocket. But, in the fullness of time he, too, became Chancellor of Florence, and on the way 'became very rich at the court of Rome' by employing the golden skills of language.

Apart from their mutual love of learning, Poggio and his patron Niccolò Niccoli differed from each other at every point. Where Niccoli was neat, restrained, gentlemanly, Poggio was large, expansive, rumbustious, 'given to strong invective' and a liking for even stronger drink. He was a born raconteur, and his collection of highly dubious stories, the *Facetiae*, was received with an enthusiasm in the Florentine equivalent of smoking rooms. He began his career, as did so many of his kind, as a notary and it was through the good offices of Salutati that he found a job in Rome as 'scrivener' at the papal court. It was a humble enough post, part copier, part writer of the innumerable letters that went out all over Christendom from Rome, but his outstanding gifts as Latin writer, combined with his easy bonhomie, took him out of the humble ranks of Chancery clerks. Pope Martin sent him to England as a courier 'where he found much to censure in the way of life of the country, how the people were fain to spend all their time in eating and drinking' – a curious criticism from Poggio Bracciolini with his passionate fondness for the white wines of Crete.

In 1414 Poggio was in the entourage of the bizarre figure of Baldassare Cossa, one of the three claimants of the papal tiara known to his adherents as John XXIII, when he was summoned to the Council of Constance. The Council had been called to end the scandal of the Schism and, unsurprisingly, 'John XXIII' was not only deposed but imprisoned, accused of an interesting variety of crimes ranging from piracy to rape. The Florentines had been among the few who recognised him as pope and it was through this link that Niccoli asked Poggio to keep an eye open for interesting manuscripts while they were in the barbaric land of Switzerland. After the pope's deposition, Poggio was unemployed and gladly devoted his time, at Niccoli's expense, to the hunting down of books. He had a remarkable flair, an instinct for the kind of place that would yield the treasure they sought. At the monastery of St Gall near Constance he stumbled immediately upon a rich vein, a collection of manuscripts some of which had been copied more than 800 years before. Among them was a veritable treasure, the complete book of Quintilian's *The training of an orator*, whose existence was known from a series of tantalising hints in other authors but of which Niccoli had despaired of ever finding a copy.

The survival of Quintilian in St Gall was due more to accident than the monks' reverence for learning, for the monasteries had long since lost their once noble reputation as refuges for scholarship. The story told of Boccaccio some seventy years before woefully illustrated that fact. He was visiting the monastery of Monte Cassino, St Benedict's own foundation, the very first fruit of that great monastic system which was to transform

Europe, and asked permission to visit the library. 'Pointing to a lofty staircase, the monk answered stiffly, "Go up, it is open." Joyfully ascending, he found the place of so great treasure without door or fastening. And having entered, he saw the grass growing upon the windows, and all the books and shelves covered with dust. And, wondering, he began to open and turn over now this book, now that and found that there were many and various volumes of many and ancient works. From some of them, whole sheets had been torn out, in others the margins of the leaves were clipped and thus they were greatly defaced ... Weeping and grieving he withdrew and asked a monk why those precious books were so vilely mutilated. He replied, that some of the monks, wishing to gain a few ducats, cut out a handful of leaves and made psalters which they sold to boys. And likewise of the margins they made breviaries which they sold to women. Now therefore, Oh scholar, rack thy brains in the making of books!'

In that brief passage Benevento da Imola, who tells the story, sums up the history of what had happened to the physical body of learning that had survived the collapse of the Empire: manuscripts were no safer in the mother house of an order devoted to learning than they would have been in an illiterate baron's castle. The monks of St Gall had not, personally, mutilated the manuscripts in their care as had the monks of Monte Cassino – they had been totally indifferent to them, as Poggio indignantly described. 'I truly believe that, had we not come to the rescue, this man Quintilian must have speedily perished: for it cannot be imagined that a man magnificent, polished, urbane and witty could much longer have endured the squalor of the prison house in which I found him, the savagery of his gaolers, the forlorn filth of the place.' In a common reaction the monks, having neglected their property, became abruptly possessive as soon as an outsider apparently saw value in it, and refused to let it out of their possession. Resignedly, Poggio set about copying it personally – a task which took him thirty-two days, as he recorded feelingly, a rare and valuable measurement of the sheer labour of the copier.

Over the next fifteen years, Poggio continued his treasure-hunting in France, Germany, Switzerland and Italy. Anything

written in classical Latin was reverently disinterred and laboriously copied. Like Niccoli before him, Poggio evolved his own
script – one which was to have even greater long-term significance than Niccoli's italic. The script in use at the time was a
spiky, rather unattractive 'gothic' which Poggio condemned not
merely for its intrinsic lack of clarity but for its base, non-Latin,
origins. In its place, he extolled a script which he believed to be
Roman in origin but was, in fact, a product of the Carolingian
court. He was not the first to mistake Romanesque for Roman
but it was a fortunate accident, for the Carolingian script was not
only beautiful but also marvellously clear. Others copied the
handwriting he developed from this and, in due course, when the
first of the Italian printers began looking for a model for their
founts, it was Poggio's now widely used script that they chose.
The direct debt that the modern world owes to him can be
perceived by comparing any Italian manuscript written before he
evolved his script, with that written afterwards: the latter is
immediately readable even to an eye that has no experience of
ancient manuscripts.

The remarkably eclectic nature of the library Poggio assembled bears testimony to the almost mystic veneration in which the
classical world was held. Books on cookery or astronomy, on
agriculture or history – all were swept into the bag, regardless of
the intrinsic value of the subject; they were in the Latin that
Cicero wrote and that was good enough for Poggio. Greek was,
for him, a closed book although, in 1396, the Greek scholar
Manuel Chrysoloras had settled in Florence at the direct
invitation of Coluccio Salutati.

There is something deeply poignant about the passionate
desire to acquire Greek manifested by the first humanists.
Petrarch, the greatest scholar of his age, could read only a few
words of it and he went into partnership with his friend
Boccaccio to set up a Greek-speaking monk, Leontius Pilatus, as
translator of Homer in Florence in 1360. Pilatus was a repulsive
old man – dirty, cantankerous, grasping. But to Boccaccio and
Petrarch from his mouth there came only gold; admittedly an
impure gold for the Greek he spoke was the bastard dialect
spoken in a few monasteries in southern Italy. The experiment
came to nothing: Pilatus took himself off to the Middle East

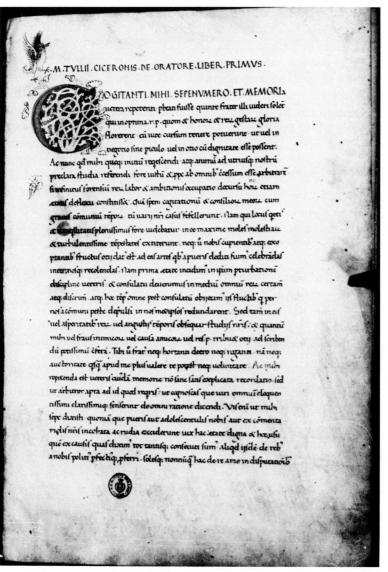

Script by Poggio Bracciolini

leaving Petrarch to kiss his copy of Homer in frustrated substitution for reading it.

Chrysoloras, unlike the wretched old Pilatus, was a genuine

scholar whose mother tongue was Byzantine Greek, and from the tiny little coterie that gathered round him in Florence during the three years he taught in the city, there developed the beginnings of a genuine school of Greek. Again, as with the Latin classics, it was not simply the language itself that magnetised the Florentine students as the fact that it was a vehicle, opening up a direct vision into the past – in particular, that segment of time which saw the fall of the Roman Republic. It was probably in response to this all-pervading interest of his hosts that Chrysoloras chose to lecture on Plutarch as representative of Greek culture rather than on one of the great dramatists or orators. Plutarch lived and taught in Rome in the last decades of the first century AD and, as the Greek-speaking biographer of Roman heroes, was an ideal link between the two ancient cultures whose fusion had created the culture of Western Europe. Centring his lectures upon Plutarch's *Lives* Chrysoloras added a potent ingredient to the intellectual brew in Florence.

Among those who attended Chrysoloras' lectures was another young man from a small town who had come to Florence to make his fortune. He was Leonardo Bruni, born in Arezzo in 1370. Like Poggio, ten years his junior, he too owed his start in life to the generosity of Coluccio Salutati for it was through the Florentine Chancellor that, in 1405, he gained a position in the papal chancery in Rome. Again like Poggio, he found that learning yielded gold in comfortable quantities. After ten years' residence in Rome, Bruni too had amassed enough capital to return to his beloved, adopted city of Florence as a private citizen.

There he began his *History of the Florentine people*, a work which Poggio was to complete and of which the bookseller Vespasiano da Bisticci made the penetrating observation, 'Among the other singular obligations which the city of Florence owes to Messer Leonardo and to Messer Poggio is this: that except the Roman Republic no republic or free state in Italy has been so distinguished as the town of Florence, in having had two such notable writers to record its activities as Messer Leonardo and Messer Poggio: for up to the time of their histories everything was in the greatest obscurity...' Machiavelli was to criticise them both for dwelling too exclusively upon Florence's wars and foreign affairs, at the cost of the description of the true inner life of the city: posterity might well find them almost intolerably mannered. 'We meet with frigid limitations and bombastic generalities, where concise details and graphic touches would have been acceptable ... striving to rival Cicero and Livy (they) succeeded only in becoming lifeless shadows of the past,'[14] is the judgement of J. A. Symonds. All this is true enough but it obscures one vital fact: through their work the Florentines became the first Italians to obtain a view of their past which, though distorted in detail, was true in perspective.

Salutati, Niccoli, Bruni, Poggio – they formed a species of apostolic succession stretching over a century from the first stirrings of self-consciousness in the mid-fourteenth century with its flowering at the end of the fifteenth. They are only four out of a dozen or more like-minded men in the city but, through them, it is possible to see the impulse being transmitted until it came to be amplified by the Medici bankers.

The House of Medici

The Medici family have suffered more than most from what might be called that Burckhardtisation process whereby characters from the Italian Renaissance become ever more colourful and larger than life. Non-Italians paid no particular interest to the family until the late eighteenth century. Edward Gibbon toyed with the idea of writing a history of Medici Florence, but abandoned it for his larger canvas, and it was not until William Roscoe published his *Life of Lorenzo de' Medici* in 1796 that attention became focused on the family. The book was immediately successful and Roscoe followed it up, in 1805, with a biography of Lorenzo's son, Pope Leo X.

William Roscoe was a Liverpool attorney and shared some of the characteristics of his subject, being both wealthy through financial dealing, and an art collector. His books, though dated, still provide valuable source material and, with their anecdotal richness and fluency of style, are still extremely readable. Certainly, for at least a century, they provided the most potent propaganda for the Medici, doing for the family what

Burckhardt and Symonds were to do for the Renaissance as a whole. As far as Roscoe was concerned, the Medici were virtually the creators of the Renaissance, and not simply enlightened patrons who used their money to promote an existing trend. Uncritical adulation produced, as reaction, uncritical condemnation with nineteenth-century liberals drawing attention to the undoubted fact that the Florentine republic became a Medici dukedom, typecasting the whole family as destroyers of 'liberty'.

The family which was to become virtually synonymous with Renaissance Florence was already solidly middle class when its members first appeared on the political stage towards the end of the fourteenth century. The founder of the family fortune was Giovanni, born in 1360. He began his career in the Rome branch of the family banking business and pulled off an outstanding coup there when he became banker to the Papal court. This was the true origin of the Medici wealth. Their relationship with the Papacy would vary over the years but, in the main, the revenues of the Roman Church passed through their hands. They were honest hands, but the commissions they honestly received on those sums were enough to establish them as Europe's major business house. In 1397, Giovanni established the headquarters of the bank in Florence and, somewhat reluctantly, became involved in Florentine politics. No Florentine could possibly avoid public service and a successful banker with widespread foreign connections inevitably was charged with important commissions, and at one time or another Giovanni held most of the highest offices in the State. As Machiavelli put it, 'He never sought the honours of government, but enjoyed them all.'

When Giovanni died in 1429 he left his son Cosimo the immense fortune of 180,000 florins. But he left him something more – a reverence for the things of the mind. He had begun the Medici patronage of the arts when he financed Brunelleschi's building of the Sacristy of San Lorenzo. As one of the city fathers he sat on two commissions which produced two significant works of art, the competition for the Baptistry doors and for the design of the dome for the Cathedral. But probably even more important than his direct patronage was the long-term effect he created by ensuring that Cosimo was educated in the new mode, rather than in the learning by rote that had so long characterised education. While still an impressionable young man, therefore, Cosimo came into close contact with those who were changing the very thought-patterns of society: with Poggio, the manuscript hunter, and Niccoli, the aesthete, and Bruni, the historian who was opening up a new perspective into the past, as well as with the Greek scholars who were suddenly widening the whole concept of civic life and responsibility.

Cosimo de' Medici has been overshadowed in the popular mind by his more obviously glamorous grandson, Lorenzo. Significantly, however, the Florentines themselves, though ever suspicious of the aggrandisement of the individual, gave to Cosimo the title of *Pater Patriae* after his death, but made no such gesture to his grandson. The title 'Il Magnifico' with which Lorenzo has gone down in history was the commonplace Italian style accorded in correspondence to any important person. It is not denigrating the achievements or personality of the grandson to observe that the grandfather travelled further. As it happens it is possible to measure the psychological distance that Cosimo travelled with curious exactness. His father, Giovanni, owned three books, all on religious subjects: Cosimo eventually owned 10,000, covering the entire existing field of knowledge.

Cosimo was forty when he succeeded his father in the family business but was already widely experienced in it. He was, first and foremost, a businessman – a banker – and remained so until the end of his life: it was, indeed, his success as banker that made all else possible. An international banking system like that of the Medici not only channelled money towards him who sat at the centre but, what was just as vital as money – information. Medici agents from all over Europe kept their principal informed of people and events: which government was strong, and which weak; which prince could be trusted to keep his word and repay a loan and which could not. Cosimo possessed that faculty of the successful businessman which to the outsider looks almost like second-sight: the ability to assess a man or a situation on minimal facts. One of the many clients who approached the Medici bank for urgently needed aid was a monk with no collateral but his face and manner. Cosimo de' Medici lent Tommaso Parentucelli the desired sum – and in due course the penniless monk became Pope Nicholas V, the humanist pope who was

Cosimo de' Medici by Pontormo

bent on transforming Rome and was willing to expend any money for that purpose. He never forgot his benefactor.

It was another humanist pope, Pius II, who left one of the most discerning portraits of Cosimo, a very friendly portrait considering that Pius was a Sienese and Sienese had very little love for their fellow Tuscans. 'He is of fine physique and more than average height. His expression and manner of speech were mild. He is more cultured than merchants usually are and has some knowledge of Greek ... He is the arbiter of peace and war and the moderator of the laws – not so much a private citizen as the lord of the country. The policy of the republic is discussed in his house: he it is who gives commands to the magistrates.'

In those last two sentences Pius shrewdly summed up the thoroughly ambiguous role that Cosimo, his son, and grandson played in Florentine society. Despite appearances, despite the careful observation of all the outward forms of democracy, Cosimo de' Medici was de facto 'lord of the country'. It had come about slowly, undramatically, deviously. During one stage of the long struggle with his political rivals, Cosimo actually found himself under sentence of death, a punishment commuted to exile. But he returned in triumph and continued the steady work of establishing the power of his party in the city. Much of his power sprang directly from his wealth: an impressively high proportion of the most influential people in the city were in his debt, or wanted to be. But the measures which he and his party took to manipulate the drawing of the lots – measures which ranged from the unethical to the illegal – were not particularly new or unusual. What was new and unusual was the skilful co-operation of the party workers. A disgruntled opponent of the regime gives some hint of the technique involved when he complained that Florence was no longer governed from the palace 'but from dinners and desks'. The complex checks and balances of the Florentine constitution were designed to spread the exercise of power while preventing the emergence of a despot. It was far less effective against the establishment of an oligarchy which would eventually act as a Trojan horse.

But that eventual development lay nearly a century in the future. Despite the opportunities open to him, Cosimo de' Medici clung to the role of private citizen. 'He acted with the greatest skill to preserve his power,' Vespasiano da Bisticci noted admiringly. 'Whenever he wished to achieve something he saw to it that the initiative came from others and not from him and so he escaped envy.' It also left him room to manoeuvre as Pope Eugenius IV found to his irritation. He had tried to persuade Cosimo to adopt a policy of which he disapproved and the wily Florentine escaped the problem by piously pointing out that he was simply a private citizen.

But political considerations apart, at the very core of the man's character was an incorruptible integrity. He really did seem to have believed that to have usurped power in a free city would have been an unredeemably wicked action. His life he modelled upon his admired Romans – the Romans of the heroic period when a man was farmer, soldier and citizen combined – a free man in a free society. The richest man in Florence, he could have commanded what luxuries he liked. Instead, he lived the simplest of lives, contenting himself for recreation with an occasional game of chess after dinner. He delighted to escape to his villa at Careggi, running its farm as though he were a peasant, digging and planting and weeding with his own hands.

Cosimo is among the first of that generation which emerged from the obscurity of time to stand as it were three-dimensional before the gaze of posterity, illuminated by the new learning, the new pattern of thought which emphasised the humanity of man, by portraits which strove to bring out the mind behind the mask of vulnerable flesh, by biographies which as yet clumsily, hesitantly but with increasing assuredness strove to understand and demonstrate their subjects' psychology instead of simply amassing pious or hostile anecdotes. Cosimo did not emerge on the public scene until his early forties and there are therefore no portraits of his youth and adolescence, but those of his maturity and old age are in abundance. They show a watchful, somewhat remote man (it is a curiosity of Medici portraits over four generations that their subjects rarely look at the observer but are glancing downwards or sideways, brooding). In old age Cosimo appears somewhat gaunt, the expression quizzical, the firm full lips slightly compressed. He had a talent for salty, pithy maxims which were repeated with delight, passing into Florentine mythology. Reproached for the number of exiles he engineered on his return, he remarked briefly, 'Two yards of scarlet (cloth) will make a citizen.' A proposal to forbid priests to gamble was met by his retort, 'First stop them using loaded dice.' He had the Tuscan love of small children. Once, a group of ambassadors was scandalised when he broke off an important conference in order to whittle a whistle on the peremptory demand of his small grandson. He smiled at the ambassadors' expressions, 'Come, my lords, are you not fathers too? It is fortunate that the child did not ask me to play it, for I would have done so.'

His friend, the bookseller Vespasiano da Bisticci, believed that one reason for Cosimo's prodigal generosity in endowing the arts in Florence arose from his own uneasiness about his trade of banker. 'He had prickings of conscience that certain portions of his wealth – where it came from I cannot say – had not been righteously gained, and to remove this weight from his shoulders he held conference with Pope Eugenius, who was then in Florence, as to the load which lay on his conscience.' Technically, Cosimo was a usurer: usury was forbidden by canon law for it was held to be an unnatural thing to make money, a dead thing, breed money. Every transaction which earned Cosimo interest – including those done on behalf of the Church – was technically under the ban of the Church, deserving punishment in this world and the next. Prudent merchants used to make provision in their wills for the return of all usuriously gained monies, but though the ban was losing its force, obliged to give ground to the realities of a booming trade system spread over thousands of miles and involving big transactions in gold, it could still be invoked to embarrass a banker, and a deeply religious person like Cosimo might well be occasionally preoccupied with the problem. Eugenius suggested he eased his conscience by building a monastery and Cosimo adopted the idea. There is no reason to believe that he was attempting to bribe God in the crude medieval manner, but a man of his cast of mind may well have reflected that he owed God a debt for his good fortune, and tried to repay that debt in a manner which came naturally to a citizen of Florence – the physical beautification of the commune which was believed to be under the direct protection of God.

Cosimo eventually spent more than 50,000 florins on the rebuilding of San Marco – the monastery which, by a profound irony, was to become the headquarters of his grandson's great enemy Savonarola. He not only built it, but endowed it, and the extent of his munificence can be measured by comparing his donation with his tax bill to the state in 1457: it was not quite 600 florins – and that was the heaviest imposed upon an individual. Fittingly, he presented Niccolò Niccoli's magnificent manuscript collection to the monastery. In the last years of his life, Niccoli had virtually an open cheque upon the Medici bank and if any man had the moral right to dispose of the library as he thought fit, that man was Cosimo. Nevertheless, he insisted that each book should bear Niccoli's name. He incidentally demonstrated his prodigious memory while checking through the library with Vespasiano. One of the books should bear the name of a certain German scholar who had once owned it, he remarked, and was proved correct though it was more than forty years since he had last seen the book. Vespasiano benefited considerably from this Florentine Maecenas. Later, when Cosimo was building the church of San Lorenzo, he discussed with Vespasiano the means of furnishing it with a truly representative library. Vespasiano was dubious: the books were just not available. 'Tell me what you would do,' Cosimo asked. 'I said it would be necessary to have the books transcribed, and he asked whether I would undertake the task.' Vespasiano agreed and Cosimo gave him freedom to act, stipulating that all costs would be paid by the bank. Eventually, Vespasiano had forty-five scribes working on the project, producing 200 volumes in under two years – the nucleus of the great Laurentian library for which, a century later, Michelangelo himself was to design the furniture.

Cosimo's grandson later calculated that he spent at least 600,000 gold florins either directly on commissioning architects, or indirectly by subsidising scholars and, less often, painters. But undoubtedly his most spectacular coup was when he brought about the transference of the great ecumenical conference from Ferrara to Florence, so that it was ever afterwards known as the Council of Florence. The conference was called to try and end the schism between the Greek and Roman Churches which had existed since 1204. The Roman Church was represented by the full panoply of the pope and the crimson-robed College of

Cardinals. The Greek Church was, if anything, even more splendid for the emperor himself had come to Italy – the real emperor, not the upstart from Germany, but the lineal, if Greek-speaking descendant of the great Caesars resident in Constantinople. The splendour was marred behind the scenes not only with squabbles about precedence and complaints about the provincial lodgings available in Ferrara but, more embarrassingly, about money. The Emperor John Paleologus and his enormous retinue of 700 officials were the guests of Pope Eugenius who very rapidly ran out of money. His friend, Cosimo de' Medici, came forward with an offer of free accommodation and a loan of 1,500 florins a month for as long as the Council lasted, if only it were transferred to Florence. Eugenius grasped at the opportunity and, on a blustery cold winter's day in 1439 the citizens of Florence had their first sight of the Byzantine Emperor and his fabled court.

Vespasiano was among those who were able to attend the inaugural mass in the cathedral and, like most Florentines, was much impressed with the strangers, in particular the Emperor. 'He was clad in a rich robe of damask brocade and a cap in the Greek fashion, on the top of which was a magnificent jewel. He was a very handsome man with a beard of the Greek cut. Round about his chair were posted the many gentlemen of his retinue, clad in the richest silken robes made in Greek fashion, their attire being most stately.' The essential Greek conservatism astonished Vespasiano: 'I will not pass on without a special word of praise for the Greeks. For the last 1,500 years and more they have not altered the style of their dress . . . '

Nothing came of the Council for the division was too deep to allow for a papering over. But it had a profound effect upon the Florentines themselves and, ultimately, upon all Italy. Florence had never been exactly a parochial city and strangers were no rarity within its gates. But the presence of some seven hundred exotic orientals for many weeks in the Tuscan city undoubtedly created a new stimulus to explore a widening world. The sumptuous garments, extraordinary headgear and frequently bizarre servants and pets of the strangers particularly took the fancy of the artists of the city and the Greek presence made its mark on many a painting, either as influence or as deliberate

Procession of the Magi: mural by Benozzo Gozzoli. Lorenzo de' Medici is the splendidly dressed youth on horseback, front right, followed by Cosimo and other members of the Medici family

recording. When Benozzo Gozzoli was commissioned by Cosimo himself to create that Medici family portrait which has since become one of the great symbols of the Renaissance, the artist's mind was evidently still awhirl with those images he had seen in the streets of Florence. He took as a theme the Procession of the Magi and with the splendid disregard of anachronism which he shared with the painters of the day he not only introduced Cosimo, his family friends and retainers in contemporary dress, but also the Emperor John Paleologus and his attendants to give a suitably oriental impression.

The long-term effect of the visit of the Greeks was even more important than the influence it had upon artists. That magical language for which so many learned Italians had yearned, which had been introduced into Florence half a century earlier by

Marsilio Ficino: bust by Andrea di Piero Ferruci

Salutati like a transference of precious fire, for a matter of weeks became commonplace in the streets of the city. The very urchins learned one or two words of Greek and at the upper levels of society the fortunate learned Greek direct from some of the foremost scholars of the Byzantine world. Amongst them was a certain Gemistos Plethon, probably the world's greatest authority on Plato. Cosimo attended his lectures and was deeply stirred, for this clear-headed capitalist and pragmatic politician shared a fundamental uncertainty with the most insecure adolescent: was there a life after death? Plato, through Plethon, provided him with an answer. He never forgot the undramatic but fundamental revelation and years later he was to found what became known as the Platonic Academy. Its beginning was informal like so many of the great seminal movements of the fifteenth century: Cosimo adopted a young medical student, Marsilio Ficino, out of friendship to his father, paying for his education. Ficino, who later became a priest, proved to be a philosopher of rare breadth and ability with an almost empathetic understanding of the great Greek philosopher who was to give shape and colour to the Renaissance. From out of Ficino's letters, from out of the eager debates that sprang up between him and his ever-growing circle of friends, grew the concept known as neo-Platonism.

There is, perhaps, nothing quite so dead as an outmoded philosophy and, in the late twentieth century, it is difficult to apprehend the impact of neo-Platonism. But in the middle years of the fifteenth century it proved to be the final solvent that dissolved the pattern of thought that had imposed itself upon Europe. European thought had been ruled by Plato's great disciple, Aristotle; European Christians had tried to frame their paradoxical faith in the exact, cold terms of Aristotelian logic. The discovery of Plato – a philosopher of equal status but one in whose system there was a place for love and poetry and imagination – was like the working of the thaw of spring upon a frozen river. Before he died, Cosimo was to see his young protégé, Ficino, become one of the towering thinkers of his day, the interpreter of the Interpreter. Of all that the old banker's wealth had provided, none was as valuable as this.

Cosimo died in 1464 at the age of seventy-four, preparing himself for death with the methodical care he used to prepare himself for a journey – he even closed his eyes 'to get them used to it' as he sardonically informed his anxious wife, Contessina. And the Florentines – who had devised an entire political system to avoid the threat of dynastic ambition – hastened to his son, Piero, begging him to take over the supposedly non-existent office of leader. Piero did so and guided his fellow citizens well for five years before succumbing to the family illness of gout. And again the Florentines begged the house of Medici to maintain that non-existent office. This time, the head of the family, Lorenzo, was only twenty years old. He was extremely reluctant, and pointed out that he was far too young. But his fellow citizens insisted and at last he gave way – though his reasons were not wholly altruistic, as he noted candidly, 'It goes ill in Florence with those who are rich and have no say in the government.'

With Lorenzo the Magnificent, we move into the realm of myth and legend – paradoxically so, for he was closely observed by his enemies and admirers alike, minutely documented. The glamour that shines upon him tends to dazzle, so that the human weaknesses are glossed over, the outstanding men who worked with him fall into the background and the whole portrait becomes suspect because it is obviously so much larger than life. But there is substance in the legend, for the man was an astonishing admixture of moods and talents, today drinking with rowdy companions in rough taverns, tomorrow engaged in deep philosophical argument with brilliant scholars. A poet of very considerable ability, recognised today as one of the creators of Italian literature, even his poems are contradictory, for some are highly bawdy and others deeply religious and others again are of great poignancy and nostalgia:

> Fair is youth and void of sorrow
> But it hourly flies away
> Youths and maids enjoy today
> Naught ye know about tomorrow

He wrote *La Giovinezza* – which centuries later the Fascists were to adopt as their anthem – for the carnival which he himself instituted in Florence. Nevertheless, he was deeply religious, while being no bigot: on one occasion when a wandering friar tried to stir up trouble against the Jews in Florence, Lorenzo had the man discreetly shown out of the city. One of his companions records how he enlivened a thirty-mile journey with a party of friends by singing all the way. In an entirely different mood, at a public reception, he became so engrossed in a conversation he was having with a peasant that he quite forgot the glittering company and walked out, still deep in conversation. At his banquets, guests sat quite regardless of rank yet, at the same time, he was very much aware of his status. 'He did not want to be equalled or imitated even in verses or games and exercises and turned angrily on anyone who did so.'

So the catalogue of talents and contradictions could be extended almost indefinitely, for again and again he was to startle his contemporaries and on each occasion there would be somebody eagerly recording for posterity. His physical characteristics come down through the centuries with even

Lorenzo de' Medici (the Magnificent) by Vasari

greater detail than his mental abilities. He was a powerfully buil
man, athletic, with broad shoulders, deep chest and wel
muscled. The jaw juts pugnaciously but the mouth is generou
and the face in repose, as with all the Medici, is remote an
touched with melancholy. The nose is flattened and he had, i
fact, no sense of smell, typically passing it off with a laugh, sayin
that most smells were unpleasant. As with all his class, he adore

hunting but with him hunting went far beyond that of merely slaughtering wild creatures. He seemed to be able to establish a rapport with animals – his racehorse, Morello, used to mope if he did not feed it regularly with his own hands and showed its joy at his approach by stamping and neighing. Not, by any means, a handsome man, for his voice was harsh and squeaking, his complexion bad, the skin sagging. But the attractiveness of his personality totally distracted from the physical defects.

For twenty-three years this bundle of contradictions guided the affairs of the free city. He neglected the family business – badly, so that the Medici bank went into a decline but he was still businessman enough to prefer peace to war, to prefer negotiations to threats. Typical of the panache with which he conducted affairs was his decision to go alone and in person to the King of Naples during the course of a bitter, long-drawn war between Naples and Florence, to try and negotiate a peace. Typical of his courtesy, too, and of the careful attitude towards the government of the State was his letter of apology to the Signoria. 'It was not from presumption that I did not notify the reason of my departure to your Illustrious Excellencies, but because it seemed to me that the agitated and disturbed condition of our city demands acts and not words.' He was putting himself in very real danger: no one knew better than he that Ferrante of Naples was a 'king by nature treacherous, unstable and bitterly opposed to him'. But it worked: Ferrante, doubtless taken aback, welcomed him and a treaty was drawn up in the very nest of the viper bringing peace back to central Italy, a peace which Botticelli was to symbolise in his curiously disturbing painting of Pallas subduing the Centaur.

Lorenzo died, still a young man, of the disease which lay in wait for all his family, gout, and Ferrante of Naples – not a man given to compliments, idle or otherwise, remarked percipiently, 'He lived long enough for his own glory, but died too soon for the peace of Italy.' And certainly within a year of his death the precarious balance of Italian power toppled over and the first of the foreign invaders entered the land.

To try and analyse the power or influence or control which Cosimo, his son Piero and his grandson Lorenzo exerted over the city-state of Florence is to try and analyse the very well-springs of

Pallas subduing the Centaur: allegory by Sandro Botticelli

human relations. They were simply the first among equals – and only scarcely the first, for their social equals included men who were only marginally less wealthy than themselves and certainly their intellectual peers. These early Medici were sustained by neither the mystique of monarchy, nor the naked force of autocracy: twice they were chased out of the city by a popular uprising – but came back by popular wish. After Lorenzo, the heroic strain came to an end. 'I have three sons,' he was credited with saying, 'one is good, one is wise, and one is a fool.' The good one died, the wise one became pope – and unfortunately it was the fool who inherited the leadership and died trying to emulate his father, unsuccessfully, during the French invasion of 1494.

But the republican impulse was growing feebler and though there was resistance Florence eventually followed the majority when, in 1537, the first Medici duke – ironically of a cadet branch – turned the citizens into subjects. There were to be Medici dukes for two centuries, some of them of great splendour and intellect, but those who worked in Florence when it was the powerhouse of the Renaissance were citizens.

3

The throne of St Peter

The Renaissance popes

Some time during the 1420s Poggio Bracciolini, wit, bon viveur and sensitive scholar was sitting with a friend among the ruins of the Capitoline Hill, that favourite spot for nostalgic musings. What he saw that day deeply moved him so that it eventually formed a powerful section in his book, *Of the variations of fortune*. 'The hill of the Capitol on which we sit was formerly the head of the Roman Empire, the citadel of the earth, the terror of kings, illustrated by the footsteps of so many triumphs enriched with the spoils and tributes of so many nations. This spectacle of the world – how is it fallen! How changed! How defaced! The path of victory is obscured by vines, and the benches of the senators obscured by dunghills ... The Forum of the Roman people is now enclosed for the cultivation of pot-herbs, or thrown for the reception of swine and buffalo. The public and the private edifices that were founded for eternity lie prostrate, naked and broken, like the limb of a mighty giant, and the ruin is the more obvious because of the stupendous relics that have survived the injuries of time and fortune.' And after this more or less obligatory threnody on the theme of sic transit gloria, he embarked on a lively attempt at a check-list or topographical guide, describing what survived in the giant city nearly a thousand years after the last true Caesar had abandoned it.

What he saw from the Capitol was an overgrown wilderness, dotted about with a number of enormous tree or bush-clad ruins, and given shape by the circuit of walls some fourteen miles in circumference. The dominant structures within those walls were

View of Rome, 1494. Colosseum left centre; Pantheon centre; Old St Peter's and Castel Sant' Angelo beyond the river

still the ceremonial buildings of the classical city – the Colosseum, the Pantheon, the various triumphal arches – many of them crowned with medieval fortifications as well as chance-sown vegetation. Sharing the skyline with these ruined structures were a number of huge churches, either brickbuilt or adorned with ill-matched marble facings and columns plundered from the older structures. In between these buildings – the ruins of the pagan city and the decidedly shabby monuments of the Christian city – lay meadows and copses, as though the surrounding Campagna had broken in like the sea. These patches of wilderness could give shelter to anything from wild animals to robbers. An English visitor recounted with incredulity how he witnessed the spectacle of dogs fighting a wolf barely a stone's throw from St Peter's. The energetic could still hunt down their food in the heart of the city, if they wished, for hares and rabbits flourished everywhere. The less energetic simply pastured their herds and flocks on the heathlands that had sprung up over the centuries. The very site of the Forum was known colloquially as the Campo Vaccino, the Cow Field: the great columns and walls that survived to mark what had been the heart of a world civilisation seemed now like organic growths springing up from the grassy fields; some of them were buried up to a third of their height by the spoil heaped up over a thousand years. The crests of the hills – those famous Seven Hills that were part of Europe's mythology – were again deserted, given over to vineyards for they became uninhabitable as soon as the high aqueducts failed. The people drifted down to settle in the valleys and the flat areas, in particular in the horn-shaped area by the river known as the Plain of Mars. It was liable to flood and, in summer, was far less pleasant than those cool heights but at least water was available. And there was no lack of space: the city which, at the time of Augustus, in the first century, held perhaps a million people, had a population of about 25,000 at the beginning of the fifteenth century. Detectably, the pulse of Rome was fluttering towards extinction.

Such was the city to which Pope Martin returned in September 1420, bringing to an end over a century of exile and schism. In addition to the physical damage had been the social decline. During the absence of the Papacy in Avignon between 1305 and 1377, Rome had had no choice but to govern itself and had evolved a variation of the old communal form of government. During the Schism the presence of the Roman pope had effectively suffocated the feeble new republic, but he had been too preoccupied in fighting his Avignonese rival to pay much attention to his titular city, and civic government had virtually come to an end.

The pontificate of Martin V, who died in 1431, emphatically marked the end of one era and the beginning of another, for the bureaucracy which he established was the foundation both of the Renaissance papacy and that which succeeded it. The most obvious measure of his success, and the success of those popes who followed him, was the spectacular improvement in the finances of the Papacy. At the end of the Schism a commission of cardinals calculated that the revenues of the Papacy had shrunk by at least a third. During the pontificate of Gregory XI, the last pope of an undivided church, total revenues had amounted to as much as 300,000 florins. Martin V was obliged to make do with an income of 170,000 florins. A century later, a Venetian estimated that the splendid, profligate pope, Leo X, had spent on an average 590,000 ducats a year during his eight-year pontificate. Admittedly, he left an enormous pile of debts which gravely embarrassed his successor and his unexpected death at an early age bankrupted many a man who trusted him. But the fact that the bankers of Siena and Florence and Genoa were prepared to allow him to run up such colossal debts was indication of the strength of the collateral – and, in turn, of the strength of the organisation that created them.

It was during the fifteenth century that the Papacy became an Italian princedom. Even during Martin's pontificate the all-powerful College of Cardinals had been international in character, with Italians only one group among the French, English, Germans, Spanish and even Dutch and Danish. By the 1450s the College was predominantly Italian – with a heavy bias towards Roman families – and became very largely an arena where the conflicting Italian interests were fought out. Every city, every great family, strained to have a representative in the College. Lorenzo de' Medici skilfully manoeuvred to have his 14-year-old son Giovanni (the later Pope Leo X) made a cardinal, laying out a great deal of money in the process. In a long letter of advice to the young man, he lamented that very change in the College which such actions as his were causing: 'The College is at this moment so poor in men of worth. I remember the days when it was full of learned and virtuous men – and theirs is the example for you to follow. The less your conduct resembles that of those who now compose it, the more beloved and respected you will be.'

The Papacy's income came from three major sources: the so-called 'spiritual' income, which included Peter's Pence and annates, and fees paid by a prelate on assuming office; the sale of offices, which were, in fact, a species of loan to the Papacy, repaid in the form of salary but nevertheless an embarrassment to would-be reformers; and taxes from the Papal States. The importance of this latter had increased immensely: before the Schism they had contributed less than a quarter, afterwards they contributed more than a half to the total papal income.

The Papal States were founded on the so-called Donation of Constantinople, the forgery made in the eighth century by which Constantine was supposed to have donated the western half of his empire to the Bishop of Rome. Whatever the circumstances of the forgery, it was good enough to take in generations of hostile critics of the Papacy, including so great a scholar as Dante:

> Ah, Constantine, of how much ill was mother
> Not thy conversion but that marriage dower
> Which the first wealthy Father took from thee

he lamented in his *Inferno*, echoing the protests of de Mussi and of all those who witnessed the Papacy's long-drawn-out battle to keep its grip on the States of the Church. Yet, in retrospect, given the then territorial origins of all wealth, it is difficult to see what alternatives the Papacy had if it wished to raise money to fund its activities. The States were divided into six regions including the Patrimony, the area immediately to the north of Rome where the Tolfa mines were situated. The pope's control over the cities of those States varied immensely: in some, such as Ferrara and Bologna, it was little more than notional, the Papacy contenting itself with an annual tribute from the leading families who were de facto rulers. In others, such as Pesaro or Forli, the popes would, from time to time, impose their own vicars – usually members of their own family.

The papal bureaucracy, the *Curia*, was run by semi-autonomous bodies whose relative importance changed from time to time, reflecting both social changes and the power of the cardinals who ran them. The Tribunal of the Penitentiary was broadly responsible for matters of conscience; in practice it handled such delicate matters as applications for absolutions and remission of penances – and the fees for them. The oddly named Sacra Romana Rota was the appeal court for ecclesiastical cases throughout Christendom generally, and for judicial matters in the Papal States. The newly established and fast growing office of Datary was concerned with the sale of offices; the Apostolic Camera handled all finances. The effective voice of the Church was the Chancery: with its hordes of protonotaries, abbreviatores, scrittori, computatori and bullatori producing some

10,000 letters annually it was the biggest single employer of humanist literary skills in Italy. And, according to a modern Italian historian, Pio Pecchai, 'It was probably from that body of cosmopolitan *letterati* that Rome was deluged with such lamentable corruption.'

The city of Rome continued, in theory, to be a separate authority from the Papacy. Twice there was an attempt to revive its former independence, the first fleetingly successful, the second disastrous. In 1347 Cola di Rienzo, reputed to be the son of a tavern keeper and a washerwoman, proclaimed himself to be the Tribune of the People and issued a resounding proclamation. 'We decree, declare and proclaim that the holy city of Rome is the capital of the world and the foundation stone of the Christian faith and that all the cities of Italy are free. From this moment on we cause, declare, and proclaim that all the citizens of all the cities of Italy are citizens of Rome and enjoy the privilege of Roman liberty.'

For a while it seemed as though there might be a genuine revival of Roman greatness, that under this handsome and urgent young man, who had learned of Rome's grandeur by reading the inscriptions on the shattered monuments of the classical city, Italy itself might move in the direction, at least, of unity. Even so great a scholar as Francesco Petrarch was moved to recognise him. But power corrupted him and he was hacked down by his erstwhile followers on the Capitoline Hill.

The second occasion when Rome tried to revive its independence was in 1453 when a band of rebels, who had drunk deeply but not wisely of those humanist writings which extolled the classic past, hankered after a cloudy Golden Age when priests would again be subordinates, not masters, in the city. Their leader, a Roman aristocrat called Stefano Porcari, carried around a golden cord with which to bind the Pope after the Curia had been overthrown. But the papal grasp on Rome was by then too firm to be prized loose by a group of scholarly dissidents and the rebellion was put down bloodily. Thereafter, the history of Rome and the history of the Papacy are inextricably intertwined until they were forcibly pulled asunder in 1870.

The problems that faced the papal monarch were wholly different from those which faced any other ruler not merely in

Italy or in Europe, but on the planet. Unlike kings, popes came to the throne as old, frequently very old, men. Their reigns were consequently short. The volcanic Julius II who transformed Rome, destroyed Cesare Borgia, halted the French advance into Italy and even bound such a man as Michelangelo to him, ruled for just ten years. By contrast, the three European kings who began their reign at about the same time as he did, ruled for more than three times as long – Henry VIII of England for thirty-eight years, François I of France for thirty-two years and Charles V of Spain for forty years before his voluntary abdication.

As supreme pontiff, too, the pope had two distinct and often conflicting tasks. He had to run an international church whose components were inextricably linked with national politics and economics and, at the same time, he had to run one of the major Italian states. And he had to do all this without the family backing which every other monarch drew upon as a matter of course. In an ordinary monarchy, self-interest alone would usually ensure the loyalty of the heir for he would hesitate to erode the basis of a power which he would, some day, inherit. No such consideration inhibited the action of those immediately surrounding the papal monarch. An isolated, ageing man, fighting to survive in a court which was either indifferent or actively hostile to his well-being, he naturally turned to the sons of his sisters or brothers for support. The papal nephew ('nipote') was an inescapable product of a system which enjoined celibacy on its ruler. Many – probably the majority – of the nephews discharged a valuable and honourable role; it was those who did not who gave nepotism its undying taint of corruption. Viewed against the perspective of their brief tenure of office it becomes evident that most popes must have wrought miracles of organisation to achieve what they did. And viewed in the historical perspective of the long sequence of apostolic succession, the corrupt popes – the Borgia, the Cibo and the Della Rovere who were intent on benefiting their 'nephews' – are decidedly in the minority. But the frisson of scandal provided by the spectacle of a compulsorily celibate religious leader providing for his children ensures that it is their portraits that dominate.

Martin V, as a good Roman, began the task of restoring his native city. But that task was so enormous, his resources so limited, that relatively little was achieved beyond the refurbishing of some of the churches. In 1447, however, Tommaso Parentucelli was elected pope, took the style of Nicholas V, and set about changing the face of the medieval city.

He was born in Tuscany of poor parents – but was the same penniless monk whom Cosimo de' Medici had helped. 'You know what great kindness Cosimo de' Medici has done me in my time of need,' he told Vespasiano da Bisticci shortly after his accession. 'Well, I am going to reward him and tomorrow I shall make him my banker.' But if a Florentine banker benefited from Roman gold, Rome benefited infinitely more from Florentine ideas, for Nicholas had absorbed the new learning in the heady atmosphere of Florence itself. Financed by Cosimo, he had organised the priceless manuscript collection of Niccolò Niccoli, creating the Medici library. As pope, backed by the resources of the Papacy, and implicitly justified by the Church's role of guardian of learning, he threw himself into the congenial task of founding what was to become one of the world's greatest scholarly institutions, the Vatican Library. Even on his tours, undertaken as part of his duties as the Church's chief administrator, he was accompanied by an army of copyists; German and French for the most part for he had the Italian's suspicion of the Italian, 'Their spirits are too high: they get too big for their station.'

In the sixth year of his pontificate, in 1453, there occurred the long-awaited catastrophe when Constantinople at last fell to the beseiging Turk. As pope and as European potentate Nicholas was appalled: as bibliophile he hastened to benefit from it, dispatching his agents to purchase the priceless Greek manuscripts, now ownerless or homeless after the death or flight of their owners. And, incidentally, he helped to create the legend that the Renaissance was 'caused' by the fall of Constantinople because it seeded Italy with the learning contained in those fugitive manuscripts.

'Greece did not perish,' a grateful scholar later recorded, 'but owing to the liberality of a pope was removed to Italy which once in antiquity was called Magna Graecia.' The Italians viewed the newcomers with decidedly mixed feelings. On the one hand as possessor of that priceless key to the past, the Greek language, they were to be admired, envied and emulated. But they were also, for the most part, a singularly unappealing lot, bewildering their hosts with their passionate squabbling about hairbreadth interpretation of doctrine, indifferent or contemptuous of the new spirit abroad, as hidebound and limited as any medieval pedant. Western scholars were by no means unfamiliar with the treasures they brought for Greek authors had been known to have been translated by the scholars of Islam. At least one western writer, the French monk Gossuin, was convinced that Plato and Aristotle were 'Sarasains'. But the entire corpus of Greek literature was now available in its original language, not simply an arbitrary section that had passed through the filter of Arabic, and it was available at precisely that point of time when the West was both hungry for it, and capable of using it. It was as though the Greeks had brought the dough for the Italians, with their restless, speculative minds, to provide the yeast.

Nicholas V was a slightly built small man, pale from endless study, simple in manner and habits so that he donned the gorgeous robes of his office with the greatest reluctance. He was, nevertheless, possessed of an iron will and 'he expected to be understood by the beck', as Vespasiano da Bisticci put it, 'so assiduous was he in regard to all the matter in hand'. And the matter in hand closest to his heart, taking precedence even over the collection of manuscripts, was the restoration of Rome. It was not so much the buried city of the Caesars that interested him – on the contrary, in one year alone he authorised the removal of 2,500 cartloads of irreplaceable material from the Colosseum to act as foundations for his new buildings. It was, rather, the Rome of the Age of Faith, whose huge but now shabby churches were a standing reproach, that aroused his solicitude. All Rome eventually was to benefit, but his most grandiloquent plans were reserved for the powerhouse of the Faith – the Leonine City on the Vatican Hill.

When the Emperor Aurelian enclosed Rome in immense walls in the third century AD he did not trouble to extend their protection across the river to the Vatican Hill, for the area was desolate and used mainly as a cemetery. Somewhere among the tombs, however, was the modest grave of St Peter and it was upon the site of that grave that the first great basilica of St Peter was built, supposedly by Constantine himself, with the high altar directly above the tomb. In the year 852 Pope Leo IV enclosed the area in its own circuit of walls and it took his own name, the Leonine City. The walls, over forty feet in height, swept up from the Tiber to the crest of the Vatican Hill and down again to join the river further downstream. The key to the Leonine City was the Mausoleum of Hadrian. Built originally as a tomb, the enormous circular building stood on the Vatican side of the river, and its size and strength ensured that it would be turned into a fortress. By the tenth century, its name and origins were forgotten and the Romans now knew it as the Castello Sant' Angelo, for legend had it that the Archangel Michael had once appeared on its summit.

In the sixth century, administrative buildings had begun to appear around the basilica of St Peter, the nucleus of the later enormous Vatican Palace. But for over half the recorded existence of the Roman Church, from the early years of the fourth century to the late fourteenth, the home of the Papacy was not in the Vatican but in the Lateran Palace on the other side of the city. This palace – the magnificent private home of a wealthy Roman family, the Laterani – came into the possession of the Emperor Constantine who after his conversion gave it to the bishops of Rome to be used as their residence in perpetuity. During one of the many tumults that took place in the fourteenth century during the absence of the Papacy, the palace was burnt and by the time the Papacy returned to Rome, the logical place to make its home was in the fast-growing locality around the tomb of St Peter. It was this complex that Nicholas planned to turn into the largest palace-fortress on earth. His plans were on an altogether pharaonic scale; contemporaries said that it would have been impossible for even a bird to enter it without the Pope's permission. If he had succeeded in his purpose, he would probably have altered the later history of Rome, for the popes, instead of being part of the hurly-burly of civic life would have been secure and remote in their immense fastness. It would have required a lifetime to have executed the plans, and Nicholas's pontificate lasted barely eight years. But he achieved miracles of construction and destruction even in that short period. Platina, the librarian who served his successor and wrote a brisk series of

Lives of the Popes, was filled with admiration. After recounting his energetic work in the City itself, Platina goes on: 'In the Vatican he built those apartments of the Pontiff which are to be seen to this day. And he began the wall of the Vatican, great and high, with its incredible depth of foundation and high towers, to hold the enemy at a distance. He also began the tribune of the Church of St Peter, that the Church might hold more people and might be more magnificent.' In that casual, throw-away remark, Platina describes the beginnings of one of the greatest acts of vandalism in history – and one which, by an irony of history, was to be the immediate cause of the sundering of that Faith whose unity it was designed to enshrine. It was Nicholas V, the passionate lover of antiquity, who decreed the destruction of the 1,200-year-old Basilica of St Peter; half a century later Leo X approved the sale of indulgences in order to pay for its splendid successor.

Nicholas summed up in his personality the dichotomy at the heart of the Renaissance papacy. He was personally austere, personally simple. Vespasiano da Bisticci has a description of him that possesses all the vivid clarity and charm of an illumination. It was just after Nicholas had been elected and Vespasiano had been summoned to wait upon his old friend, now Vicar of Christ on earth. 'According to custom I kissed his feet. Afterwards he bade me rise and rising himself from the seat, dismissed the court. He then went to a private room where twenty candles were burning, near a door which opened into an orchard. He made a sign that they should be taken away and when we were alone began to laugh and said, "Do the Florentines believe, Vespasiano, that it is for the confusion of the proud that a priest only fit to ring a bell should be made Supreme Pontiff..."' But the same little man who delighted to stroll in the gloaming with an old friend, laughing at himself and talking about old times, that same man it was who ordered that another circlet be added to the double crown of the popes, creating the triple tiara as a sign of lordship over all created things. His death-bed speech was a model of modest piety; but in life, when crowning Frederick III, the last Holy Roman Emperor ever to be crowned in Rome, he had insisted upon and received the most abject reverences from the man on whose head he had placed the

crown of empire. Under Nicholas V the papacy blazed forth in
temporal splendour – but the bill for that splendour was to be
presented by a German monk half a century later.

Nicholas's election proved to be a breakthrough for the new
learning. There was a temporary hiatus with his successor,
Calixtus III, a dour, sour Spaniard who was shocked by the
godless waste of money on manuscripts and architecture and
drove the thronging artists and scholars from the court. But
Calixtus's reign was brief and the man who then picked up the
burden of office was cast in almost the same mould as Nicholas.
Almost, but not quite, for Aeneas Sylvius Piccolomini possessed
all the talents except that of being really serious about anything.
In appearance, he looked like a peasant, and a not particularly
intelligent peasant at that – a burly man with a heavy, impassive
face. In fact he was a member of a noble, but impoverished
Sienese family and was possessed of one of the quickest, lightest,
most charming minds of his day. He was one of those men whom
scholarship had rescued from some dull career: he had become
private secretary to a high-ranking prelate and travelled widely
through Germany and Britain, fathering at least one child on the
way for he was a passionate admirer of women. But in truth, he
was a passionate admirer of every manifestation of life: he loved
travelling; he loved talking; he loved the world of nature and in
this he was very considerably ahead of his time for most of his
contemporaries simply disregarded that aspect of nature that
could not be hunted or eaten. Books poured from him, not only
the solemn, sober treatises expected from a humanist scholar but
also light-hearted essays, children's stories, histories, travels. He
was forty-one years old before, reluctantly, he took Holy Orders
to ensure his advancement and was just fifty-three when he
became pope.

Characteristically, it is through him that posterity gains the
first real glimpse of what went on in a conclave, the very human
wheeling and dealing through which the will of the Holy Ghost is
finally made manifest. He described it at length in his *Commentaries*, a species of diary written in the third person, openly
modelled on the Commentaries of Caesar and displaying a vanity
which, though colossal, oddly enough does not repel the reader,
so open and almost childish it is. Vividly he portrayed the

claustrophobic atmosphere in which a group of men, each in pursuit of a separate goal, try to come to a common decision. The voting had gone in favour of the Frenchman, Estouteville. 'A number of cardinals, seeking a private place, met in the latrines and agreed together that they should elect Estouteville pope. Relying on them, he straightaway began promising priesthoods, magistracies and offices ... A worthy setting for the choice of such a pope.' He goes off to try and drum up support for himself, and finds the young Spanish Cardinal, Rodrigo Borgia, sitting pensively in his cell. Borgia says that he intends to vote for Estouteville: 'What would you have me do? Many of the cardinals have met in the latrines and decided to elect him. It is not to my advantage to remain with a small minority out of favour with the new pope.' Piccolomini exploded, 'You young fool! Will you then put an enemy of your nation in the Apostle's chair? And will you put more faith in a man who is faithless? Will a Frenchman be more friendly to a Frenchman or to a Catalan? Take care, you inexperienced boy? Take care, you fool.' His homily in fact persuaded the young man to change his mind and it is largely as a result of that change that Piccolomini emerged as pope, taking the name of Pius.

'Forget Aeneas, welcome Pius,' he pleaded with his old friends and with that engaging habit of self-mockery which went side by side with his vanity, he scribbled a piece of doggerel:

> Quando ero Enea
> Nessuno mi volea
> Ora che son' Pio
> Tutti mi dicono Zio

(When I was just Aeneas nobody wanted to know me; Now I am Pope Pius, everybody wants to call me Uncle.)

As was to be expected from a pope, he lavished patronage upon his birthplace, the little village of Corsignano not far from Siena. He raised it to the status of a city, commissioned the architect Rosellino to build a cathedral and a bishop's palace for it, urged his cardinals to build their own palaces there, for he intended it to be another home for the Curia, and called it Pienza, immortalising – or hoping to immortalise – his pontifical name.

Pienza: Piazza Pius II

His vaunting plans for the little hill village is one of the most vivid illustrations of the passionate Italian attachment to a locality, that genius loci which the Romans themselves were the first to identify and define. Pienza, on its hilltop 1,500 feet above sea level and well off the highway between Siena and Rome, could obviously have little future as an administrative centre. The cardinals made half-hearted plans to follow their pope's lead, but as soon as he died they forgot them with relief, and Pienza went back to the quiet obscurity it had known as Corsignano, a monument to ill-directed local patriotism.

'Forget Aeneas: welcome Pius.' He meant what he said and it was, perhaps, in atonement for past frivolity that he, quintessentially a pope of the Renaissance, should adopt that most sterile of medieval objectives – the Crusade. Admittedly, emphasis had changed since the eleventh century when Christian knights had carved out their brief-lived Latin kingdom in the Middle East.

Departure of Pius II for Basilea: detail from a mural in the Cathedral Library at Siena by Pinturicchio

Since the fall of Constantinople, five years before Pius's election, it was not simply a question of regaining the Holy Places but of doing something to stem the remorseless northward advance of Islam. Even so, Pius's desperate campaign to stir the nations of the west to a realisation of their danger met only yawns and polite attention. Europe was already forgetting the ancient lure of the east, preoccupied with its own affairs or beginning to speculate as to what lay to the west, beyond the rolling grey waters of the Atlantic. Pius was able to stir only two other European rulers, the Duke of Burgundy from some antique notion of honour, and the Doge of Venice, moved by very modern notions of commercial value, old men both of them. That did not deter Pius. 'We shall be three old men, and our trinity will be aided by the Trinity of Heaven.' He was papal monarch and an urgent and eloquent man, and in his travels around Italy he was able to fire a sufficient number to provide at least the nucleus of a crusading army and the Doge of Venice agreed that, if this somewhat motley army would assemble at Ancona, a Venetian fleet would carry them off to the war. Pius planned to accompany his Crusade, despite his age and the increasing physical debility of the illness that would kill him. 'We do not go to fight but to pray. We will stand on the prow of our ship, or upon some hill and with the Holy Eucharist before your eyes, we will ask from our Lord victory for our soldiers.' He travelled painfully to Ancona and there discovered the hollowness of Venetian promises and, before he died, must have become aware that the world had changed. Tradition has him standing on the headland looking out to sea, waiting at first hopeful, then with increasing despair, for the Venetian fleet. The Crusaders lost heart and began to melt away and it probably broke his heart for he never left Ancona but died there in 1464.

Pius had been an essentially innocent, an essentially 'decent' man and his death marked a moment of real change in the Papacy. The new learning was not necessarily everywhere a universal good. It had dissolved much of the medieval heritage that had been sterile and frozen and limited. But it had dissolved, too, an ancient pattern of morality which had helped shape the Papacy. Among the scores of popes that had occupied the Throne of St Peter there had been evil men and weak men as well as honourable men and saintly men. But in the main, their concern had been for the aggrandisement of their office, not their person. In the thirteenth century Innocent III had as goal the subjugation of all the world to the Roman Papacy; in the fifteenth century Innocent VIII had as goal the successful marriage of his son –

significantly, it was the same pope who first dropped the polite fiction of the papal 'nephew' and openly acknowledged his depraved young son, Franceschetto.

The freedom which in Florence produced the Medici, in Rome produced the Borgia because Rome had no tradition of debate. There never had been a Roman middle class to act as buffer between plebs and nobles, to absorb what was best from each and reject what was malignant to the corporate good. From the days of the Caesars onwards, Rome was a city of parasites; when it became the Holy City of western Christendom, the parasites merely changed their objectives. With the establishment of the Papacy as a major continental power, the parasites had rich pickings supplying the wants of both an expanding ecclesiastical court, and the envoys and ambassadors and their hundreds of followers who, perforce, had to come to Rome in order to negotiate with the only supra-national power on the continent. As late as the seventeenth century a Venetian ambassador, Luigi Mocenigo, noted that, 'Almost all the native-born inhabitants of Rome are without a trade, whence almost all live in poverty – for which reason the women mostly sell their honour easily and that of their young daughters. The dishonour is, for the most part, the result of need,' he added charitably. A society which was, in effect, split in two with a small, immensely wealthy and powerful clique at the top, and a vast mass of people whose major talents lay in wheedling or in corporate violence would almost inevitably develop into the Rome of the High Renaissance, all glitter without, all corruption within.

It was in the reign of Pius's successor that the change of direction became pronounced. Pietro Barbo, a wealthy and remarkably good-looking Venetian, wanted to take the name of Formosus (Handsome) when he was elected pope but when the shocked cardinals objected, settled for Paul after the great architect of Christianity. As cardinal, he built one of the biggest private palaces in Rome, the Palazzo Venezia, plundering the Colosseum of its stone to do so, and filling it with treasures. A strong-minded, sardonic dilettante who slept during the day and worked at night, whose greatest delight was to sit for hours fingering his collection of gems, it is arguable that Paul II was only formally a Christian. But only arguable, for his character as bequeathed to posterity has been thoroughly blackened by the papal librarian and biographer, Platina, a classic example of the power of a vengeful humanist. According to Platina, 'When Pius was dead and Paul created in his place, he proceeded to dismiss all the officials elected by Pius, on the grounds that they were useless and ignorant and deprived them of their dignity and revenues without permitting them to say a word in their defence.' Still according to Platina he and a deputation of humanists visited the pope to protest, were bawled out, were then unwise enough to threaten him with an appeal to a Council, whereupon all were arrested and imprisoned, Platina in particular being subjected to torture.

Although Paul doubtless was an unpleasant, bullying autocrat, it is not too difficult to read between the lines of Platina's carefully polished account to see an admittedly unsympathetic character energetically rooting out what he honestly believed to be a nest of traitors, heretics and hangers-on, all battening on to the Curia because they could claim an acquaintance with a dead language. Undoubtedly Rome was a magnetic attraction for any hungry pedant who could put together a few pages of Ciceronian Latin or declaim on Plutarch or Plato. Like helped like, and the corridors of the Chancery were full of bustling men whose scholarly skills and output of work did not bear too close an investigation.

But the scholars who occupied the higher levels of the Chancery, or enjoyed the extramural patronage of 'enlightened' popes were, for such a man as Paul, far more dangerous. These learned rebels with their taste for antiquarian research, burrowed down into the very roots of society, questioning values which had always been taken for granted. One of the first of them, Lorenzo Valla, had exploded the mine that had lain under the Papacy for over 800 years when he conclusively proved that the Donation of Constantine was an impudent forgery. The Papacy was far too firmly entrenched in its temporal position to experience anything more than mild embarrassment at this disclosure, and Pope Nicholas had even encouraged the man, employing him as a translator of Thucydides. Valla, at least, had been a good Christian – but what, Paul might well have wondered, was one to make of such a man as Pomponius Laetus.

He had been christened Julius but so infatuated was he with all things classical that he had rejected his baptismal name in favour of the orotund Pomponius. And, it was creditably rumoured, as well as his baptismal name he had rejected baptism and wandered about Rome preaching the virtues of paganism. So passionately fond was he of that long-dead world that he literally haunted the cemeteries, poking around for inscriptions and on more than one occasion was taken for a ghost. A great scholar undoubtedly, he lived solely for learning: at dawn he could be seen, unkempt, shabbily dressed, carrying a lantern for the first of the lectures that would draw hundreds of students. That was the danger of these 'humanists' from the point of view of a traditionalist: they were an infection in the social body, spreading their pernicious doctrines through society. Even Platina, who earned his bread in the Curia, had affected a Roman name in place of the sober Italian name, Sacchi of Piadena, that had been his father's. Others followed the self-conscious custom: Buonoaccorsi, a good, solid Tuscan name became Callimachus Experiens; perversely, the Roman Marcus took the Greek name Asklepiades; others flaunted the style of Glaucus, Volscus, Petreius. They met in Pomponius's house on the Quirinal, calling themselves the Roman Academy and plotting mischief, Paul was convinced. Had he not seen, personally, a letter which Pomponius addressed to Platina – that papal official – as Pater Sanctissimus? Humanist affectation, or straw in the wind, to use a name by custom reserved to the Holy Father himself? Who was to say? Pope Paul II took no chances and threw all of them into Sant' Angelo castle and prison. The Angel knew how to tame the spirit of the most haughty. Later, after Paul was conveniently dead, Platina was to boast how Pomponius defied the Inquisition, tying them up with his witty ripostes. The truth was less gallant than that: after a few weeks in the dreadful dungeons of Sant' Angelo, Pomponius was only too eager to exculpate himself, to blame others, to do anything that would take him into the open air. He was freed after the trial, but Platina was doomed to remain nearly two years in gaol before Paul's rage was abated.

With Paul's successor, Sixtus, the Papacy began its plunge to those depths of moral degradation that marked its Renaissance period, while simultaneously Rome began its climb to the summit of the greatest splendour it had known since the days of Augustus. The two phenomena were closely linked, for both were the product of the personality of Francesco della Rovere who became pope in 1471 and adopted the style of Sixtus IV. With Sixtus, nepotism became a policy of state: three of his eleven nephews became cardinals – Girolamo and Giuliano della Rovere and Pietro Riario – while Pietro's brother became lord of one of the papal cities. The doting, insensate favouritism which Sixtus lavished on Pietro Riario gave rise to the strong suspicion that their relationship was rather closer than that of uncle and nephew. The 25-year-old monk who, until his supposed uncle's election, had not a penny to his name, suddenly had an income of 60,000 gold florins derived from his offices as Patriarch of Constantinople, Archbishop of Seville, of Florence, of Mende. Enormous wealth, and the sensation of unlimited power as parasites grovelled for his attention, turned the young man's head. He threw himself into a career of self-indulgence, amassing debts of nearly a quarter of a million florins in a little over two years. Not surprisingly he killed himself with excess, dying two years after being elevated to cardinal. Sixtus wept, then sought another member of the family upon which to lavish his love. Curiously, he ignored the dignified young man standing beside him, that Giuliano della Rovere who, a few years hence, would be one of the greatest of all popes and, instead, his eye fell on the other Riario brother, Girolamo, a crude young man of limitless appetites and limited intelligence. He found a bride for him – Caterina, the illegitimate daughter of the great Sforza duke of Milan. He installed him in a city-state of his own – Forli, carved out of the States of the Church: he cherished and pampered him and even, when it seemed that the Medici were getting in the way of young Girolamo, he entered a plot to have them assassinated even though Lorenzo was his banker...

But at the same time, he devoted himself to the task of rebuilding Rome. He threw a much needed bridge over the Tiber, repaired the great Cloaca Maxima so that Rome's sewage was again swept away. He restored the aqueducts so that for the first time in many centuries the cold, sweet water that nourished Rome was carried to the tops of the hills. Then having purged and cleansed the city's arteries he began to build. King Ferrante of Naples gave him a useful lesson in town planning. As the chronicler Infessura described it, 'He went all over Rome to see the great buildings ... And when he had seen all these things, he turned back and talking to Pope Sixtus said that he (the pope) could never be lord of the place, nor ever truly reign over it, because of the porticoes and balconies which were in the streets. If ever it were necessary to put men-at-arms in possession of Rome, the women in the balconies, with small bombs, could make them fly. And nothing could be easier than to make barricades in the narrow streets. And he advised him to clear away the balconies and the porticoes and to widen the streets, under pretence of improving and embellishing the city.' Ferrante, a ferocious king and a skilled survivor, knew what he was talking about on the subject of repressing a population and Sixtus followed his advice, doing for Rome what Haussmann would do for Paris – and for the same reason – three centuries later.

In his own palace, the Vatican, Sixtus built a large and somewhat gloomy chapel whose prime purpose was to allow a conclave to be held in relative safety. His Sistine Chapel was in two main sections: the upper was decorated by some of the leading artists of the day – Perugino, Botticelli, Ghirlandaio, Rosselli and Pinturicchio, drawn to Rome like so many before and after by the promise of gold and creating what, it seems, the Romans were totally unable to create themselves. They painted their 'stories' upon the walls in ten great murals. The ceiling of the chapel was painted, when it was consecrated in 1483, by a certain Pier Matteo d'Amelia, who decorated it simply with gold stars: his work would last barely thirty years before being superseded by Michelangelo's work.

The floor beneath the chapel was to be the new library. The lust for power had not wholly eroded the love of learning which had carried Sixtus so far up the ladder and his re-establishment of the Vatican library was probably his most important single contribution to the new learning. He was tolerant enough – or confident enough – to reinstate Platina as librarian and the painting which he commissioned Melozzo da Forli to commemorate the occasion echoes every aspect of the man's violently contradictory nature, so that it becomes a species of leitmotif of the Renaissance papacy, to be echoed again and again.

TEMPLA DOMVM EXPOSITIS·VICOS·FORA·MOENIA·PONTES·
VIRGINEAM TRIVII QVOD REPARARIS AQVAM·
PRISCA LICET NAVTIS STATVAS DARE COMMODA PORTVS·
ET VATICANVM CINGERE SIXTE IVGVM·
PIVS TAMEN VRBS DEBET·NAM QVAE SQVALORE LATEBAT·
CERNITVR IN CELEBRI BIBLIOTHECA LOCO·

Sixtus IV gives audience to Platina: by Melozzo da Forli

It is, essentially, a family portrait. The pope is seated in an informal but splendid chair, his hands firmly grasping the great gilt knobs, looking at the group before him with a somewhat brooding expression. Standing beside him is Cardinal Pietro Riario, and it almost seems as though the artist is determined to emphasise the very close blood relationship for the old man and the young are both in profile and the Cardinal's heavy, fleshy face with its contemptuous expression could come from no other mould but that of the pope's. Immediately facing Sixtus is the nephew for whom he had no particular liking – Giuliano della Rovere – a remote figure whose strong, handsome face disassociates him from his relatives. Kneeling is Platina, a grey-haired, keen-faced man pointing at the plaque recording the establishment of the library and immediately behind him is the other Riario brother, Count Girolamo, with the petulant, arrogant expression so clearly drawn from life. The family and their scholarly retainer is set as a group in one of the splendid, recently painted halls of the Vatican but, eerily, none of the six figures is aware of any of the others. Each stands brooding in his own capsule of space and time, sheltered physically by the same golden roof of the Vatican but, individually, eternally alone.

Sixtus made a determined attempt to turn the Papacy into a family corporation, promoting his nephews to positions of power regardless of their merit. His successor Innocent VIII carried the process a stage further by celebrating the marriage of his son and granddaughter actually in the Vatican. But it is Innocent's successor, Rodrigo Borgia, who took the name of Alexander VI, who provides material for the archetypal legend of the Renaissance Papacy. Born in Jativa, Spain, in 1431, he was summoned to Rome in or about 1455 by his uncle, Calixtus III. He rose rapidly and high in the Curia, and gained a reputation as a hard-working, competent man. A papal official gives a very favourable portrait of him at the time of his election in 1492. 'It is

Alexander VI (Rodrigo Borgia) worshipping Christ: detail from a mural by Pinturicchio

now thirty-seven years since his uncle Calixtus III made him a cardinal and during that time he never once missed a Consistory, except when prevented by illness and that was most rare. Throughout the reigns of Pius II, Paul II, Sixtus IV and Innocent VIII he was at the centre of affairs. Few understood etiquette as he did. He knew how to dominate, how to shine in conversation, how to appear dignified. Majestic in stature, he had the advantage over lesser men. He was just at that age, sixty, at which Aristotle says men are wisest. He was robust in body and vigorous in mind and so was perfectly suited to his new position.'

Apart from the result of transient affairs, Borgia had two families. History has largely ignored the first, to concentrate upon the second. This consisted of three males and one female. Juan, the second son, was a bragging bully who was probably murdered by the oldest, Cesare. Cesare survived his father's death in 1503 by four years, escaping to Spain where he was killed, in an obscure mercenary skirmish, at the age of thirty-two. The third son, Joffre, was a nonentity who was married off to the illegitimate daughter of the King of Naples. The daughter, Lucrezia, after various adventures became Duchess of Ferrara where she died,[15] aged thirty-nine, in 1519.

Lord Acton's resounding dictum that 'the Borgia are beyond hope of rehabilitation' has now entered the canon of Renaissance history. But it only answers part of the question, only tells part of the story. The really intriguing question is: Why did this family achieve its fantastic reputation both in their own day and for posterity? For fantastic it is. That famous Borgia poison, for example, supposedly capable of striking down at the moment required perhaps days or weeks ahead, belongs strictly to the realm of mythology. The Italian mind was fascinated by this devious, secretive means of murder and every death not obviously attributable to natural causes or obvious violence was immediately assumed to be poison. But the Borgia had access to no other form of poison more lethal than the crude preparation of arsenic generally available. Cesare, the true murderer in the family, preferred the more certain methods of stiletto or garrotte.

In terms of personal morals Alexander, the father of the brood, was scarcely the ideal Holy Father. But it is difficult to see in what manner he really differed from other morally degenerate popes: from Innocent VIII who married his family in the Vatican; from Sixtus IV who ran the Papacy like a family business, even launching a war and arranging an assassination to establish his nephew Girolamo Riario in the Romagna; from Innocent X who allowed his appalling sister-in-law to take over the business of the Vatican. Viewed purely as an administrator, Alexander did well by the Curia. And, though the brutally efficient campaign that his son Cesare conducted in the Papal States undoubtedly had as objective the creation of a power-base for that son, one of its by-products was the chastening of a turbulent province, subjecting it to a discipline from which Alexander's successor would benefit.

The probability is that the family's reputation suffered from the fact that they were foreign, and that they were successful. Xenophobia has never been an Italian characteristic – except during the Spanish invasions. Italians managed to establish a modus vivendi with most of the swarms of the foreigners who, for one pretext or another, settled in Italy – except with the Spaniards. People from the harshest, most austere of European countries perhaps inevitably despised a people from the most voluptuous, most civilised – a compliment which was heartily returned. The Borgia were Spanish from beginning to end: they spoke Spanish among themselves, dressed like Spaniards, ate Spanish food and fought with the devastatingly successful Spanish weapons and tactics. And they were successful. Cesare and his father, whatever their private opinions of each other, worked together as a highly efficient team using Spaniards as their tools – men who, aware of the bitter hostility around them, closed ranks to advance their compatriots' interest. As, one by one, the little princelings fell to this utterly ruthless efficiency, so the legend grew as defeated men sought to explain and excuse their defeat. The charge of incest, for example, sprang directly from such a cause. With considerable skill Alexander had brought about Lucrezia's divorce from her first husband, Giovanni Sforza, using as pretext the completely false accusation that Sforza was impotent. Humiliated, enraged, defeated, the wretched young man blurted out that the reason why Alexander wanted his daughter divorced was in order that he could enjoy her himself. It was a demonstrably ludicrous charge for Lucrezia was immediately married off to her second husband. However, when that second husband was, in due course, murdered by Cesare and Lucrezia was betrothed to the heir of the powerful Duke of Ferrara, that whispered charge was brought out into the open as a useful weapon by those who hoped to prevent the matrimonial alliance.

The growth of the Borgia legend was a classic example of the mythopoeic process. Accusations against the whole clan had only to be voiced in order to flourish, regardless of their inherent improbability or manifest inaccuracy. Years after Alexander's death the Florentine art historian, Giorgio Vasari, described how one of the murals in the Borgia Apartments of the Vatican showed Alexander worshipping his mistress under the guise of the Virgin Mary. The only portrait of Alexander in the Apartments shows him, quite unmistakably, worshipping the risen Christ, a fact which could be established by anyone troubling to enter the apartments. Nevertheless, the accusation was repeated, century after century, entering the received catalogue of Borgia crime.

It was Cesare Borgia's misfortune that Cardinal Giuliano della Rovere, who succeeded to the tiara as Julius II in 1503, should have a deep, personal and most bitter hatred for the Borgia stem. He spent the opening months of his pontificate dedicated to one objective, the total destruction of Cesare Borgia. Succeeding in that, he turned his attention to the chasing of the French out of Italy with the war cry, 'Out, out with the barbarians.' He succeeded in that, though only temporarily, and then turned to making Rome a fitting capital for the new majesty of the Roman Pontiff.

With Pope Julius II, both Rome and Papacy enter a Golden Age. The new pope had an appearance and character to equal his ambition. The good looks of his youth, as captured by Melozzo da Forli, had gone but the introspection remained and deepened, the white-bearded, powerful face when seen in repose resembled that of an Old Testament prophet. But periods of respose were rare; men felt they were in the presence of a briefly dormant volcano:

Julius II (Giuliano della Rovere) as a young man: detail from group portrait by Melozzo da Forli

Julius II by Raphael

He has not the patience to listen quietly to what you say to him, and to take men as he finds them. But those who know how to manage him, and whom he trusts, say his will is good. No one has any influence over him and he consults few or none ... It is almost impossible to describe how strong and violent he is and how difficult to manage. In body and soul he has the nature of a giant. Everything about him is on a magnified scale ... there is nothing in him that is small or meanly selfish.[16]

'Papa terribile' the Italians called him with their ear for a nickname, an 'awesome pope', as often to be seen in armour as in the soft vestments of a priest. He continued the work begun by Cesare Borgia, drawing the Papal States firmly under the control of the Papacy. In Rome, he followed the lead of Sixtus IV, placing his imprint upon the architecture of the city. Above all, it was he who gave the final impetus to the plan devised by Pope Nicholas V nearly half a century ago – the demolition of old St Peter's and the rebuilding of a new.

Work of demolition began in 1505. There was strong and indignant opposition both within and without the Curia, Michelangelo being particularly opposed to the scheme. Even Julius felt it necessary to defend and explain his action: the old basilica was in a dangerous condition and he was merely following proposals that had long been in the air. Despite the protests the measure went through and the oldest, largest, most sacred building in Christendom was knocked down as though it were a peasant's hovel. Demolition was to continue for nearly a century before the last traces of the 1,200-year-old building quite disappeared. In those first few months the most important part of the basilica disappeared in a fury of destruction that did not spare the very tombs of the popes. Donato Bramante, the great and sensitive architect whose design for the new building had nerved Julius to his decision, acted like some Goth or Vandal. Indeed, he went about his work of destruction with so passionate a dedication, so total an indifference to what he was destroying that he gained the nickname of 'Il Ruinante' – The Destroyer. Neither pope nor architect were ever to see the building which took its place. When Julius died in 1513, only the four great piers of the central crossing had been completed. Bramante himself died the following year; other men inherited the work, including

Old St Peter's, interior: mural from the Church of S. Martino ai Monti

Old St Peter's, exterior: detail from the Return of Gregory XI from Avignon by Vasari

*New St Peter's in course of construction. The rotunda of the new
basilica can be seen rising behind the façade of the old*

Raphael and Michelangelo, each modifying what had been
planned. Money ran short and in 1517, the reigning pope, Leo X,
conceived the idea of raising money by selling indulgences.
Among the sellers of these indulgences was the monk, Johann
Tetzel, whose activities came to the attention of the monk Martin
Luther.

The resurrection of Rome

In 1444, thirty years after Poggio Bracciolini had made his
threnody on the top of the Capitoline Hill, another immigrant,
Flavio Biondo of Forlì, provided the first archaeological survey
of the city in his *Roma instaurata*.

The Rome of the Caesars had not been forgotten during the
long centuries but it had retreated underground, literally and
figuratively. The memory of its political greatness was transformed into magical tales where fact and fiction, myth and
reality, Christian belief and pagan tales were mixed. Legends

The Colosseum as quarry by Silvestro da Ravenna

crowded like ghosts in every street, linked to the city's past by shattered marble columns, nameless porticoes, enigmatic fragments of statues each with its legend, distorting history. In the first decade of the Christian era – during the years of Augustan splendour – there had been a tremendous upsurge in building, culminating in the reign of Nero when vast, gleaming structures swallowed whole areas and streets. By the time that Poggio made his lamentation and Flavio began his painstaking pedestrian survey, all those countless tens of thousands of tons of marble had wholly disappeared. The modern visitor to Rome can gain some faint idea of the sheer level of destruction by visiting the Forum. Despite a century and more of careful reconstruction, an area that was once crowded and flanked with enormous public buildings, the very heart of an enormous empire, looks like a builder's yard littered with a few worn blocks of stone and fringed with cavernous brick ruins. Not until the aerial bombardments of the mid-twentieth century has a great city been so gutted. But though, over the centuries, Rome had indeed been put to the sack more than once, it was the Romans themselves who dismantled the classical city and that for the most humdrum of reasons. The marble of which the city had been built when burned, yields lime, which can be used for plaster. An entire profession of lime-burners (the Calcarii) developed whose stock-in-trade was the city itself, the scores of lime-kilns being fed by irreplaceable fragments of past glory. And what the Calcarii might have spared, the Marmorarii – the marble-cutters – claimed by slicing up priceless coloured marbles for their exquisite but destructive art of inlay.

Again and again over the centuries, emperors and popes issued draconic measures to halt the vandalism, although they were, themselves, the worst offenders. The process began at the very beginning of the Christian era when, under Constantine's benign gaze, the builders of his vast basilica of St Peter dismantled a number of ancient structures, taking what was required to hasten the structure of the new Christian temple, no matter how inappropriate it might be in its new context. Thereafter, every state visit of a Byzantine emperor to his titular city finished up as

A present day view of the Forum, Rome

a plundering expedition. The last of these took place in AD 663 when Constantius II, in a brief visit of twelve days carried off every bronze statue he could lay his hands on, and finished up by plundering the venerable Pantheon of its beautiful gilt-bronze tiles. The imperial edict of AD 425 decreeing that pagan temples could be used as Christian churches gave some protection to those that were so transformed, but the popes continued to regard Rome simply as a vast quarry from which conveniently cut stone could be obtained for their own building. Even Nicholas V, with his love of ancient Rome, hacked vast amounts of stone out of the Colosseum to act as foundation for his buildings in the Vatican. A few years later his successor, Paul II, renewed the onslaught on the Colosseum, extracting enough stone to build his impressive palace. No surviving building more clearly demonstrates the titanic scale upon which imperial Rome had been built than this Flavian amphitheatre, known popularly from its sheer size as the Colosseum. For century after century, Romans treated it as an accessible quarry – yet even in the twentieth century it remains the biggest single structure in central Rome.

But while the Romans themselves, or those in whose keeping Rome had been confided, continued their onslaught on the city, visitors began to look behind the substance seeking the form. It was, perhaps inevitably, two Florentines who first began to look at the ruins of Rome neither as a quarry nor as a gallery of sculpture but as the physical expression of a potent idea. Brunelleschi and Donatello came to Rome some time after 1401. Brunelleschi devoted the better part of twelve years to the study, clambering over the great ruins, burrowing deep into their foundations, measuring, sketching, finding out for himself just how it was that the Romans had been able to build their titanic buildings, roofing them over with domes bigger than had ever been built before or since. The citizens of Rome might, themselves, be a parasite but the city itself was a vast reservoir of ideas filled by the genius of half a dozen races. Brunelleschi was among those who had the patience and skill to tap that reservoir and what he took from it was to alter the face of his native city, Florence, years later.

Treasure hunters had long been aware that, some ten or fifteen feet below ground level, there lay the city of the Caesars. Every so often a householder, sinking a well or preparing foundations for an extension to his house, would bring up a pot of gold or silver coins or a small statue of precious metal. Sculptures in marble were, in the main, ignored except in so far as they provided material for the kilns. Lanciani, the Roman archaeologist, described one of these kilns he found in February 1883.[16]

That kiln could have been packed any time over a period of a thousand years or more. Only a disaster of some magnitude would have led its owners to abandon the result of so much work and the probability is that it was the sack of Rome of 1527 that inadvertently saved these particular sculptures. But even before that, marble statuary was beginning to acquire a monetary value as interest in antiquity increased and it was in quest of these new treasures that, sometime during the 1490s, the buried Golden House of Nero was discovered – a discovery which was to have a far-reaching effect on the revival of antiquity as an art form as well as an historical source.

The vast palace of Nero, near the Colosseum, had disappeared from human view partly as a result of deliberate demolition, partly from the action of time. In AD 104 Trajan levelled part of the site, filled in the lower floors and built his own enormous baths upon them and they were forgotten until the last decades of the fifteenth century. The treasure hunters found their way into the buried halls, choked up to three quarters of their height with rubbish; news spread, and exploring the buried house of Nero became a popular diversion for those who possessed good health and strong nerves. A Milanese visitor to Rome left a rhymed description of the perils and excitements of one of these subterranean expeditions. It was advisable to travel with a party and to take provision and to go with a guide. Torches were essential, and the writer described graphically how the advancing noise and chatter and lights disturbed the bats and owls and rats in their immemorial hiding place.

Among the many visitors was a little, wizened man, 'deaf and undersized, mean in person and appearance' as a contemporary contemptuously described him. He was the painter Pinturicchio, native of Perugia and now court artist to His Holiness Alexander VI, the Borgia pope who was energetically building a home for his family in the Vatican. Fashion rather than artistic sensitivity probably led Alexander to choose Pinturicchio for, at thirty-eight, the little man with the big head had emerged from the ranks of anonymous immigrant artists and was much in demand among the wealthy, more conservative patrons. Apart from his physical appearance, he had the misfortune to be married to a shrew and altogether passed as a figure of fun among the swaggering gallants of Rome. But it was this same stunted, hesitating, henpecked little man who explored the buried past and brought back, at considerable physical danger, a lost art. The walls of the Golden House were richly decorated with 'designs which are called by the ignorant "grotesques" because they were found in certain subterranean caverns (grotte) in Rome, the said caverns having been in ancient times bath houses, studies and the like', as Benvenuto Cellini later explained condescendingly. It was these paintings which fascinated Pinturicchio. He had no gift for words; he spoke with his brush and his brush traced on the new walls of Rome those designs he had seen upon the buried walls of Nero. Most of his work is conventional – that was why he earned good money, for his employers were mostly conventional men. Three of the four chambers he decorated for the Borgia pope are also conventional enough, but in the fourth and last chamber of the series, the one entitled 'Room of the Saints' after the dominant formal theme, it is as though he gathered all his confidence together and, in one great swirling act of creation, transmuted into his own idiom the essence of those long buried murals before which he had stood entranced, candle in hand, for so many hours. The 'Room of the Saints' gains its name from the legends of the saints which are depicted in formal frames but it might be better called the Shrine of the Bull. On the ceiling and in all the spaces between the paintings of the legends, the bull – the emblem of the Borgia – is repeated hundreds of times. Unequivocally, it is the Bull of Osiris and the smaller decorations that link this sacrificial animal together are the enigmatic monsters from the buried halls.

Although it was non-Romans who began the re-discovery of Rome's past, the passion for antiquarianism permeated Roman society. In other communities, the search for the past might be conducted as an intellectual enquiry; among Romans it became a

reaffirmation of their lost status, a device to conceal or compen-
sate for their present undeniably ignoble lot. The extraordinary
scenes that took place on the discovery of a young Roman
maiden's body in 1485 seem to owe more to religious emotion
than to achaeological interest. The body was discovered in a
sarcophagus in an astonishing state of preservation. It was
brought from its grave on the Via Appia to a public building
where men in their thousands passed by it to – what, adore? So it
would seem from the reaction of the reigning pope, Innocent
VIII, who, fearful of the possibility of a new heresy, ordered the
body to be moved and secretly re-buried. But whatever the cause
of the emotions generated by the discovery of this long-dead
Roman girl, it was a symbol. Romans were again aware of their
real, as opposed to their legendary, past.

4

The paradox of Venice

On 4 April 1423 Tommaso Mocenigo, Doge of Venice, lay
dying. As was the custom, he delivered – or was reported as
having delivered – a well-rounded speech to those who stood
about his bedside. Being a Venetian, however, his speech differed
in some surprising details from that normally given – or
supposed to have been given – by a dying man.

'Your city has, every day, some ten million ducats put out as
investment throughout the world: the profit which our traders
gain from this is four million ducats. Our housing is valued at
seven million ducats, the annual rental being 500,000. Some
3,000 merchant ships carry out our trade and they are protected
by 43 major warships and 300 smaller ones, manned by a total of
19,000 seamen. Our mint coins one million ducats each year...
If we go on as we are doing we will become masters of all the gold
in Christendom. The Florentines send us 16,000 pieces of cloth
each year, which we dispose of in the Barbary, Egypt, Syria,
Rhodes...'

So the torrent of figures pours on in one of the earliest
statistical summaries of the life of a great commercial and
industrial city. Mocenigo's speech is unlikely, for a dying man
could scarcely have managed the long periods and sustained
arguments. It may, perhaps, have been composed beforehand
and issued afterwards like any other political speech, or a core of
fact may have been embroidered. But however it was delivered, it
tells two profound things about the Venetian character: his love
of exact order as expressed by statistics and his near-deification
of the State so that it was not thought inappropriate to put an
accountant's summary into the mouth of a man taking his
farewell of the world.

But then, Venetians had always been a law unto themselves. Venice was an anomaly among Italian cities: she was not a daughter of Rome. She owed nothing to anybody except her own sturdy citizens who had built their improbable city with their own hands.

Sometime during the fifth century, when the rule of law was collapsing throughout Italy and the barbarians were sweeping down from the north, a group of people fleeing the invaders found refuge of a sort on a group of mud and sandbanks in the north-west corner of the Adriatic. The action of sea and rivers upon a flat coastline had carved and fretted out a wide but shallow bay or lagoon. A number of sandbanks had survived the action of water, 117 of them in all. Most were scattered around the lagoon but two of the largest – long narrow strips later to be known as Lido and Palestrina – acted as a kind of natural breakwater guarding the lagoon from the open sea. The first-comers established themselves on the northernmost of these strips, Lido, but gradually moved inward to settle upon the other islands – Murano, Torcello, Burano and the closely connected group known as Rialto.

Over the following decades other refugees followed. There was nothing on these drab little islands in their grey lagoon to tempt the cupidity of greedy, armed men. The jewelled cities of Italy lay defenceless before them: why bother about a handful of islands inhabited by poor but remarkably pugnacious fishermen? So, over the years, the refugees turned into a community. They hammered down wooden stakes into the mud and sand and built upon them and, by one of those strange quirks of history, the city they built upon those fragile foundations would prove physically more durable than that built upon the solid rock foundations of Rome. Close to hand were two easily obtained, but extremely valuable items – salt and fish. And with this stock in trade the inhabitants of the islands went out and built an empire. They traded first with their neighbours on the mainland – the 'terraferma' as they were to call it, as though speaking of a different order of earth, of reality. But gradually they extended their sphere of operations and interest eastward and southward, creating what they called the 'stato da mar', the state or empire of the sea. By the opening of the fifteenth century Venice owned, or

Plan of Venice attributed to Jacopo de' Barbari

Venice: details from the Nuremberg Chronicle 1496

controlled, most of Dalmatia, Corfu, the coasts of the Morea,
islands in the Aegean, and Crete. In the sixteenth century one of
her private citizens, Caterina Cornaro, through her marriage
was to become Queen of Cyprus, giving Venice a foothold on
that great Mediterranean stronghold. They had acquired,
absent-mindedly it seemed, Athens itself – though that provincial

town with its few thousand poor inhabitants had little value apart from its name.

Few cities show their physical origins so clearly, so unequivocally as does Venice – but fewer still retain in their citizens' characters, as well as in their laws, those impulses which founded it. This group of people living on lands eternally at the mercy of the sea had a dual characteristic: the need to co-operate and the desire for independence. A group of farmers scattered over a similar area can exist happily enough with no more than casual contact with each other. A group of fishermen need, again and again, to combine effectively against their common enemy, the sea. At the same time, because they were living on islets which though separated from each other by only a matter of yards were nevertheless separated by the living sea itself, such a people would have a passionate sense of individuality, of independence.

The major Venetian characteristic, therefore, was the ability to act almost instinctively as a group while yet retaining individuality. It was, in a sense, the same kind of characteristic that must prevail on any ship. And, just as the crew of a ship is divided into two, officers and men, so the population of Venice was rigidly divided into two, aristocrats and plebs. This people, who made a policy and a virtue of welcoming foreigners, among themselves practised the most rigid mutual exclusion for political purposes. But it worked.

'The constitution of Venice can be considered eminently successful for it endured 500 years, whereas the much admired constitution of the U.S.A. has not yet lasted 200' the American scholar, F. C. Lane,[17] noted in 1966. If the whole of Italy can be regarded as a laboratory where political combinations were endlessly permutated, Venice was the place where, by accident of time or place or personality or just plain luck, a durable combination was struck. 'Our commonwealth has attained that which none of the former hath, though otherwise honourable and famous for from the first beginning till this time of ours (c. 1520) it hath remained safe and free this thousand and two hundred years, not only from the domination of Strangers, but also from civil and intestine sedition of any moment or weight,' wrote the Venetian political theorist, Gasparo Contarini. It depends, of course, on how the term 'of any moment or weight' is interpreted and, during that long period of time calculated by Contarini, Venice was by no means free from all 'civil and intestine sedition'. But certainly the state was not only tranquil, compared with any other Italian political unit but it outlasted all the other free republics. The stability of the Venetian constitution gave rise to what has been termed, by Italians themselves, the 'myth of Venice', a myth so potent as to influence people centuries in the future and thousands of miles distant.[18] Even Florence in the crisis of 1494 after the expulsion of the Medici, looked to the Venetian constitution as a possible alternative to her own restless experiments.

The Venetians accepted what appears to be an inalienable factor in human society – that that society is pyramidal in shape, and the apex must be occupied. They devised a system which, in the idiom of the day, combined the rule of the One, the Few, and the Many – the monarch (doge), the nobility (the patriciate) and the plebs. In practice, it contained only two of those elements, the doge and the patriciate, and the power of the former was very firmly under the control of the latter.

The patriciate was limited to those who could sit in the Grand Council. In 1315, the famous Golden Book of the Nobility totally and permanently disfranchised all who were not regis-téred within its pages – in other words, only those whose ancestors had sat in the Grand Council since 1176 were recognised as full citizens. Historians have disagreed as to the exact significance of the Serrata, or 'closing' of the Grand Council. There was certainly a relaxation in 1381 when a number of families were admitted, and there are indications that the numbers were topped up from time to time as families died out. But whatever the social subtleties, the political fact was that power had passed finally into the hands of some 2,000 adult males out of a population of 120,000. Not the least remarkable aspect of this transition was the passive manner in which it was accepted by the populace as a whole. Even Contarini thought it 'a matter surely strange and scarcely credible, that the people being so many years deprived of the publique governement, did never yet refuse nor unwillingly support the government of the nobilitie, neither yet did ever attempt any thing whereby the form of the common-wealth might be altered, but have always hetherto faithfully loved and willingly obeyed the Nobilitie'. Contarini provides a clue to that apparent passivity: the ordinary people, he thought, were content to be excluded from political power for they were provided with ample opportunities to run the great non-political institutions, such as the guilds and the charities known as the Scuole Grande, which were a feature of Venetian society.

The Grand Council was far too unwieldy in size to practise daily government, and a body – the Senate – was therefore chosen from the Council. Composed of something between 200 and 300 members it was, for all practical purposes, the Government of Venice. 'The whole manner of the commonwealth government belongeth to the Senate,' Contarini said firmly. 'That which the Senate determineth is held for ratified and inviolable.' It was the Senate who appointed ambassadors and created the cabinet, known as the Collegio, which in its turn set up a number of what might be termed ministries under Savii or 'wise men'. The Doge, with his six Ducal Councillors, was a member of the Collegio.

Parallel to this organisation was the body which, more than any other of Venice's political institutions, has attracted the attention of posterity – the Council of Ten. It came into being to counter a conspiracy in 1310 and was, quite simply, a committee of public safety. The consideration regarding exactly how, and where, this somewhat sinister body fitted into the Venetian system exercised Venice's friends and gave ammunition to her enemies. Its members were chosen from the Senate by the Grand Council and so, to that extent, the Council of Ten was under control. But its operations were in secret, its powers extended into every department of government and it would not be an exaggeration to regard it as the KGB of its day.

Although the totality of political power was in the hands of a minority of noblemen, the Venetian nobleman differed from all others of his class in Italy, and from most outside. By no means all Venetian noblemen were wealthy: on the contrary, special charitable provisions were made for a class recognised as being composed of 'poor nobles'. The Venetian nobleman was neither a parasite nor a sword-wielding bully, but a hard worker. Far from his disdaining trade, it was reserved for his class – though in general it was expected that a Venetian nobleman would deal either in bulk, or in valuables. It was he who officered the State's galleys and who took his turn at the tedious minor offices of government.

The young nobleman's progress through the various levels of Government followed a fairly standard pattern. He might begin by being elected a Savio ai Ordini, responsible for the coming and going of the sea-going convoys. A more responsible post would be membership of the Quarantia al Criminal, the chief criminal court. One of the vital but unattractive offices of this court was the splendidly named Lord of the Night (Signore di Notte) in charge of the nightly police patrols. The young man could, in due course, become an ambassador, a ducal councillor and, ultimately, Doge.

Of all the remarkable institutions of Venice the office of Doge was the most astonishing. As early as 1303 the Tuscan constitutional theorist, Tolomeo of Lucca, praised the Venetian system, remarking that, 'In the regions which are today called Lombardy no one has been able to hold office for life, other than by tyranny, except the Doge of Venice. He, however, has a limited power.' The Venetians anticipated the nineteenth-century concept of constitutional monarchy by over 500 years, creating a ceremonial figure who ruled with great splendour for life, in whose name laws were transacted, who had very considerable influence but whose power and actions were subjected to the minutest, most suspicious scrutiny.

The shaping of the dogeship was a long, painful and delicate process. In the beginning, as with all other monarchical rulers, the Doges had aimed for power to go with their ceremony. Some had succeeded in the early years but, as the centuries went by and the community grew ever more certain of itself, so the Venetians began to trim back the power of their titular head. The battle showed clearly in the grim statistics of the dogeship: by the early fifteenth century seven Doges had been assassinated, one beheaded, twelve abdicated under pressure, two deposed. The Venetian technique for electing a Doge consisted of a complex process of alternating lotteries and nominations. At a special ceremony in the basilica of San Marco a young boy, chosen at random from the congregation, took thirty names from a golden

Francesco Foscari: portrait by Giovanni Bellini

urn. These thirty were reduced to nine by lot who in their turn chose forty – who were reduced to twelve ... the process continuing until an electoral college emerged who finally chose the Doge. Yet even this system was capable of manipulation and the Ten were utterly merciless in their reaction against any suspected of monarchical ambitions, as the story of Francesco Foscari demonstrated.

The tragedy of Foscari and his son Jacopo – 'the two Foscari' – is one of the great set pieces of Venetian history. Its dramatic content was powerful enough to attract a poet of Byron's status: its inherent contradictions has attracted the attention of generation after generation of constitutional historians, and the sheer vulgar splendour and colour of the Doge's reign has ensured its place in any popular account of the Venetian renaissance. But even with this concentration and maintenance of attention, a mystery remains. Was Foscari victimised, or deservedly punished? Did he really attempt to transform the dogeship into an hereditary crown, or was the evidence rigged by those who had their own axes to grind?

Foscari's election in 1423 was a close-run thing. To begin with, he was one of the 'poor nobles' and regarded as something of an outsider. More importantly, he belonged to the 'war party' – those who believed that Venice should pursue a policy of aggressive expansion on the western terraferma. It had been, specifically, to block his election that the dying Doge Mocenigo had made his 'state of the nation speech', ending it with an unequivocal warning. 'Many of you are inclined to Messer Francesco Foscari and do not, I think, sufficiently know his impetuous character and proud, supercilious disposition. If he is made doge, you will be at war continually. Those who now possess 10,000 ducats will have only 1,000. Those who possess ten houses will be proprietors of one. You will lose your money and your reputation and will be at the mercy of a soldiery.'

Nevertheless, Foscari succeeded Mocenigo and threw himself with gusto into the business of being Doge. His wife, now the Dogaressa, was brought to the Doge's Palace in the Bucentaur, the crimson and gold state barge. It happened that the superb murals of the new Sala del Maggior Consiglio (Hall of the Great Council) were completed during the first year of his office and he caused it to be opened with great ceremony.

The probability is that the majority of the ordinary citizens believed that the murals were his personal contribution to the glory of Venice. Certainly, during his reign, the city began to blaze forth in its Renaissance splendour. The Rialto Bridge was

Corpus Christi procession in the Piazza San Marco by Bellini

re-built in a more fitting form. Artists were brought from all over Italy to work in the churches of Venice. And above all were the splendid pageants and processions which were to become a hallmark of the city.

All Italian cities tended to be used as stages, living theatres, where the ceremonies of church and state were enacted like so many plays. But none, not even Sistine Rome, could equal the richness of the Venetian background – that extraordinary backcloth composed of Gothic and Byzantine architecture bathed in that living, glowing light reflected from the lagoon. Venetians were accustomed to such gorgeous confections as that Corpus Domini procession which Gentile Bellini depicted, but Foscari was able to match even the skilful ecclesiastical choreographers. There was the visit of the Prince of Portugal in 1428 when the Bucentaur brought the Prince across a lagoon which seemed to be merely an extension of the land, so crowded was it with gaily decorated vessels. And at the banquet in the palace the Prince's eye was able to feast upon the sight of 250 Venetian beauties clad in cloth of gold and silver. Ten years later there was an even more splendid occasion when no less a person than the

Eastern Emperor, John VIII (Paleologus), condescended to visit this child of Byzantium. Admittedly, this outwardly god-like emperor was inwardly desperately worried for the Turk was now battering almost at the gates of Constantinople and he was here not as autocrat but as one suing for aid. Foscari had no intention of diverting Venetian energy towards the east but he made the most of this occasion to display yet more glitter and splendour to the world, the emperor being entertained with endless banquets and concerts and routs before travelling on, still empty-handed, to Florence where Cosimo de' Medici was awaiting him. And after that visit was the visit of the other emperor – the Holy Roman Emperor of the German Nation – come to pay his careful respects to the city of the lagoon and in particular its doge.

Behind this dazzling display of crimson and gold and purple Francesco Foscari pursued his policy of expanding to the west. He refused to send aid to Constantinople and though its fall was foredoomed – a hollow shell collapsing at last under ruthless pressure – yet the Byzantines blamed him for it. And meanwhile his fellow nobles were regarding his career with speculation, noting the waves of popular hysteria when it seemed that the Doge had contracted a mortal disease, the no less hysterical delight when he recovered. Was this, then, where Venice was heading, the seven-hundred-year republic to become an orna- ment for yet another despot? They began to move in on him – or so it appears with hindsight. His weak link was his son Jacopo, the only surviving one of his five sons. Doge Francesco had brought about a brilliant match for his son, marrying him into the Contarini, one of the oldest in that city of long-established patricians. But the Contarini were unable, or unwilling, to protect their newly acquired kinsman when the Council of Ten accused Jacopo of negotiating with Venice's most deadly enemy, the Duke of Milan. There then began a cat and mouse game which went on for twelve years – up to a few days before Foscari's death. Jacopo was exiled, allowed to return, impris- oned, tortured, exiled again. His father, as Doge, was forced to sign the instrument of banishment. On the last occasion the wretched young man appealed to his father to use his power to save him from that fate of exile which every Italian regarded as scarcely preferable to death. Foscari reacted like a Roman: 'Go and do your country's bidding and ask no more.'

But it broke the old man, now in his eighty-fourth year. No longer ebullient, aware of the depth of the hatred directed against him, grieving for the virtual extinction of his family, he pleaded to be allowed to abdicate. The Ten refused: no Doge could abdicate without the consent of the members of the Grand Council. Then came news of Jacopo's death and, presumably feeling that there was no more profit to be gained from tormenting the Doge, the Ten demanded his resignation. The resolution incorporating that demand can be read either as a heartlessly cynical exercise, or as an example of the Venetian veneration of the State and of the office of doge which symbolised it. Opening with a succinct statement as to why a community like theirs needed a head, even a figurehead, it went on to deplore the fact that their 'most illustrious Prince' was incapable by reason of age and infirmity of carrying out his office and therefore 'we, the Council of Ten, have decided to request his Serenity, for the evident good of the State – his patria – freely and spontaneously to resign his power, which he ought to do as a good prince and father of his country'. With a return of his old spirit, Foscari refused to do so – on the same grounds as they had earlier refused to allow him to remove his burden. The Ten then resorted to naked threats: if he did not resign, he would be thrown out, all his goods confiscated and his pension rescinded. He bowed to the inevitable; but went out with style, insisting on descending by the great ceremonial stairs, clad in his scarlet robes of state, instead of slipping out discreetly as he was ordered. He was dead within a week – some say he died of rage on hearing the bells proclaiming his successor. But even now, the malice – or the passion for form – of the Ten had not been satisfied. Foscari's widow wanted to give him a private funeral. The Ten insisted that, as an ex-Doge, his body in effect belonged to the State and therefore must be given a State funeral. And the body was taken away despite her passionate protests.

What was the truth behind this remarkable series of events? There is little doubt that Foscari rigged his election, but there is equally little doubt that every would-be Doge went to great lengths to sweeten his potential electors. Foscari did carry out a remarkably aggressive policy on the terraferma; but it was a policy that had been initiated by his predecessors. The Grand Council – and the Council of Ten in particular – may have been genuinely perturbed by his popularity and his clear delight in ceremony and splendour, but by exiling his only son they had virtually eliminated any danger of the Foscaris establishing an hereditary dogeship. It may be that the Ten wished simply to create a memento mori, an unequivocal object lesson that would deter any future Doge with dangerous ambitions.

Certainly a major effect of the destruction of Doge Francesco Foscari was to eliminate, finally, any possibility that a Doge of Venice would ever emerge as a true monarch. Oligarchic power was firmly and finally established in the city. In a country, and during a period, which apotheosised the individual, emphasising the concept of individual excellence and fame, the Serenissima opted for personal anonymity. Those Venetian names which stand out from the general background belong, for the most part, to people like Foscari himself, or to those like an earlier doge, Faliero, who gained fame of a sort, being beheaded for treason – or to foreigners. Elsewhere in Italy, the brilliant names soar above the horizon to provide some sort of scale and direction in a crowded landscape: Medici in Florence, Sforza in Milan, Malatesta in Rimini, Gonzaga in Mantua, Este in Ferrara, Montefeltro in Urbino, Borgia in Rome – every city from the smallest to the largest had some family name as a species of tutelary deity. But not in Venice. The names of the great nobles appear year after year, century after century, in the records as serving their city-state as ambassadors or merchants or admirals or soldiers. Rarely, however, in their own right, and though the historian might regret the absence of those three-dimensional figures which, elsewhere, provide a frame of reference the advantage to the Venetian himself is unequivocal. Long after the other free city-states of Italy had succumbed to the despot, emerging finally as merely the appanage of a prince, Venice retained its freedom, the Serenissima Repubblica which suffered no man as master.

Foscari's aggressive policy of advancing to the west into the terraferma was one of the factors which probably led to his downfall. He had chosen that policy deliberately, but it would have been forced upon any Doge of Venice during the fifteenth and sixteenth centuries. The Stato da Mar and the Stato del Terraferma – the known mother against the uncertain neighbour – these formed the conflicting choices that faced the Republic as soon as it had advanced beyond the little circle of sandbanks to become an empire. The Stato da Mar, the world of water whence their city was born and across which they drew their wealth, was the Venetians' natural element. Their relationship with the Greek world, in particular Byzantium, was apt to be ambivalent. Long ago they had wrested their independence from the Byzantine emperor and, indeed, in an act of quite outstanding treachery they had teamed up with the Crusaders in 1204 to bring about the first fall of Constantinople. But at the same time they retained a strong tincture of Byzantium. Officials of the State carried resounding Greek titles; the great basilica of San Marco was a Byzantine church; the Greek scholars who fled to Venice after the fall of Constantinople in 1453 declared that they felt as though they were returning home.

Until the mid-fifteenth century, Venetians more than held their own with that other great seaborn power, the Ottoman Turks. It was commonly assumed, by the Turks as well as the Venetians, that a single light galley wearing the lion of San Marco was the equal of four or five blundering Turkish warships. But the fall of Constantinople in 1453 demoralised the Christians as much as it encouraged the Turks. The first great clash came in 1470 when the Venetians were not only defeated at sea but lost Negroponte, as they called Euboea, tearing open the whole of their southern defences. The Venetian admiral, Niccolò da Canal, was brought home in disgrace, forced to repay his salary and exiled, but the once distant threat was now immediate and permanent.

A similar state of affairs had been developing on the mainland. Throughout the early centuries, Venetians had been able to turn their backs upon their unpredictable fellow-Italians, interfering on the terraferma only when the press of squabbling city-states threatened their own equilibrium. Venetian policy there was admirably simple, the maintenance of a balance of power by the judicious use of Venice's most potent weapon – gold. Rarely did Venetians join in fighting the land wars: their skills were those of the sea and to put an army in the field would mean relying on the most dangerous and double-edged of tools, the professional soldier.

Such a policy worked well while northern Italy had consisted of small independent states all jostling for dominance but when, in the late fourteenth century, the state of Milan fell under the control of the Visconti family, the balance of power altered. Under Gian Galeazzo Visconti, the first Duke of Milan, the Milanese state extended eastward, city after city being absorbed until at last Milan and Venice shared the same frontier. Reluctantly, the Venetians embarked on a terraferma policy, at first intending to do little more than strengthen and police that frontier. But how far should they advance in the treacherous world of the terraferma? The moderates wanted simply to secure a foothold: the radicals preached a doctrine of a Lombard empire.

The radicals won. By the end of Foscari's dogeship in 1451, eastern Lombardy was a Venetian state. By the year 1499 the Serenissima Repubblica had transformed itself into a dual empire, straddling land and sea, towering over north Italy, threatened by the Turk but still sending her shadow far down the Adriatic. Then, in swift succession, the republic suffered three blows which would have destroyed a less resilient state: total defeat at sea; total defeat on land; and the relegation, as a maritime trading power, to a backwater in consequence of the opening up of the Atlantic routes.

Preoccupied with her struggle on the mainland Venice had ignored the warning of one of her own admirals that the Turks 'having now put their maritime affairs in order were not to be trifled with'. The defeat of the Venetian fleet at Zonchio should not, in itself, have been a humiliation. The fleet, though formidable and consisting of nearly a hundred ships carrying a total of 25,000 men, was outnumbered by the Turkish fleet. What was shameful and shaming was the manner in which the great galleys backed away from the fight and fled. In the subsequent trial of the wretched admiral, Antonio Grimani, his enemies made much of the charge of cowardice. More likely it was the disastrous result of trying to control a battle from the rear, from Venice, at a time of great technological change. The chain of command, evolved over a centuries-long tradition, was unable to cope with a situation in which new weapons, cannon, and new ships, the great carrack, were involved.

Battle of Zonchio

But even this disaster was as nothing compared with the consternation felt in Venice at the news of the triumphant return of the Portuguese caravels from India in 1501. As early as 1455 the Venetian, Alvise da Ca' da Mosto, who accompanied a Portuguese expedition to the equator was warning his fellow citizens that a new world was in process of being opened up. Involved in their own universe at the eastern end of the Mediterranean, the Venetians paid no particular attention until the opening up of the route to India. Then, in the words of the merchant banker Girolamo Priuli, 'There were still many who did not wish to believe it, even when the aforesaid caravels had arrived . . . because they did not wish it to be.' The Venetians were better equipped than most to realise just what had happened: they were, after all, members of the same race from which Marco

Polo sprang. The Mediterranean was no longer the centre of the world and the unique link between East and West which the Venetians had controlled, and grown rich in doing so, was suddenly drastically devalued. 'Venetian merchants will be like a baby without its milk,' was Priuli's opinion. 'I see the ruin of the city. It was the worst news the Venetian Republic could ever have had, excepting only the loss of their freedom.'

And eight years later, the Republic came the closest she ever would to losing that freedom, until it was extinguished entirely in the eighteenth century by Bonaparte. Throughout the fifteenth century Venice had steadily transgressed the first – indeed, the only – law of Italian political morality. She had become too successful, was too dominant and, in consequence, provided the only catalyst which could make Italian states combine for a particular end. The so-called Holy League against Venice owed its adjective to the inclusion of the pope, Julius II, who was prepared to ally himself with the hated French in order to bring down the power of the arrogant Venetians. It was signed, in December 1508, at Cambrai in France – a geographical fact of ominous significance for the future of Italy – and, apart from Pope Julius II, included the rulers of Spain, Savoy, Ferrara and Mantua. At Agnadello in May 1509 the Venetian army was totally defeated, leaving the island city for the first time in its maturity at the mercy of an enemy. Priuli's diary vividly conveys the sense of despair that swept through the city in the panic-stricken days following the battle. He was himself a member of the nobility and a merchant banker by profession and was only too aware of the implications of defeat on this scale. As he described it, venerable senators were to be seen tottering like drunks in the street. Those who could were already packing their bags, sending their valuables not merely out of Venice but out of Italy. Some, he noted disapprovingly, were even prepared to run to the Turks. There was even talk within the city as to whether Venice should not appeal to the Turks for aid. But to do so would be to introduce a most terrible neighbour on to the already threatening terraferma and, as Priuli put it pithily, 'No one cuts off his virile member in order to injure his spouse.'

Venice survived, her diplomats exploiting with consummate skill the inevitable rifts that appeared among the ill-assorted members of the 'Holy' League. The ordinary citizen must have at times found himself wondering just who was the current enemy, who the current eternal ally. Two years after Agnadello Papal and Venetian troops were fighting side by side against the French; three years after that French and Venetian troops were swearing comradeship and together fighting the Spanish. But whatever the change, after the dust had settled the Serenissima Repubblica was seen to be just a little more firmly in control than before.

Venice's increasing involvement on the terraferma, the increasing extent to which she was obliged to entrust her very existence

Bartolomeo Colleoni: detail of equestrian statue by Verrocchio

to condottieri, notoriously the most venal and unpredictable of men, is clearly demonstrated by the changing terms of contract. The usual contract with a mercenary leader was divided into two parts: the 'firma' and the 'di rispetto'. During the period that the firma was in operation, the condottiere and his company were deemed to be on active service; during the di rispetto the contracting employer had the right to renew the option, while the soldiers in effect went on the reserve. In 1404 Malatesta di Malatesti, Venice's first Captain-General in the climacteric fifteenth century, received a six-month contract – four months firma, two months di rispetto and allowances for 300 lances, each 'lance' consisting of three soldiers. Half a century later, in 1457, Bartolomeo Colleoni received a contract that was measured in almost as many years as Malatesta's had been measured in months: firma of three years, di rispetto of two years and funds for a thousand lances. The fact that Colleoni's family was granted permission to erect the great statue of the condottiere and his horse created by Verrocchio was also testimony to the enhanced status of the condottiere.

Florence had been the first of the Italian states to solve the problem of the employment of mercenaries as virtually a standing army. But the Englishman John Hawkwood, who served her for over twenty years and actually became her Captain-General, was in many ways an unusual man in his profession. Venice succeeded in turning the unusual into the norm: with few exceptions her condottieri served her faithfully and well over a period of some twenty-five years during which she was almost continually at war. Following that principle of hers in drawing in new blood, she actually granted her condottieri citizenship by making them honorary nobles with a seat in the Great Council. They were given palaces and estates on the terraferma, were treated with great ceremony and dignity and, even after they had ceased to be of effective use to the State, they were granted pensions.

One of the most delicate areas in the chain of command was the link between the civil power and the mercenaries carrying out the orders of that civil power. The usual practice was to include a number of high-ranking officials in the condottiere's headquarters, who would go on campaign with the army, ready to give on-the-spot political advice. Arrogant or incompetent agents could imperil their principal's policy: the Visconti of Milan once lost a campaign through a quarrel between John Hawkwood, then in their pay, and the Milanese agents who injudiciously tried to give him advice regarding the conduct of a seige. 'I do not choose to regulate military affairs according to the counsel of scriveners,' he announced and stalked off. The Venetian 'provveditori' never made so crass a mistake because they themselves usually had considerable military experience, the Venetian training system of ensuring that a young nobleman made his way upward through the ranks paying considerable dividends. In an emergency, it was even known for the provveditori to take over temporary command of the army, if necessary.

But even Venice could not ensure the total loyalty of a mercenary, as was shown by the famous incident of Carmagnola. By the beginning of the fifteenth century the old-fashioned foreign mercenary with his unimaginative tactics, his lack of motivation and his total untrustworthiness was being superseded by a new breed of men. Carmagnola was typical of such: native born – in his case, into a peasant family – dedicated to his profession, and utterly ruthless. He rose swiftly in his profession, becoming Captain-General to Filippo Maria Visconti, duke of Milan. He even married into the ducal family but, after a quarrel with Visconti, he offered his sword to Venice. Foscari was the reigning doge and he was delighted to accept the services of so outstanding a general.

At first, Carmagnola served his new employer well and, in return, received signal tokens of honour, including a splendid palace on the Grand Canal. Then he unaccountably began to drag his feet, finding one excuse after another to postpone action against Milan. In retrospect it is almost impossible to decide why he acted as he did, well knowing, as he must have done, that to arouse the suspicion and irritation of the Serenissima in this manner was about the most dangerous thing he could do. It began to be believed, probably with some justification, that Carmagnola was using Venice as a cat's-paw to gain his ends with his late employer.

By the spring of 1427, the Serenissima were convinced that they had concluded a very bad bargain indeed. In the previous

September, Carmagnola had informed his astonished employers that he was 'going into winter quarters' at least two months before it was customary. He was ordered into the field, and did so reluctantly, but the Serenissima had had enough.

It was one thing, however, to reprimand a dilatory commander but quite another to remove him for he could not possibly be arrested in the middle of his own men. Nevertheless, the bureaucracy of the Serenissima disposed of this, as it had disposed of other difficult problems. The Commander-in-Chief was respectfully invited to attend a conference at the Ducal Palace and on arrival in Venice was welcomed with the deference he had come to expect. The Doge was expecting him to dinner in the Palace, he was informed: would he give himself the trouble of proceeding thither. At the palace he dismissed his bodyguard and, accompanied by eight polite noblemen, entered an ante-chamber where they engaged in desultory conversation. An official then appeared, informed the still unsuspecting mercenary that, alas, the Doge was indisposed and asked him to return on the morrow. The whole charade had been designed simply to detach him from his bodyguard for as he returned – in the midst of his still polite escort – to the courtyard where his gondola awaited, he was suddenly seized and thrust towards one of the entrances to the dungeons. 'I am lost,' he cried as he was dragged away and thus, decorously, the Serenissima negated a potential danger. The rest was a foregone conclusion. Years later Machiavelli was to explain, and tacitly approve, the Serenissima's decision: 'Perceiving that Carmagnola had become cold in their service, they yet neither wished nor dared to dismiss him from a fear of losing what he had won for them. And so for their own security they had no option but to put him to death.' In order that the proprieties be observed, it was necessary to have a confession and he was scientifically tortured, his feet being burned and one arm broken until he confessed what was desired. There was only death for him now. But still he had been a great servant of the state and the Venetians put great store by ceremony and protocol so he was to be ushered out of the world in a fitting manner. His sentence was that 'today, after nones, at the usual hour ... he should be led between the two columns of the Piazza San Marco, to the usual place of execution and that his head be struck from his shoulders, so that he die'.

The event went off well. Francesco Carmagnola, Captain-General of the Serenissima Repubblica, was allowed – obliged – to wear the splendid costume that betokened his rank: scarlet cloak and crimson tunic. The cloak decently hid the fact that his hands were tied behind him, and only those close could see that a wooden gag had been thrust into his mouth to prevent treasonable utterances. At that 'usual place', between the columns of the Winged Lion of San Marco and the crocodile of St Theodore, he was unobtrusively forced to his knees. His last sight on earth would have been, successively, the waters of the lagoon glittering under the westering sun, and then the marble pavement under his knees.

From the fifteenth century onwards, political necessity forced the Venetians to establish themselves upon the Italian mainland, becoming a major terraferma power. But, to the end, she remained literally wedded to the sea. The ceremony of the casting of a golden wedding ring was more than just one of those

The Arsenal

colourful civic rites in which this somewhat dour people excelled. The Wedding of the Sea commemorated Ascension Day 997 when the then Doge, Pietro Orseolo II, led a Venetian fleet to victory over the Dalmatians. Each Ascension Day thereafter the reigning Doge and his court were rowed in the great state barge, the Bucentaur, out to the misty horizon where the sea met the lagoon and there threw a golden ring into the water, intoning the words, 'I wed thee in sign of dominion.'[19]

The Wedding of the Sea was the ceremonial expression of the significance of the Stato da Mar. The practical significance is shown by the fact that the first major Renaissance architecture in Venice was the handsome approaches to the Arsenal, the State shipbuilding yards. The Arsenal itself was one of the first great industrial enterprises of Europe. In 1104, at about the time when the rest of Europe was still engaged in building a feudal society based on an armoured man's fighting capacity, the reigning Doge, Ordelafo, laid the foundations for an industrial organisation which would survive for centuries, at its peak employing over 2,000 highly skilled workers. Here, in one area, was established in an inter-related system all the trades that were necessary for the construction and outfitting of every kind of vessel from rowing boats to the great galleys that could be used as fighting or trading vessels. Foundries, rope-makers, blacksmiths, sail-makers, shipwrights, chandlers were all to be found on two marshy little islands which, originally known simply as 'the Twins' (Zemelle), came to be known by a variation of the Arabic phrase Dar Sin'a, or house of construction and which, entering the Venetian dialect as Arsenal, was eventually to pass into every European language. By the 1300s the great Arsenal was famous throughout Europe, so much so that when Dante wanted an image for the furious activity prevailing in the Circle of the Barrators in *Inferno*, he turned to

> ... the Arsenal of the Venetians
> (where) Boils in winter the tenacious pitch
> To smear their unsound vessels o'er again.

Even as the Venetian dogeship anticipated nineteenth-century constitutional monarchy, so the Venetian shipbuilding techniques anticipated the mass production of the industrial era. It was calculated that the Arsenal could produce a ship in a hundred days. A Spanish observer described how one of these galleys was fitted out for sea. 'Out came a galley towed by a boat, and from the windows (of the buildings lining the canal) they handed to the occupants, from one the cordage, from another the arms and from another the ballistas and mortars, and so from all sides everything that was required, and when the galley had reached the end of the street (the canal) all the men required were on board, and she was equipped from end to end.' The entire operation was completed in less than two hours.

During the great formative years of the Republic and until well into the fifteenth century, it was the Venetian boast that the crews of her galleys were free men, their conditions of service carefully regulated by law. It was not until the mid-sixteenth century that it began to be necessary to conscript men. The reason, according to the great Venetian seaman, Cristoforo da Canale, was because the citizens' fibre had been sapped by wealth and good-living. 'The people are so comfortable and well-off,' he complained, 'that nothing less than overwhelming necessity would oblige them to take service in the galleys.' Such a complaint from a professional seaman is familiar in all ports at all times but there was an undoubted element of truth in Canale's remark. Certainly a graph could be drawn, showing the correlation between increased wealth and an increasing degradation among the crews.

All sea-going craft belonged to the State and on board every major ship that put to sea were at least two officials, the provveditori, whose role was essentially that of commissars – men appointed by the Grand Council as representatives of the government. Officers were invariably drawn from the nobility, but those appointed to the merchant galleys had a distinct financial incentive for they, as with the crews, were permitted to use part of the deck space for their own private enterprise goods, an excellent example of the Venetian ability to mix private and public activities.

Trading on the great galleys of Venice could make a man wealthy overnight – provided he escaped the perils of shipwreck, war or slavery. Many a hopeful young man who took his place on a well-found galley as she glided across the lagoon and out to the open sea for the first time could find himself tugging a Turkish or, later, a Genoese oar as a slave a few months hence. But the rewards were correspondingly immense. Cargoes were of small bulk and high value – the spices and silks of the East taking precedence – and leaving home with a few hundred golden ducats the merchant could obtain goods in Alexandria or Aleppo which could be sold for thousands of ducats in northern Europe.

A typical career was that of the young nobleman, Andrea Barbarigo who, in 1420, went to sea for the first time with a mere 200 ducats in his wallet – and even that had been scraped together with great difficulty by his mother. Young Andrea was a nobleman – but a poor nobleman: his father had had the misfortune to lose the galley entrusted to his command and the 10,000 ducats fine imposed upon him had bankrupted the family. Apart from those 200 gold coins, all that Andrea possessed was his skill as a crossbowman, and it was as a 'bowman of the quarterdeck' that he obtained passage to Alexandria. Evidently he laid his small capital out to good purpose, for a year or so later he is to be found as a merchant on the Rialto, that peerless school of commerce where could be met merchants from every trading nation of the civilised world. Ten years after he had embarked as a crossbowman he had increased his capital to 1,600 ducats, doubled that by judicious borrowing and embarked on a full-scale trading operation. He bought and sold anything that would make a profit, and following his activities over the next two decades is to become aware of how much of the trading lifeblood of Europe was provided by Venice. On his first major venture he bought pepper in Alexandria and sold it in Bruges; with the proceeds obtained there he crossed to England and bought cloth and pewter. This was sold at a handsome profit in Venice – but that profit was promptly ploughed back into his expanding enterprises for he bought a large cargo of cotton in Alexandria. Unfortunately for him, Venice had embarked again on its endless military struggle with Genoa, and his cargo of cotton fell into Genoese hands. Fortunately, he had taken to heart the lessons learned on the Rialto and did not put all his eggs in one basket: he sold a subsidiary cargo of gold thread at a high profit in Constantinople. So the tale goes on: sometimes he was unfortunate, his rich cargo falling as booty to an enemy or the pirates that swarmed in the Mediterranean. Sometimes war obliged him to switch his kind of trade, investing in such bulk cargoes as wheat rather than in the more obviously profitable luxuries as silk or wine. But steadily his capital expanded. He married his partner's sister who brought a substantial dowry with her and, in 1442, a little over twenty years since he set out to sea with borrowed money, he had some 10,000 ducats in circulation.

Venice's wide-ranging trading interests, together with that identification of the citizen with the State, ensured that the Serenissima was probably the best informed of all governments, including that of the Vatican. Even cardinals were, as a matter of course, expected to break their vow of secrecy and provide a detailed account of who voted what and why during the election of a pope. The ambassadors themselves were undoubtedly the best in Europe: drawing upon that common pool of confidential information they were able to thread their way through the labyrinthine paths of European politics with the confidence created by foreknowledge. And in return, they contributed to that ever growing pool.

Ambassadors reported back to their government through two clearly different media, 'dispacci' and 'relazione'. The dispacci were the formal letters, the balanced reports emanating from the man on the spot more or less at the same time as the incidents reported in the dispacci. Relazione were more informal – and, in the long run, probably more valuable – accounts which the ambassador rendered in person on his return home. 'Everyone who returns from any mission comes to this most wise Senate, not to render account of his actions (which can clearly be grasped from the letters written by him from time to time) but to report if he had learned anything of the country from which he comes worthy of being heard and pondered by prudent senators for the benefit of the fatherland.' It makes an impressive picture: the returning diplomat rendering his report to his fellows in one of the gorgeous rooms of the Doge's Palace, filling in the details that he had only sketched in the dispacci, answering the probing questions of other, veteran diplomats. Venetian diplomats knew as much, if not more, about the internal conditions of the country to which they were accredited as did the government of that country. After the massacre of St Bartholomew in France, when the Huguenots were on the edge of a massive uprising the Venetian ambassador provided his government with a precise statistical breakdown of the Huguenot ability to finance a major civil war – details which were certainly not available to Huguenots outside Paris and which were known only to the inner circle around Caterina de' Medici, the Italian-born queen mother.

The ambassadors excelled at what can only be called psychological studies, analysing not only how a powerful man would react, but why. Marco Foscari, the Venetian ambassador in Rome in the 1520s, provided a vivid pen portrait of the vacillating Pope Clement VII, whose indecisiveness largely contributed to the sack of Rome in 1527. 'The Pope is forty-eight years old and is a sensible man, but slow in decision, which explains his irresolution in action. He talks well, he sees everything but is very timid. He suffers no control in state affairs – he listens to everyone then just does as he pleases . . . He is very abstemious, and is a stranger to all luxury. He gives largely in alms, but nevertheless is not liked . . . ' Contarini in France leaves an unforgettable description of the unfortunate Charles VIII of France. 'He is twenty-two years of age, small and badly formed of person, ugly of face with eyes great and white and much more apt to see little than enough, an aquiline nose much larger and fatter than it ought to be, also fat lips which he continually holds open and ugly, spasmodic movements of the hands.' Superficially, the fact that a pope gave alms but was not liked, that a King of France was ugly and seemed to suffer from adenoids may seem mere gossip unworthy of a diplomat's consideration. But centuries of dealing with foreigners had taught the Serenissima that anything about them was of potential value, that a man's appearance modified his personality, his personality modified his actions. So the great archives grew, to become in time one of the treasure houses of European history.

Venice resembled Rome, and differed from Florence, in one very significant detail: she was mainly an importer, not a producer, of talent. It may have been the result of that deliberately eclectic immigration policy of hers, but certainly most of those who created the beauty that dazzled visitors came from the despised terraferma. Of the scores of immigrants who made their fortune in the city – and incidentally contributed to its expanding wealth and influence – three can perhaps be taken as representative of the rest: the printer Aldus Manutius, the writer Pietro Aretino and the painter Titian.

'Venice was the first city in the world to feel the full impact of printing, and to experience the most important revolution in human communication between the development of letter symbols, and the emergence of electronic mass media in our own day,' is the opinion of Aldus's biographer, Martin Lowry.[20] Born in Rome about 1450, Aldus established his press in Venice during the 1490s and the success of his career there reflected not only his skill as scholar and printer but as businessman. Printing introduced not only a revolutionary new communication technique, but demanded the administrative ability to exploit a whole new range of social, technical and financial skills. The would-be printer had to raise capital, assemble a workforce that was both literate and manually skilled, obtain and assemble a wide range of materials and then finally market an end product many miles distant from its point of production. Aldus encountered at an early stage the problems of organised labour. 'Four times now my hired men and workers have conspired against me in my own house, led on by that mother of all evils, Greed: but with the help of God I so smashed them that they all thoroughly regret their treachery.' He was by no means an easy person to work for, or with, as Erasmus's famous letter testifies. Erasmus was preparing a book for the Aldine Press in 1508 and was living-in as was customary. His account of his experience gives a vivid picture of the establishment – part printer's workshop, part study, part private house. The house itself still survives, a shabby-looking building marked with a modest plaque near the church of Sant' Agostin. When Erasmus was working there, it seems to have had a household of around thirty people, of whom half were operatives. As a good Dutchman, Erasmus held his stomach in respect and was appalled by the quantity and quality of food that the parsimonious Aldus deemed adequate for visiting scholars, guests or workmen. But on his side, Aldus was endlessly complaining about costs: he claimed that he was spending 200 ducats a month to keep the establishment going. And if Erasmus, the author, was critical of Aldus the entrepreneur, Aldus was equally scathing about the troublesome tribe of authors, complaining about the habits of scholars who would pester him with lengthy letters, and poetasters who would turn up without appointment, waste his time with reciting their effusions and then demand that he print them. But while Aldus was certainly not disposed to accept fools gladly or otherwise, he was a good friend of genuine scholars and writers, prepared not only to publish work by living writers but even to commission in advance.

Pietro Aretino was born in Arezzo in 1492. 'The scourge of princes' he called himself, and it was true enough: certainly there was more than one prince who would have been delighted to lay his hands on this swashbuckling, blackmailing scribbler who happened to be gifted with an enviable talent. He was perfectly prepared to turn that talent to eulogy or invective, the one taking the place of the other according to the presence or absence of a bribe. A big, burly man with an unquenchable thirst for good living, an ability to inspire amusement and outright affection among his boon companions, he could perhaps be described as the first of the journalists, the first of the gossip columnists. In an active life of over forty years he wrote thousands of letters, personally selecting 3,000 of them for publication in book form. In style and content his literary output covered an astonishing range from pornography to diplomacy, from topographical description to prescribing a cure for the pox.

It was natural that a man of Aretino's talents should gravitate to Venice for he had exactly the kind of skill the Ten most valued – the ability to extract information from confidential sources. Not the least of his skills, perhaps, is that he – who made a profession of indiscretion – not only survived but flourished in a society where every man was reasonably supposed to be acting as a government spy upon his neighbour. But no denunciation of Aretino ever found its way into one of the lion's mouths that dotted the city – or, if such a paper came into the hands of the Ten, it was ignored.

Nothing less than a palace was good enough for Pietro Aretino, the son of a shoemaker, and he moved into a splendid

Pietro Aretino by Titian

new building near the Rialto. His vivid description of life on the
Grand Canal has the same kind of precision and colour that
Canaletto was to express in paint two centuries later -- peasants'
barges loaded high with melons; foreign tourists so crammed
into a little boat that it capsizes; courtesans passing in a shimmer

of gold and silk. His style is racy and casual, but behind the letters was a precision of language and thought that makes it possible, for instance, to identify the locality of his house to within a few feet in twentieth-century Venice.

Aretino's letter to his friend Titian, congratulating him on a child's portrait shows the other side of his contradictory character, a warmth and tenderness and artistic insight that seems out of keeping with the rest of him. Technically, Titian was a Venetian, for he was born within the boundaries of the state. But his birthplace was on the terraferma and, like Aretino, he was an immigrant in the city which was to be his headquarters and workshop until his death in 1576, reputedly at the age of ninety-nine. Titian, the realist, the pragmatist, exactly echoed as artist the pragmatic city which he adopted, or that adopted him. It was fitting that his first commission, as a lad of eighteen or nineteen, should have been painting decorations on the Fondaco dei Tedeschi, the trading establishment of the German merchants in Venice, for trade and aesthetics, realism and idealism were never far apart in the Venetian mind. Even in his allegorical subjects Titian retains that down-to-earth quality which marks out the Venetian. In the *Bacchanalia*, the central figures hold up against the sky a real Venetian glass jug filled, one suspects, with wine from the hills around Verona or the plains of Padua, real wine with a colour range as exact as the crystal that contains it. And though he made his fortune painting portraits of the great, presumably arriving at a compromise which satisfied his clients' vanity while not compromising his own artistic integrity, there is one searing group portrait which has the ultimate word upon the corruption wrought by absolute power. It is the portrait of Pope Paul III and his two nephews. The foxily senile pope is flanked by his obsequious nephews, the one peering defiantly at the observer, the other humbly genuflecting, smirking at his uncle, the source of all power, clearly prepared to undergo any humiliation, betray any principle so long as he can hold on to the fruits bestowed by that power. It is typically a Venetian who shows the realities of political power quite so unequivocally, quite so ruthlessly. Significantly, the painting is unfinished.

Fondaco dei Tedeschi

5

The warrior princes

Like three suns blazing simultaneously in the sky, Renaissance Florence, Rome and Venice tend to blind the view of posterity to the activities of their contemporaries. The golden-tongued apologists of Florence, many of whom became enshrined in the national literature, the stability and longevity of Venice and the sheer mystique of Rome attract attention away from their neighbours. In the introduction to his study of Ferrara, Werner Gundersheimer remarks on the phenomenon and observes feelingly: 'To choose to spend years in the study of a relatively little-known, medium-sized Renaissance despotism in a period when many of the best Renaissance scholars of one's own and immediately past generations have devoted their energies to illuminating the history of its greatest republic, Florence, has sometimes seemed an idiosyncratic and perhaps somewhat marginal undertaking.'[21]

The 'despots', as individuals, have had a bad press or no press at all. Nineteenth-century historians, with their preoccupation with cultural, ie 'courtly', history, perforce had to recognise the world of the prince. But they tended to do so with an air of disdain. Burckhardt, their doyen, revels in the cultural details of the princely courts but is at pains to point out their vices, both moral and political. One of the reasons why earlier historians tended to concentrate on the republics, or to laud them, was either because they were themselves republicans, like the Swiss J. C. L. Sismondi (whose *History of the Italian Republics in the Middle Ages* has been described as 'one long hymn to liberty followed by a funeral ode'), or because they were sympathisers. Ferdinand Gregorovius, the German scholar whose magisterial *History of the City of Rome in the Middle Ages* still provides the major link between the classical and Renaissance city, for all his

aristocratic background cannot hide his revulsion at the autocracy of the papal monarch. The Englishman J. A. Symonds is an
excellent example of what might be called the crypto-republican.
He rationalises his standpoint by quoting the Florentine republican Matteo Villani: 'The crimes of Despots always hinder and
often neutralise the virtues of good men . . . ' and then goes on to
pen the standard portrait of the despot which has become a
stereotype. 'The life of the Despot was usually one of prolonged
terror. Immured in strong places on high rocks, or confined to
gloomy fortresses he surrounded his person with foreign troops,
protected his bedchamber with a picked guard, and watched his
meat and drink lest they should be poisoned. He had no real
friends or equals, and against his own family he adopted an
attitude of fierce suspicion . . . his timidity verged on monomania.'[22]

The nineteenth and twentieth centuries' condemnation of the
'despot' and praise of the 'republican' is an excellent example of
the dangers of judging by hindsight, of applying terms evolved
for the use of one society, to that of another. In the twentieth
century 'democracy' as a word has the kind of moral weight
earlier centuries would have applied only to religious terms. The
republicans of Florence and Venice and similar 'free' cities,
though they might use the word 'popolo' as a rallying cry, would
have been appalled at the idea of a genuine democracy. The
fourteenth-century political theorist Tolomeo of Lucca, made
that quite clear, republican though he was, specifically condemning the idea of extending power to 'those of the lowest condition,
because they at once turn it into a democracy. For when they
think themselves on top, forgetful and ignorant of government,
they are swept under the false leadership of low scoundrels . . . '

And if changing political terms act as a trap for the unwary, so
do changing cultural styles. Werner Gundersheimer sums up that
problem: 'Scholars have always been sceptical, and with good
reason, of the lavish praise heaped upon Renaissance rulers
by the humanists who surrounded them. Yet we have been
much less cautious about accepting the sometimes comparably
extravagant of inflated rhetoric of those humanists who surrounded the great men of the republics . . . Can we be certain
that their ideals were invariably higher, and their achievements

always superior to those of their counterparts elsewhere?'[23]

It is not difficult to find princes to fit Symonds' description of the criminal but timid despot. Neither is it difficult, also, to find examples of men who moved freely among their subjects, who contributed richly to the new culture as patrons, and whose dynasties outlasted many of the famed republics. The members of the three dynasties who form the subject of this chapter contradict their stereotype at almost every important point. The Este of Ferrara were not usurpers and oppressors but were invited by the citizens to take up the burden of office and ruled the city well for four hundred years: Francesco Gonzaga in Mantua and Federigo da Montefeltro in Urbino, far from being timid to the point of monomania, pursued successful careers as condottieri. Federigo da Montefeltro had a very happy family life, and was a generous and enthusiastic patron of the arts, as were most of the Estensi. In the fifteenth century all three dynasties were closely linked in matrimony when Federigo's son, Guidobaldo, married Elisabetta Gonzaga and Francesco Gonzaga married Isabella d'Este, neatly illustrating in family terms the common sense of identity that lay behind the outward regional variations of contemporary Italian culture.

In one respect, however, the leading members of the dynasties conform with their stereotype: they are excellent examples of Burckhardt's thesis of 'the state as a work of art', that is, of the state being created and maintained by an outstanding man. It is possible to imagine Florence without the Medici or Rome without the Borgia: it is not possible to imagine Urbino without Montefeltro, Ferrara without Este or, to a lesser degree, Mantua without Gonzaga. In the twentieth century it is their palaces, not the palaces of the communes or even the cathedrals, which first catch the eye in their respective cities.

The Montefeltri of Urbino

Federigo da Montefeltro, Duke of Urbino, is enshrined for all time in the unforgettable portrait by Piero della Francesca. Piero shows a man in whom strength is combined with tolerance: a man who would be surprised by nothing, expected nothing and was well able to defend his own. The hooded eyes are deceptively sleepy, the firm mouth will smile easily but the great, broken nose and jutting chin thrusts aggressively forward. All his portraits are, like this, in profile for he lost an eye in a tournament and, with an engaging touch of vanity, preferred that his best side only should be shown.

Federigo was illegitimate by birth but, according to the humane Italian custom of the day, he was brought up with his father's family. In due course his younger, but legitimate brother Oddantonio succeeded to the title while he himself went off to

Federigo da Montefeltro: portrait by Piero della Francesca

make his fortune as a mercenary. Young Oddantonio, however, fell victim to the corruption of power. For fourteen months he acted the part of the classical tyrant in the small state, taking the wives and daughters of the citizens as he chose, contemptuously overriding the advice of his counsellors. Oddantonio forgot, however, that the despot had to have certain survival skills as well as unlimited appetites and in due course was assassinated by his enraged subjects. His half-brother Federigo was summoned to take the title, but before he was allowed in the city a committee of citizens subjected him to a rigorous cross-examination as to how he proposed to rule. At the gates of Urbino, in the July of 1444, was very clearly demonstrated the transitional nature of power in Italy. The citizens of Urbino recognised their need for a lord, but they were not so far removed from their free past that they would abjectly accept whatever that lord decreed.

The new lord of Urbino divided his time between soldiering for other princes, and building up in his little hill city one of the centres of the Renaissance. As condottiere, he was outstandingly successful without being brilliant. He turned loyalty into a marketable asset. During one of the wars between Venice and the Este of Ferrara, for example, Ercole d'Este retained Montefeltro: hearing of this, the Serenissima promptly offered him 80,000 ducats not to fight for them, but simply to stay at home. He declined the offer. Such unusual integrity, coupled with good, solid professional competence, enabled Montefeltro to flourish at his chosen trade for over forty-five years, and to include the Papacy, the kingdom of Naples and the republics of Florence and Milan among his many employers. At his peak he was earning 165,000 ducats a year and, although he personally had only 45,000 of these, because the bulk of his troops came from Urbino, most of the money eventually circulated through his dukedom.

Soldiering was only the means of earning a living as far as Montefeltro was concerned and in this he was very much an Italian, declining to invest the military life with the glamour and mystique that the northern nations saw in it. Federigo's interests were intellectual and cultural, using his little State as the means of working out his political and cultural theories. Urbino was small even among the miniature Italian states. There were only two cities of any standing – Urbino itself and Gubbio – and their combined population was probably a quarter of that of Florence or Venice, most of the people living in the 400 or so hill villages and small towns that made up the state. Baldassare Castiglione, who lived in Urbino for some years and later enshrined it in his book *The Courtier*, left a glowing picture of the locality. 'Although situated in a mountainous region, less pleasant than some we may have seen, it is favoured by heaven in that the country is exceedingly fertile and rich in the fruits of the earth. And besides the pure and health-giving air of the region, all things necessary for human life are to be found here in great abundance.' But Castiglione's affection led him to exaggerate somewhat. Certainly Urbino and its immediate locality was beautiful and the intellectualism of the little court charged the atmosphere so that a number of excellent artists developed in the city, Raphael predominant among them. But Urbino was somewhat off the beaten track, of no particular importance to anybody, owing its place in Renaissance culture entirely to Federigo and, to a lesser degree, his son Guidobaldo.

Federigo had been educated by the humanist Vittorino da Feltre whom Lodovico Gonzaga had established at Mantua. He called his school the Joyous House where rich and poor, girls and boys enjoyed the same education, merit alone being the test of entry. Federigo was a Latinist of no small ability, a Greek scholar of skill and depth – as well as an historian and mathematician. His major personal passion was book-collecting, and Vespasiano da Bisticci found in him one of his most profitable customers; in return, he left a vivid portrait of the man so that, between Vespasiano the Florentine bookseller, and Castiglione, the Mantuan diplomat, it is possible to build up a clear picture of an unusual and most attractive character. In one matter he was suspicious of innovation – and that was regarding the products of the printing press. 'In his library all the books were superlatively good, and written with the pen and had there been one printed volume it would have been ashamed in such company,' Vespasiano noted. He also described the minutely detailed rules which were drawn up for the selecting of the librarian and running of the library. The books were to be available to all 'but when ignorant or merely curious people wish to see them, then a

glance is sufficient – unless it be someone of considerable importance.'

The palace which Federigo had inherited was typical of its period – a gloomy, depressing place whose major attraction was its strength. In 1450 he turned to the task of transforming this Gothic fortress into a home and did it with such great panache that, even in the twentieth century when the building has suffered the fate of similar places and become a museum, it still has that indefinable atmosphere of home. Castiglione, who lived in it, was ecstatic about it, 'It seemed not a palace but a city in the form of a palace, and he furnished it not only with what was customary such as silver vases, wall hangings of the richest cloth of gold, silk and the other like things but for ornaments he added countless ancient statues of marble and bronze and rare paintings...' In this twofold role of admirer of ancient art and patron of modern artists Federigo was very much a man of his day.

Federigo da Montefeltro died at the age of sixty in 1482 and his son inherited. It was Guidobaldo's misfortune rather than his fault that he lacked the characteristics of his father. He was a martyr to gout; in him, too, the intellectualism of the father had become transformed into introspection. Piero della Francesca's portrait of him brings out his essentially gentle, rather melancholy nature and it was one of life's ironies that such a man who would have been happier working in his splendid library was obliged to follow his father's profession. The name of Montefeltro was sufficient to ensure his employment and he acquitted himself honourably, but misfortune followed him. Fighting for the Borgia pope, Alexander VI, he was captured and the pope, instead of ransoming him as was customary, merely washed his hands of his unsuccessful general. Guidobaldo would have languished indefinitely in captivity had not his subjects, who genuinely loved him, rallied and raised the heavy ransom.

Militarily, Guidobaldo made the profound mistake of judging others by his own honourable standards. He therefore fell easy victim to Cesare Borgia during the latter's tempestuous campaign in the Marches, for Borgia first lulled him into a feeling of false security and then pounced, invading the state with

Federigo reading: portrait by Melozzo da Forli

overwhelming force. Guidobaldo had to flee for his very life, wringing his hands with bewilderment and dismay. 'I cannot understand why I have been so treated for I have always sought to please the pope and Cesare.' He was particularly indignant at the Borgia propaganda story that his subjects were glad to see him go. 'They say that Cesare claims that my people drove me out. I swear they wept when they heard of my plight.' It was probably true for, after Cesare's brief hour of triumph, Guidobaldo returned to an enthusiastic welcome. 'Troops of children flocked out to meet him with olive branches in their hands, singing for joy at sight of their beloved prince. Old men, tottering under the weight of years, hurried out to meet him with tears of joy streaming down their cheeks ... The very stones seemed to dance and exult at his coming.'

It was under Guidobaldo's wife, Elisabetta, that the little court achieved its fame as a species of sixteenth-century salon, establishing that code of courtly behaviour which Baldassare Castiglione enshrined in his book *The Courtier*. Samuel Johnson gave the book his benediction some 200 years after Urbino had ceased to exist as a state: 'The best book that was ever written upon good breeding, *Il Cortigiano*, by Castiglione grew up at the little court of Urbino and you should read it.' Castiglione was in residence for some four years from 1504, mingling delightedly with the beautiful and the witty and the famous who were attracted to the beautiful palace presided over by its charming mistress. The picture that he presents is of a group of brilliant minds, familiar with each other and therefore at ease, who have turned briefly aside from the cares of state and seek refreshment in conversation. There are feasts and entertainments of wide variety: during the day the members go about their business but each evening they meet again under the presidency of the duchess, for Guidobaldo is now grievously afflicted by gout and retires as soon as decently possible. The group talk into the small hours, pursuing each topic informally but with sobriety and order – and merriment too – fashioning between themselves the concept of the perfect man, much as Plato fashioned the concept

Palazzo ducale, Urbino

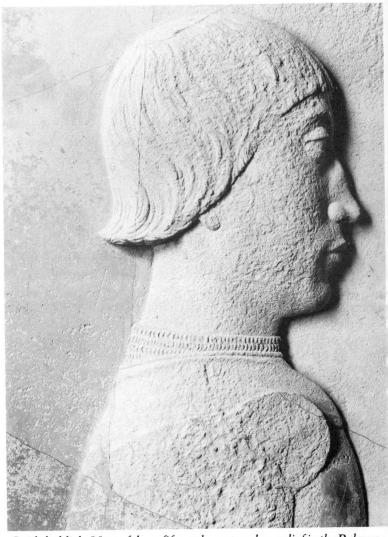

Guidobaldi da Montefeltro: fifteenth-century bas-relief in the Palazzo ducale, Urbino

of the perfect state through dialogue. So vividly did the memory stay with Castiglione that, twenty years afterwards, he could describe the end of one of these sessions with the poignancy of a paradise lost.

Then every man rose to his feet, and not one of them felt any heaviness of sleep. When the windows were open then upon the side of the Palace that looked towards Mount Catri, they saw already risen in the East, a fair morning, rose coloured, and all the stars gone save only Venus from which seemed to blow a sweet blast that filled the air with biting cold and began to quicken the notes of the pretty birds among the hushing woods of the hills nearby. Then they all, taking their leave with reverence of the Duchess, departed towards their lodging without torch, the light of day sufficing.

The idyll came to an end with the death of Guidobaldo, at the early age of thirty-six, in 1508 the state passing to his nephew – who was also the nephew of the martial pope Julius II. Guidobaldo's widow was inconsolable. Her sister-in-law, Isabella d'Este, sent an ambassador to convey her condolences. He found the duchess in a room draped all in black with a single candle in the middle of the floor. 'I was led in by my cloak like a blind man. She offered me her hand and I stood for a time like a mute, unable to speak, for we were both sobbing.' There are worse epitaphs for a prince of the Renaissance.

The Gonzaga of Mantua

Guidobaldo's wife, Elisabetta, came from martial stock, for she was a Gonzaga of Mantua and the Gonzaga of Mantua gained their power in the marshland city by means that were only too familiar. On 13 August 1328 they murdered the heads of the ruling family and established themselves in their place. But that was over a century and a half earlier and in the interim the family had not only achieved respectability, but a title to go with it. Following the lead of the usurping Visconti in Milan, Gianfrancesco Gonzaga purchased his title of marquis from a venial emperor in 1433 and, despite their violent entry upon the national stage, the family was to prove one of the longest lasting of princely families, surviving into the eighteenth century. Like the Montefeltro of Urbino they were heavily dependent upon soldiering to subsidise the Mantuan budget: unlike the Montefeltro each of the succeeding marquises was a tough, unscrupulous soldier. No Gonzaga would have fallen victim to the blandishments of the Borgia as did the unfortunate Guidobaldo da Montefeltro.

They were cultured men as well as professional soldiers. The same Gianfrancesco who had no hesitation in bribing the Emperor Sigismund to obtain his title was also the prince who sponsored Vittorino da Feltre, foremost humanist teacher of his day. And Vittorino da Feltre was not disposed to modify his system in order to please a sponsor, no matter how influential. When the marquis offered him the post of tutor to his children with a handsome salary and a private establishment the scholar said bluntly, 'I accept, but only on the understanding that you require nothing from me that would dishonour either of us. And I will serve you only as long as you deserve service.' It says much for both men that Vittorino remained in Mantua until his death twenty-three years later, their mutual affection remaining unaffected even when Vittorino interfered in a family quarrel between the marquis and his eldest son, Lodovico. The marquis preferred his second son, a violent, headstrong young man, and actually disinherited Lodovico and condemned him to death. Vittorino, who knew the worth of both youths, reproached the marquis to his face and it was very largely as a result of Vittorino's coldly energetic defence that Lodovico was restored to his inheritance and, in due course, emerged as ruler.

Lodovico Gonzaga, Marquis of Mantua, is probably best known to posterity through two murals in an unassuming little room buried deep in the enormous palace. The room is the so-called Camera degli Sposi (Bridal Chamber) and the murals are of the marquis and his family, painted by Andrea Mantegna. The Camera degli Sposi is a dark little room with only one window set asymmetrically high up in the thickness of the great walls. Two of the four walls are in fairly deep shadow and these are decorated with a simple tapestry design. But on the other two walls that are flooded with light from the window the observer can see two family groups, caught in unstudied, casual poses. Unlike the Medici who, at about the same time, had their family portrayed in the form of a Biblical allegory, Lodovico Gonzaga instructed his painter to show them as they were in reality and the result is one of the warmest, most intimate family portraits of all those produced in Italy at this time. In the domestic interior, the

Palazzo ducale, Mantua

Camera degli Sposi: general view. The painting on the left hand wall shows Lodovico Gonzaga welcoming his son, the cardinal, on the latter's return from Rome

Lodovico Gonzaga and secretary: detail

marquis is shown in his great chair, half turned to converse with his secretary who listens attentively and respectfully but certainly not humbly. The subject of conversation would appear to be the letter in the marquis's hand and this is probably related to the appointment of his son Francesco as cardinal – the first Gonzaga to be raised to this honour, and a matter of very considerable importance to the family and the State. Beside the marquis is seated his wife, Barbara of Brandenberg (it was for the two of them that this Bridal Chamber was originally created), and by her skirts is posed, in an attitude of comical arrogance, one of the dwarfs for which the palace is famous and around them are the members of the family and staff. In the other mural, the marquis is shown welcoming the new cardinal on his return home. As

Lodovico Gonzaga and family

Mantua itself is set in a completely flat plain, the hilly region in the background is probably one of the passes of the Appennines, the city itself being Mantegna's somewhat fanciful idea of Rome – a place he had not in fact visited. The artist placed himself, discreetly but clearly, to the right of the picture. He had earned his position as technician, quite apart from his right as artist. The murals are only a little above eye height: for over two centuries – from the flight of the last duke in 1707 to the beginning of the twentieth century – they together with all else in the great palace were at the mercy of casual or determined vandalism. But though now seen to be scarred and pitted when viewed close-up, from even a short distance they seem as fresh as the day the artist left them.

The relationship between Duke Lodovico and his talented, loyal but undeniably short-tempered court painter is highlighted in a delightful letter that Lodovico wrote to him; a letter that not only throws light on the duke's character but on the somewhat hand-to-mouth finances that characterised the court. Mantegna had evidently been complaining that he was owed money and Lodovico replied, 'Andrea, we have received a letter from you which it really seems to us you need not have written for we perfectly remember the promises we made when you entered our service ... But you cannot cannot take from us what we have not got. Since we have not received our usual revenues during the past few months, we have been obliged to defer certain payments such as this which is due to you. But we are seeking by every means in our power to raise money to meet our obligations – even if we are forced to mortgage our own property, since all our jewels are already pawned and you need not fear that, before long, your debt will be paid gladly and readily.'

Lodovico ruled his small state for thirty-six years, dying in his bed at the age of sixty-five. His son, Federigo, was also a condottiere, brave enough and competent enough but best known to history because of his children. One of his daughters, Elisabetta, became the duchess of Urbino; another, Chiara, became a duchess of Bourbon and, hence, mother of the man who triggered the sack of Rome in 1527. And his son, Francesco, who succeeded him as marquis had the double distinction of commanding the first attempt at a federal Italian army at the battle of Fornovo, and of being married to the foremost blue stocking of his age, Isabella d'Este, though he himself was largely indifferent to the arts.

Francesco Gonzaga, Marquis of Mantua, was commonly reputed to be the bravest man in Italy. He was also, indubitably, the ugliest, bearing a strong resemblance to a Pekinese dog with his flat face, thick lips, snub nose, bulging eyes and very bad temper. As a soldier, he found himself in a decidedly complex position. For the better part of a century Italians had been accustomed to fight out their battles among themselves without much interference from outside powers. Occasionally, one of the Germanic emperors would descend upon the peninsula with lordly but largely empty claims to suzerainty; more frequently

Francesco Gonzaga

one or other of the free-booting lords of Europe would conduct a species of plundering raid dignified by the title of crusade. But, until the latter part of the fifteenth century the great northern nations were too much preoccupied with their own affairs to go adventuring in Italy. With increasing stability at home, however, these nations developed foreign ambitions, Spain and France in particular producing dusty claims to this or that part of Italy, based on earlier conquest or matrimonial alliance.

The year 1494 marked what the Florentine historian, Guicciardini, was later to call 'the last of the happy years', for that was the year in which young Charles VIII of France launched the first French invasion of Italy. An impetuous, idealistic young man, reputed to be even uglier that Francesco Gonzaga, Charles was the victim of his own imagination and unscrupulous Italian politicians. Pre-eminent among them was Ludovico Sforza, the usurping lord of Milan who, engaged in a feud with the Neapolitan relatives of the true Duke of Milan, was among those who persuaded Charles to enter Italy and lay dynastic claim to the crown of Naples – altogether an object lesson in the complex, short term and suicidal nature of Italian city-state politics. Naples fell at a touch, the French enjoyed a year's dalliance in that beautiful, treacherous southern city whose endemic diseases proved far more dangerous to the French than its military defences and, in due course, Charles and his depleted army turned back to the north – to find that the Italians there had made some sort of common cause and were disposed to dispute his return passage. Venice was the leader of the ramshackle alliance and Francesco Gonzaga, as Venice's Captain-General, commanded the Italian army which clashed with the French at the battle of Fornovo. The French escaped, though badly mauled, and the Italians promptly claimed a victory. It was a propaganda, rather than a military victory and Gonzaga's role, as general, could fairly be described as second-rate. He nevertheless displayed great personal courage and was welcomed back to Mantua as a hero.

The Serenissima, however, was regarding her commander-in-chief with a distinctly unenthusiastic eye. Gonzaga, it seemed to the Senate, was altogether too fond of France and French ways, even accepting an invitation from the new king, Louis XII, to stay at his château of Loches. Abruptly, the Serenissima revoked Gonzaga's condotta, an unprecedented action which enraged and humiliated him. He did have an opportunity for revenge some years later when the terraferma powers, under Pope Julius

II, launched their concerted attack upon Venice. The Serenissima was then forced to eat humble pie, sending an envoy to Gonzaga, actually pleading with him to assume control again. He enjoyed the situation to the full, forcing the Venetian envoy to increase his bid from 60,000 to 100,000 ducats, and then contemptuously dismissing him.

It was only a temporary triumph, however. During the war that followed he was captured by his late employers and released only when his son Federigo was handed over as hostage. His wife, Isabella, was reluctant to allow her 10-year-old son to be entrusted to the enemy and found excuses to postpone the exchange until Francesco, beside himself with humiliation and frustration, wrote her a stinging letter, saying that if the boy were not handed over he would personally strangle her.

A compromise was reached by entrusting the little boy to the custody of the pope as intermediary. Francesco returned home, but if Isabella expected to be congratulated for the highly efficient way she had run the state during his absence, she was disappointed. She was absent on one of her many tours of the state when her husband returned and his letter to her is a monument of ingratitude. 'We are ashamed that it is our fate to have as wife a woman who is always ruled by her head.' But Isabella d'Este could give as good as she got, and spiritedly she replied: 'Your Excellency is indebted to me as never husband was to wife, nor must your Excellency think that, even did you love and honour me more than any person in the world, you could repay my good faith.'

Isabella d'Este, Marchioness of Mantua, is one of the great figures of her epoch, however she is viewed. Her copious, fluent letters form such a readily accessible, and colourful source of social history as to give her, in historical terms a decided advantage over other, less loquacious figures. But even allowing for this distortion, she was a remarkable woman whether considered as a wife, mother, marchioness – or art patron. In 1499 Leonardo da Vinci stopped in Mantua, on his way to Florence, to study Mantegna's frescoes. While there he was summoned to the marchioness who, in her usual impetuous manner, urged him to paint her portrait.

He probably demurred, for painting Isabella d'Este's portrait

Isabella d'Este by Leonardo da Vinci

was an occupational hazard. 'Ah, how difficult it is to find a painter who will really hit off a natural likeness,' she had grieved in one of her letters. Even Mantegna himself had proved unsatisfactory and she had declined to send the finished portrait to the friend for whom it was intended: 'the painter has done it so badly that it is not in the least like us'. Giovanni Santi, father of Raphael, fared no better 'although he has a reputation for producing good likenesses it seems that this one might well be more like us than it is'. Whether or not Leonardo was reluctant to join that slandered company, he was unable to resist either the blandishments, or the hinted threats, of the wife of the powerful marquis of Mantua. In due coursee he produced a preliminary sketch in charcoal. Like so much else that Leonardo began, he did not finish it and Isabella had to be content with this hasty sketch. It seems to have satisfied her, however, and so survives.

Leonardo's portrait speaks for itself, showing a rather plump, undeniably self-satisfied but indubitably highly intelligent and vivacious woman. The manner in which she dismissed the attempts of earlier, outstanding artists, and then doggedly pursued Leonardo da Vinci until he overcame his habitual procrastination long enough to produce at least a cartoon speaks worlds for the woman herself. Isabella d'Este was a woman who knew what she wanted, was undeterred by a total lack of specialised knowledge, and invariably got what she wanted whether it was a portrait for herself, a cardinal's hat for her son, or freedom for her husband.

Born in 1474, Isabella was sixteen when she married Francesco Gonzaga. The marriage was undoubtedly happy in the early years – probably because she made it very clear that not even Francesco Gonzaga was going to ride rough-shod over her. Early in the marriage, when she was barely twenty-two, she put up a determined fight to protect her jewels which Francesco wanted her to pawn. 'Most of them are already in pawn in Venice – not only those which you yourself gave me but also those which I brought to Mantua as part of my dowry ... If I pawn these, I shall have nothing left and I see myself obliged to wear black – for I should look ridiculous in coloured silks and brocades with no jewels.' Neither did she hesitate to give her husband advice. In 1502, when Cesare Borgia was engaged in his whirlwind campaign in the Romagna, alarming all the small neighbouring states, Francesco Gonzaga had evidently disburdened himself of some pithy opinions about the Borgia. Isabella heard about this and promptly wrote to him. 'There is a rumour here (in Mantua) that your Excellency spoke ill of Valentinois (Cesare Borgia) in the presence of the King of France and some of the pope's household. Whether this is true or false, it will come to the ear of the Valentinois. Since the latter is the sort of man who has no scruple in conspiring against anyone of his own blood, I am certain he would not hesitate to plot against your person ... For this reason, I beg and implore you to take more care of your person and make Alessandro carry out the duties of your carver with the utmost care' [in order to frustrate any Borgia attempts at poison].

Posterity possesses this three-dimensional portrait of Isabella d'Este because of her passion for writing letters, and many of these in turn arose from her passionate love of travel. Here, this restless woman was very much in advance of her day: where most of her contemporaries, both male and female, travelled only from the strictest necessity, she anticipated the twentieth-century tourist. Her intoxicated response to the invitation from Louis XII and Anne of Brittany to visit them in France in order to be godmother to their baby is very much in character. Her letter to her sister-in-law, Elisabetta, in Urbino is bubbling over with an almost schoolgirlish delight at the treat: 'Let me tell you that His Most Christian Majesty thinks that his Queen cannot bring a son in the world unless I am present and that, in consequence, he begs me most persistently to be with her for this event ... O, what splendours, what pomps and what glories I am about to take part in! I shall not only visit Paris, the flourishing university and the most populous city in the world, but the whole of France, Burgundy and Flanders and perhaps I shall go as far as Santiago in Galicia. Oh, what a number of new countries and royal spectacles I shall see in this journey!'

When away from home, she wrote constantly to her family and officers in Mantua, when in Mantua she wrote constantly to those abroad. She took every opportunity to get out of the claustrophobic confinements of the small lakeland city, travelling to Venice, where the jewellers and furriers welcomed this free-spending bluestocking: to Milan, to enjoy the somewhat ambivalent hospitality of her younger sister Beatrice, now queening it as the effective duchess of one of the most powerful

Italian states. Now it was towards Urbino that she made her way, towards the person with whom she was perhaps closest of all, the gentle, beautiful sister-in-law Elisabetta. She went to Rome to acquire a cardinal's hat for her son and grimly stayed there even during the sack of 1527 until she had got that hat.

Affection for her intimates, fierce loyalty for her family were her dominant emotions – yet she did not scruple to benefit from her sister-in-law's misfortune in order to acquire a coveted work of art – and acquiring it from the hands of no other than that same Cesare Borgia against whom she had warned her husband. After Borgia's conquest of Urbino, Isabella had approached him through an intermediary asking for the gift of two exquisite marble statues which had been the property of her sister-in-law Elisabetta and now fell to Borgia as booty. Anxious to ingratiate himself with Isabella, Borgia passed the objects on to her and when, in due course, the Montefeltro family recovered Urbino, Isabella did not feel it necessary to return the art treasures.

Isabella's bad-tempered exchange of letters with her husband were probably the result of the stress to which both were subjected during the time of his captivity. Certainly behind Francesco Gonzaga's autocratic front there was a warm enough personality. He loved his sisters and went to considerable trouble to arrange good marriages for them and when he died, still a comparatively young man, his children were deeply grieved. His true monument lay in the continued survival of his miniature state. It lay exactly between the two great and mutually inimical states of Milan and Venice, and the fact that Gonzaga was able to fight now for one, now for the other and yet retain his essential independence is no small tribute to his courage and skill. It was precisely this ability of the princes of these small states to play off their neighbours one against the other, retaining their own identity by the exercise of intelligence, that allowed the cross-fertilisation of culture within a larger society that characterised the Renaissance in Italy.

The Estensi of Ferrara

Gonzaga's neighbours and relatives, the Estensi of Ferrara, might have been type-cast for that role of a degenerate princely family of the period which has coloured the imagination of northern nations. Even the temperate Burckhardt lets himself go when describing them. 'Within the palace frightful deeds were perpetrated: a princess was beheaded (1425) for alleged adultery with a stepson; legitimate and illegitimate children fled from the court and even abroad their lives were threatened by assassins sent in pursuit of them (1471). Plots from without were incessant: the bastard of a bastard tries to wrest the crown from the lawful heir, Ercole I: this latter is said afterwards (1493) to have poisoned his wife on discovering that she was going to poison him. This list of tragedies is closed by the plot of two bastards against their brother, the ruling duke, Alfonso I, which was punished with imprisonment for life.'[24] The state run by such a family should, on this evidence, have been an anarchic hell where only the brutal survived. In fact, Ferrara was a model of good government, in advance of most cities in terms of administration and, under its energetic duke, Ercole I, the first planned town of modern Europe.

Time has dealt badly with the city, compared with its two peers. Urbino is still essentially a mountain city, splendidly crowning its double peak, its modern development discreetly tucked away. Mantua's centre, though spanning the centuries, is still essentially homogeneous, with the great palace as background. In Ferrara, Ercole's exciting town plan has been swallowed up by the twentieth-century system whose passion for wide, straight, endless roads has exaggerated the Renaissance formalism. The Este palace is still distinctive, surrounded by its water-filled moat and the great walls, created by Alfonso d'Este in response to the menace of artillery, still encompass the city. But because there is no rock substrata, Ferrara is a low-built sprawling city with no one building or group of buildings to make a definite statement of identity. The pre-Renaissance city was notorious for its darkness, its mosquito haunted streets, for no part of Ferrara is more than ten metres above sea level. A branch of the Po almost washes its walls, and the great river itself is alternately threat and highway, a major means of communication but also a very real danger in times of flood.

In October 1419 the anonymous contributor to the *Diario Ferrarese* noted that the Po had broken its banks. 'And it was decreed, under penalty of death, that every man should go to repair the (breach) so that waters would not pass beyond.' Ferrara's geography contributed, in no small part, to its adoption of a 'despotic' form of government: land reclamation and flood protection demands a high level of centralised control.

Unlike most of their contemporary fellow princes who tended to be parvenu, coming to power by fraud or violence, the Estensi were not only long established, but had been freely placed in their position of power by the citizens themselves. The family were of Lombard origin, tracing themselves back to the ninth century. They held the title of marchese from the emperor, and their name from one of their castles, that of Este, in the nearby Euganean Hills. In 1264, after nearly a century of the usual factional in-fighting, the citizens of Ferrara recognised, by general vote, a certain Obizzo d'Este as heir to his grandfather and, hence, as legal lord of the city. Ferrara might have been chosen to illustrate the tangle of rights in an Italian urban community. The citizens had freely chosen their lord, but the city itself was a fief of the Papacy and the lord held the title of the emperor. By the time the family were driven off the political stage, in 1598, they were doubly ducal, invested as dukes of Ferrara first by the emperor and then by the pope. Throughout their career they were in an unusual position – at times advantageous, at other times decidedly dangerous – of simultaneously holding power by grace of Europe's two mutually exclusive supra-national authorities.

Ferrara's maximum population was 30,000. Unlike its much bigger neighbours Milan and Florence, it had no great industry: unlike Venice, no world-wide trade. It possessed an excellent agriculture, created through reclamation of the rich alluvial lands; and its position on the major trade routes – in particular on that great highway the Po – gave it a very considerable income in customs dues and transport fees. This local source of income was augmented by resource to that universal milch-cow the Jew, who found in Ferrara a particularly safe refuge. And the trade of condottiere which most of the family followed from time to time brought in more funds: for example, Ercole d'Este as Lieutenant-General of the League of Naples, Milan and Florence had a stipend of 50,000 florins in peace and 80,000 in war. The maintenance of the brilliant Este court, however, must have been a very heavy strain on these not particularly prodigal sources of income. Manipulation of finances, in particular the creation and extraction of novel forms of taxation, was a skill the Estensi learned at a very early stage. They were helped by the fact that the city was totally under their control: there was no middle class created by trade wealth to question their decrees, and one of their first acts on assuming power had been to crush the guilds. In Ferrara, a citizen was either a pleb, or he worked for the court.

Ferrara's Golden age lasted perhaps a century from the reign of Niccolò III d'Este, who died in 1441, to the death of Alfonso d'Este, husband of Lucrezia Borgia, in 1534. Niccolò played, in Ferrara, much the same role that his contemporary Cosimo de' Medici played in Florence – strengthening and widening the base of his dynasty's power, ruling cannily, ruthlessly if necessary but always sensibly, and infusing a genuine enthusiasm for the new culture in all that he did. Like Cosimo de' Medici he, too, gained that rarest of accolades on his death –*Pater Patriae*. He came to the throne as a child in 1393, ruling for more than forty-eight years. He followed the lead of Gonzaga in Mantua by setting up a foremost humanist as tutor to his son Leonello. The man he invited in 1429 was Guarino da Verona, a friend of Vittorino da Feltre who introduced the same technique of education into Ferrara. Merit alone dictated the choice of pupils and frequently Guarino would support the young student from his own resources. Niccolò recognised the quality of the man, and later backed his appointment as professor of Greek and Latin at the university of Ferrara, an appointment which took the university at one step into the leading ranks of Italian centres of learning.

It was popularly supposed that Niccolò d'Este's bastards were uncountable, a fact which was to create considerable confusion over the next generations' rights of succession. Niccolò recognised twenty-seven, and with that flair of his for detecting genuine merit, he declared that two of these bastards – Leonello and his half-brother Borso – should be his direct heirs until the legitimate heir, Ercole, was of age. It was a good choice. Guarino da Verona's tutorship had made of Leonello a person who combined gentleness with responsibility – one, moreover, with a deep, informed love of the new learning and the arts. The brilliant Florentine exile Leon Battista Alberti, that genuine 'universal man' with equal talents as writer, architect and social commentator, became a personal friend of the young marquis. The court at Ferrara rivalled that at Urbino for the number of artists and craftsmen who found a good living at it. One of Leonello's first acts on coming to power was to give reformed statutes to the university, altering its balance away from law in favour of the arts – there were over 300 arts students as against thirty or so in law during his reign, although the importance of law studies continued to be reflected in the salaries of its professors – far higher than for those in the arts. The success of Leonello's reforms can be measured by the increased popularity of the university, students in all faculties increasing tenfold.

Inspired by the same passion for dissecting and analysing social behaviour that moved Machiavelli and Castiglione to write their treatises on the prince and on the courtier one of the Ferrarese humanists, Angelo Decembrio, attempted the same for the literary man. His book *De politia litteraria*, takes the form of a series of dialogues supposedly taking place between Leonello and his friends and is an attempt to portray the man of general culture and good taste. The modern art historian, Michael Baxandall, describes Decembrio's work roundly as 'a badly written book that repels attention in several ways' and certainly the rhetoric, which is both verbose and cloying, is scarcely to the taste of the late twentieth century. His portrait of Leonello carefully – anxiously – choosing his clothes according to the astrological code for the day, is almost a caricature of the precious, self-conscious aesthete. But the book itself gives a good picture of the interacting personalities that produce a court and, through that court, produces a distinctive cultural pattern.

Leonello died young and his brother Borso succeeded. Pius II knew the young man well and included a friendly, if somewhat tongue-in-cheek portrait in his voluminous *Commentary*. 'He was a man of fine physique and more than average height, with beautiful hair and a pleasing countenance. He was eloquent and garrulous and listened to himself talking as he pleased himself more than his bearers. His talk was full of blandishments mixed with lies ... During his lifetime the people erected in the piazza a statue which represented him seated administering justice. It bore an inscription composed in flattery and adulation for Borso loved nothing so much as praise.' A rather shallow, vain man with a passionate liking for luxuries, he was also highly competent as an administrator, operating a tax system that squeezed the maximum from his subjects yet did not drive them to despair so that, as so often happens, they revelled in the splendour of their prince, unmindful of the fact that most of the financing of that splendour came from their own pockets. For Borso eschewed the trade of condottiere as vulgar and danger- ous, preferring such fiscal experiments as selling public offices. But he had, too, a strong sense of responsibility towards his house. According, again, to Pius, 'He never took a wife with the right excellent intention of leaving to the rightful heirs the sovereignty, which he had occupied in their stead while they were children.' It was a remarkable exercise in self-restraint when the ambition of most illegitimate claimants was to usurp the legitimate, all the more praiseworthy when it is considered that, in 1471, he became duke, converting his already impressive dynasty into a dukedom.

But it was at this apogee of its fame that the Este dynasty nearly fell apart for, with the death of the illegitimate Borso, the legitimate Estes began a vicious infighting to gain the ducal biretta. Ercole, eldest legitimate son of old Niccolò, emerged triumphant at the age of forty. He could have stood as model for Machiavelli's *Prince* – a handsome, cold, cynical opportunist. The Ferrarese, with the Italian fondness for the vivid nickname, called him the North Wind or the Diamond, as testimony to that cold, hard character. Yet he was the kind of man that Ferrara needed at precisely that point. He began his rule with a wholesale spate of executions, eliminating the nearest and most dangerous of the possible claimants like a cuckoo fledgling clearing the nest. Then he stopped. On a certain Christmas Eve one of the city's magistrates approached him with yet another list of pro- scriptions. Duke Ercole took the paper from him and without deigning to glance at it, threw it into the fire and thereafter, apart from criminal executions, the headsman remained unemployed in Ferrara. He shared the Este intellectualism, but with him it took the form of a passion for architecture. It was he who replanned Ferrara, extending it and imposing a grid system of straight, wide streets that is still a feature of the city, upon the

Ercole d' Este by Dosso

medieval chaos, and building palaces for himself and his family.

The Este matrimonial network spread across Italy from north to south, from east to west, involving directly or indirectly most of the leading families, a fact that was to have a profound significance for the future peace of the land. Ercole was married to the beautiful Eleanor of Aragon, daughter of the Spanish king of Naples – an enchanting girl with black hair and startling blue-green eyes whose charm and spirit succeeded even in warming the North Wind, melting the Diamond. He had five children by her, three of whom were in due course linked into the matrimonial network: three boys, of whom Alfonso was married to Lucrezia Borgia, much against his will, and two girls Isabella and Beatrice, the first becoming the bride of Francesco Gonzaga of Mantua, the second the bride of Ludovico Sforza of Milan.

Beatrice died at the age of twenty-two before her character was truly formed; her portrait bust by Cristoforo Romano shows an almost childish roundness and softness. Yet she was anything but soft by nature and the fact that she was able to attract the respect of a woman like her sister, and the love of a man like Ludovico Sforza argues that there was much more to her than the impetuous, rather spoilt adolescent she appears to be. Born in 1475, she was a year younger than Isabella and spent the greater part of her childhood away from her, in Naples. Their mother, Eleanor, had taken her children to pay their respects to her father, and King Ferrante of Naples had so taken to the little girl, so much an Aragonese in every way, that she remained there for eight years. By one of the ironies of history one of her playmates was her cousin, Isabella d'Aragona, who would in due course marry the true heir to Milan, Gian Galeazzo Sforza and, as a result, come into direct opposition with Beatrice, herself by then the wife of the usurper Ludovico Sforza.

With Alfonso d'Este, who became duke on the death of his father in 1505, the martial spirit returned to the Este family. He had a surprisingly sensitive taste for music, but ignored all other arts: the collecting of jewels and sonnets, the building of great palaces and libraries – the whole new world of culture – was subordinated by this grim young man to one passion, artillery. He spent his days in foundries and proving grounds, dressed in the same greasy clothes as his workmen, sharing a democracy of labour for this one object, that of producing bigger and better guns. He redesigned the fortifications of Ferrara, drilled and drilled and drilled again until he was, by all accounts, the foremost artilleryman in Italy. The only women he had any time for were prostitutes, declining to spend valuable time away from his guns on fashionable dalliance. He was therefore profoundly irritated when his father announced that he had found a bride for him – the daughter of Pope Alexander VI. Alexander Borgia had good reasons to want to tie the state of Ferrara close to him for his son, Cesare, was engaged in building a principality near by. Duke Ercole disliked the idea as much as his son but, aristocratic though his house was compared with the upstart Borgia, even he could not resist the pressures that the papal monarch could bring to bear. The pope mixed bribes with threats, offering substantial subsidies, reduction in the dues Ferrara owed as a fief of the Papacy, as well as an enormous dowry provided by the papal Curia itself. Alfonso still resisted whereupon his father threatened that if he did not marry the girl then he, Ercole, would do so. As Ercole was at that time a widower, but still in the prime of life, there was little doubt but that he could carry out his threat, creating yet another Este genealogical tangle, jeopardising Alfonso's own succession by procreating a brood of Borgia-Este. Reluctantly Alfonso d'Este agreed – and, in fact, got a far better wife than the girl's reputation argued.

Looking back over the hundred years of Estensi rule during this climacteric period is to see, despite republican propaganda, that a succession of intelligent princes with a secure base could create something as durable as a republic. Each of these Estensi princes contributed something, inherited something. Niccolò had begun by providing a firm base and employing the humanists who had very considerable administrative as well as decorative value. Leonello, the aesthete, had built on his father's pragmatic foundation, making Ferrara a cultural centre, giving the university an unrivalled reputation for literature and philology. Borso, who followed, seems almost a buffoon by contrast – a tough, cheerful philistine whose only passion seemed to be that of the chase. But it was he who undertook a massive programme in land reclamation that was to benefit Ferrarese agriculture for centuries more. And, with that touch of incongruity that characterised so many of the Estensi, he had a passion for the theatre, adding another potent ingredient to the Ferrarese cultural brew. Ercole contributed town-planning to the family heritage, creating the so-called Herculean Addition that is still a distinctive feature of the city. And finally his son, Alfonso, maintained and developed the family love of music and contributed his skill as artilleryman to protect the wealth that had developed under the dynasty.

In the eyes of republicans, Ferrara was a despotism, an offence to the natural law. But the extraordinary hold that the idea of 'the prince' held upon the minds of its citizens was demonstrated by the occasion in 1482 when the city was under assault by the Venetians. The duke, Ercole, lay apparently dying; the despondent citizens were on the verge of surrender when the duchess Eleanor opened her husband's sickroom to the people, nobles and plebs alike. They filed through, and the sight of their duke fighting for his life apparently gave them heart to go on fighting the city's external enemy. Worship of the signore might be unpalatable to republicans, but it was a potent fact of life.

And, as though the whole Ferrarese story had been set up to be an experiment in civics, a working model of urban politics, when the grip of the Estensi was lessened in 1598 and the city passed under the control of its lawful suzerain, the pope, it returned to the dowdy provincial town that it had been before the Estensi established themselves as its lords.

6
Domestic interior

The family

The concept of the family was the bedrock upon which Italian society, from the time of the Romans onward, was founded. There was very little sentiment about the concept, nothing resembling the Teutonic mystic nonsense of *blutbrüderschaft*: a race that found a need to coin words for the actions described by matricide, parricide and fratricide obviously did not place excessive value upon the emotional link. But the importance of the idea of the family is evidenced by the remarkable number of names describing blood and marriage relationships – casa, schiatta, stirpe, nazione, casato, progenia, famiglia, consorteria – and, for the more distant but still connected relationship: lignaggio and agnato. The idea of the family can contract to signify little more than a direct blood relationship between parents and children and between siblings, or expand to include clan, tribe or even race.

Leon Battista Alberti's *I libri della famiglia* provides a species of blueprint for this vital subject, a sociological dissection as priceless as *The Prince* or *The Courtier*. Alberti goes far beyond considering the simple, nuclear family and its household needs: he is, in fact, describing the operation of a federation of groups that bear the same name, discussing their whole sequence of roles from the economic to the political and as such reflecting the complex nature of the family in Italian society. In its dealing with real, named people in credible situations *I libri della famiglia* far more closely resembles *The Courtier* than the bloodless political treatise, *The Prince*. Alberti, indeed, drew so directly on living

Leon Battista Alberti

material, and presented it in so lively if frequently uncomplimentary a fashion that his relatives strongly objected to the book. The

Albertis were a noble Florentine family who were thrust into exile as part of the city's endless jockeying for equilibrium in the late fourteenth century. Alberti himself was born in exile, in 1404, and did not see his native city until he was twenty-four years old. His treatise, cast in the fashionable form of a dialogue, was drafted some time before 1434 but was not printed until 1474. It therefore reflects, as do most of such treatises, what the inner circle of people were thinking rather than the wider public.

The family forms an island of certainty in a treacherous sea and the heart of that island is the house itself. Buy rather than rent, Alberti exhorts his readers, for the money stays in your own pocket. All the branches of the family should live under one roof, eat at one table for purposes of economy. Money is of little value by itself – land is what is required, for land never goes away never loses value. Don't buy produce, for the seller only sells the worst and keeps the best for himself. Get hold of a farm, if you can – but keep down the number of peasants you must employ – and here Alberti is the authentic urban snob: 'It is hard to believe how much wickedness there is among ploughmen raised among the clods.'

The farm is for the family's sustenance – but it will be necessary, too, to have a trade – 'working wool or silk or something similar'. Keep it in the family, don't bring in a partner if it can possibly be avoided. There is no need to give an allowance to the children for the father feeds and clothes them and they should have no use for cash. Clothes should be of 'joyous' colours – but of good cloth and conservative cut and Alberti mocks the growing new fashion of multi-coloured and slashed garments 'fit only for clowns'.

The picture that Alberti paints of the family's relationship with the outside world is decidedly bleak. Friends? It is better to be friends with the prosperous rather than the poor. Lend money if it is quite unavoidable – but only if you are sure of getting it back. And as far as the nobility is concerned, Alberti's advice is succinct: avoid them, avoid the great ones of the land. Don't lend money to a noble lord at all, it is far better to give him twenty florins as a gift than a hundred as a loan. Never expect gratitude from a social superior – they are surrounded only by flatterers. Courtiers are a breed of parasites that will waste an honest man's time as well as their own. Don't believe that it is possible to buy the goodwill of the great with lavish presents and entertainments. 'They treat your loans as gifts and regard your promises as obligations.'

Alberti's portrait of the perfect wife is, for posterity, less than pleasing. He is speaking in the persona of Gianozzo, a man in his sixties, but explicitly records his admiration of Gianozzo's bleak precepts. A wife is, at best, a loyal servant: under certain very limited conditions she can be regarded as a partner but on the whole, it is safer to treat her as a kind of Trojan horse sent in by that vast, inimical outside world. Gianozzo describes in detail how he broke in his young wife. After she has been settled in the home, for all the world like a young puppy getting over the loss of her mother, he takes her round the house. He shows her everything – except his books and papers. He records his pleasure at the fact that, even had she seen them, she would have been unable to read them, being illiterate. Men who take business counsel with their wives are simply asking for trouble: 'I did not doubt that my wife was most loving, but I still considered it safer to have her unable, and not merely unwilling, to harm me.' He then proceeds to drum precept after precept into the stunned ears of the poor girl: precepts on chastity, on housekeeping, on the iniquity of cosmetics (his hearers are particularly interested in this as they have been quite unable to prevent their wives using unguents). He touches on theology, on the necessity of having everything in its due place, on the virtues of obedience, prefacing every precept with an unctuous, 'Dear wife'. At the end he is asked, 'Did she seem willing to follow your advice?' and he replies, with unconscious irony, 'She seemed quite lost in thought for some time.' The reader is not surprised.

It is difficult to reconcile this approval of the humourless, pedantic, nagging Gianozzo with Alberti's undoubted charm and humanity. Apart from the fact that Alberti's book is composed, literally, of dialogues in which strongly differentiated characters advance idiosyncratic ideas, the explanation for his somewhat jaundiced view of marriage lies perhaps in his own personal circumstance. He was illegitimate by birth and though he benefited from the humane Italian view of illegitimacy in which the child was proudly recognised by the father, and brought up

by him, it must have affected his character. He was, too, a
lifelong bachelor, eventually taking Holy Orders and his view of
marriage is therefore that of one who understands how the
machinery works but not why. The poverty of his student days
would probably colour his opinion of property and money, but
here he certainly did not share Gianozzo's philistine outlook.
Later in the book, Gianozzo appears as the epitome of the
'hard-headed businessman', a man endowed with many of the
social virtues – thrift, self-reliance, industry, but also with the
lack of vision of such a man. He scoffs at those who give time to
public service – only a fool, or a knave undertakes public office
for the office holder is either bowed down under responsibilities
for which he will receive no gratitude, or is tempted to use his
power for corrupt purposes. As an honest author, Alberti allows
his character to develop his distasteful argument but, through an
attractive, young interlocutor, he implicitly condemns such an
approach.

Alberti was writing for publication, not in the modern sense,
certainly, but in the knowledge and desire that his book would be
circulated at least in his peer group. It is, to that extent, a
polished, literary example of a fairly common genre, the family
'ricordi' or memoir. An outstanding example of this was the
commonplace book or *Zibaldone* which Giovanni Rucellai, of
the aristocratic Florentine family, began in 1457, and which was
continued by his sons, grandsons and great grandsons until well
into the sixteenth century. The ricordi was to the family what the
chronicle was to the city: like the chronicle, its literary value
varied according to the skill of its current compiler. Like the
chronicle, its historical value is incalculable for it was an
unselfconscious reflection of day-to-day family life. In the earlier
periods there was an obsession with genealogy, a desire to
establish the antiquity of one's own house – again, much as the
city chronicles strove to prove the establishment of their city by
Julius Caesar or Aeneas. Meditations on the problems of
bringing up children, proud asides as to the achievement of a son,
snippets of family history, interpretations of law and politics all
bear testimony to the overriding importance of 'the family' in the
Italian mind. No man is wholly alone: always he had the support,
grudging or otherwise, of the family network. He who brings

honour, or dishonour, upon himself brings it upon the family. There is a dark side to this sense of cohesion, of belonging, and that is the vendetta. The Italian blood feud with its drama and high tragedy captured the imagination of northerners, but they had little need to exaggerate. Montagues and Capulets could be found in every city, avenging some frequently forgotten first cause in the name of family solidarity.

Women and the home

Within the all-embracing net of the family, women were relatively free and the regard in which they were held was much warmer than Alberti admitted in his treatise. And they were considerably more important than the ricordi, with their obsession regarding male inheritance, were prepared to concede. The position of women in society, and the customs that marked their passage through life, differed from region to region, giving additional colour to the picture of Renaissance Italy as a universe composed of island universes. But, again, their common italianità allows a composite picture to be built up, even as the wealth of documentation for all classes gives vivid detail to the picture.

First communion was taken at seven and nubility was reckoned as starting at twelve years. Although the legal age of marriage was at least twelve, betrothal could take place literally from the cradle onwards. And betrothal was a ceremony scarcely less binding than marriage itself. The squalid tactics adopted by Francesco Sforza to break the betrothal between his son and the eldest daughter of the marquis of Mantua demonstrates just how strong was that ceremony. After the betrothal it was discovered that the unfortunate girl suffered from curvature of the spine and both parties agreed that her sister Dorotea should be substituted. Then, for political reasons, Sforza wanted to break off the Gonzaga match and began to make quibbling objections. He was worried that Dorotea might suffer from the same affliction as her sister. Would the marquis kindly agree to having the girl inspected by independent medical authorities? Gonzaga agreed, with reluctance, and there then followed an unedifying correspondence regarding the degree to which the girl should be stripped. Sforza insisted that she be entirely nude: Gonzaga wanted to protect her from humiliation. After prolonged fencing of this nature Gonzaga at last acted with considerable dignity, saying he did not wish to subject his beloved daughter to more humiliation and offering to break off the betrothal if that was what Sforza wanted. It was precisely what Sforza wanted, and the engagement was annulled forthwith.

In the lower, as in the upper classes, arranged marriages were the norm but there was still room for spontaneous decision as Bandino's delightful story proves. A broomseller entering Genoa from the country caught sight of a woman leaning out of an upper window. 'Hey, Madonna,' he called out, 'Can you find me a girl?' The woman was indignant. 'Scoundrel! Do you take me for a bawd?' He hastened to reassure her: 'You mistake me, I want a wife.' The woman's attitude changed immediately and she told him to return on the morrow. He did so, and the woman introduced him to a pretty girl, they were promptly married and presumably lived happily ever after.

However, the carefully arranged marriage was by far the more common with the young man's mother discreetly but expertly assessing the bride. Lucrezia Tornabuoni's description of the bride-to-be of her son Lorenzo the Magnificent is a classic of its kind. 'She is reasonably tall,' she wrote to her husband Piero de' Medici, 'and fair-skinned. She is gentle in manner without the ease we are used to, but she is obedient and will soon conform with our ways. Her hair is not blond: they are not blond here (in Rome) but it is reddish and plentiful. Her face is on the round side. Her neck is slender – almost perhaps on the thin side – but graceful. We didn't see her bosom, the women cover it here, but it gave the impression of being well-formed.' In other cases it is the prince's ambassadors who have the delicate task of assessing the bride. Thus the ambassadors of Duke Ercole of Ferrara sent back a carefully worded report on the character of Lucrezia Borgia, the intended of their master's son, Alfonso. 'She is of incontestable beauty and her manners add to her charm. She seems so gifted that we cannot, and should not, suspect her of unseemly behaviour. Apart from her perfect grace in all things, she is a Catholic and shows she fears God.'

In the lower classes bride and bridegroom usually came from

the same locality and were likely to have known each other, if only by sight. In the upper classes they probably did not meet until the day of signing the contract. In Venice, that day was as great an event as the wedding itself. The bridegroom and his friends were received on the steps of the bride's home by her father and conducted inside. There would be a general atmosphere of celebration with the choicest food and wines and music until an appropriate moment when the inner door would be thrown open and the bride appeared, with her hair down and dressed entirely in either white or peacock blue. She was ceremonially introduced to her betrothed, but almost immediately afterwards was escorted to a splendidly decorated gondola and there, accompanied by all her female relatives and friends, the brilliant little fleet would set off for a round of visits to acquaint the world with her change of status. The unmarried girl lived in a kind of limbo, marriage conferring freedom as well as dignity upon her.

The bride's assent was taken for granted. Nevertheless, the Christian contract of marriage conferred a rare dignity upon her, for her specific assent was essential before the contract was signed. A stubborn girl could withhold her refusal – and occasionally win. Thus, in Siena, the notary who was engaged to draw up the contract thought it prudent to publish the fact that, 'I find the parties stiff-necked, especially the girl, who yesterday morning before the people cast herself on her knees, praying me to do her any injury but that man's wife she will not become.' The matter came to the ears of the Bishop of Siena who wrote to the Captain of the People, the city's chief law officer, asking him to put an end to the marriage proposals and so avoid a public scandal.

Second only to the girl's formal assent was the problem of the dowry she would bring. At the upper end of society, the dowry was one of the major means of creating political alliances. Indeed, the claim to bridal lands was one of the main sources of conflict, among others precipitating that wave of foreign invaders which began with Louis XII's claim to Milan as a French descendant of Valentina Visconti, the duke's daughter who was married to a French duke. The actual cash transaction included in the dower was only too often a means of 'buying' the heir to an aristocratic house for a parvenue. Galeazzo Visconti of Milan paid over 300,000 florins, as well as ceding five cities, in order to marry his daughter Violante to the son of the King of England. It was a bad bargain for the unfortunate young man succumbed to the Italian climate within three months and there was much bitter and undignified squabbling about the return of the dowry. Taddea d'Este brought Francesco Novello of Carrara a dowry of 180,000 florins whereas her sister, married off to a minor prince, took only 20,000 with her.

The dowry was a burden through all classes of society: in the early fifteenth century St Bernardino of Siena roundly condemned it as a tax on fathers. In the lower levels of society, there was a considerable justification for such a crippling burden on the parents, for it did ensure that a young couple embarking on married life were backed by hard cash during the first crucial years. But a poor man, or a mean one, or a man who had several daughters, could condemn a luckless girl to a wasted life by refusing, or being unable, to dower her. At the birth of his daughter, a prudent man would establish a fund through one of the banks or moneylenders against the day of that daughter's marriage. In most cities, too, charities provided dowries for fatherless girls, or girls of poor parents and these helped to reduce the number of unmarried girls. But only too often the local convent would be increased by more teenaged girls, condemned to a convent life without the smallest vocation for it, merely because it was impossible to buy them husbands.

The dowry was returnable on the wife's death, or when the couple separated – a very fruitful source of dissension and litigation. It was simple enough to legislate for the case of a girl who died shortly after marriage, or before having children but it was what happened in later years that caused the greater discord. In general, the husband was allowed to use the dowry, having given proper security for it. Sometimes even during the wife's lifetime, the capital could be sacrificed for pressing needs: thus a particular peasant woman applied for permission to dispose of a portion of her dowry because she and her husband and children did not have enough money even for food.

Until the mid-sixteenth century, when the Council of Trent enacted that marriages had to take place in church, the wedding ceremony was, as often as not, a purely civil affair and took place with a marked absence of ceremony, compared with the betrothal. The exchange of a ring, a kiss and a promise before witnesses were all that was required.

Not all welcomed the decree emanating from the Council of Trent. As late as 1580, when a friar was preaching in a church in Treviso emphasising the need to obey the decree, an elderly gentleman rose indignantly and said that it needed no priest to make an honest woman of his daughter. At the other extreme, however, were those who were attracted by the novelty and insisted on such a wedding, though clearly in arrears. Among those was the citizen of Rovigo who appeared before the town's chief magistrate accompanied by his wife and string of children, demanding a wedding.

The wedding ceremony itself might be simple, perfunctory, but the celebrations were invariably on the most lavish scale possible, the sumptuary laws being broken in city after city to accommodate the prodigality. At the marriage of Ercole d'Este with Eleanor of Aragon in Ferrara, the banquet lasted from 8 am to 3 pm: entire oxen roasted in sweetmeat coverings were followed by courses of gilded sheep and every possible kind of game. Edible pies, on being cut open, disclosed children in fancy dress. At the wedding of Annibale Bentivogli in Bologna in 1487, the celebrations went on for four days. The feast itself went on for as long as the Este banquet when 800 barrels of wine, 30,000 pounds of meat – excluding game – and 350 pounds of sweetmeats were consumed. Entire structures of sugar encased living birds and, in one case, a live pig which irritably broke its way out. When Lucrezia Borgia came to Ferrara there was an incredible display of rope dancing with men sliding down a rope fixed to the towering pinnacle of the cathedral. The marriage of Beatrice d'Este and Lodovico Sforza (il Moro) in Milan was enlivened by the remarkable mechanical devices of Leonardo da Vinci who, like other artists, did not disdain to waste his talents on what amounted to fairground amusements. Some of the entertainments provided spoke of a crueller, cruder past barely hidden by the current sophistication. Bullfights and tournaments were commonplace but at Urbino the celebrations designed to welcome the gentle Elisabetta Gonzaga included a naked man struggling with a wild cat. The injuries he received were so severe that the duke felt obliged to give him a pension. Lorenzo the Magnificent spent 10,000 florins for the joust alone at his wedding to Clarice Orsini.

After the wedding, the bride might remain in her father's house for anything up to a fortnight, but thereafter she was conducted to her husband's home with the utmost pomp. The bridal procession was not only a means of display, but it also provided the very important opportunity to tell the world that the girl had passed from her father's to her husband's protection. In Florence, spectacular torchlight processions were particularly popular, bride and groom being preceded by trumpets and drums. In Bologna, it was the father who brought the girl to her husband's house, she sitting pillion behind him on horseback. In Naples, the bride rode alone on a snow-white horse, followed by a mounted escort. In Rome, the ancient custom of sword and honey was still enacted: on arrival at the bridegroom's house he and the bride were given honey as a foretaste of marriage's sweetness, but a sword was meanwhile held over the bride's head as warning of the perils of adultery.

The actual bedding was a public affair, reports of the wedding night being circulated afterwards not simply out of salacity or masculine egotism but to establish the simple, vital fact that the marriage had been consummated. The grave, withdrawn Pope Clement VII attended the bridal chamber of his grandniece Caterina de' Medici on the occasion of her wedding to the Dauphin, and seemed disposed to accept evidence of pregnancy right away. In Urbino, the delicately brought up, beautifully behaved Duchess Elisabetta burst in on her niece's bedchamber the following morning with the enthusiastic remark 'Is it not wonderful to sleep with the men!'

In theory, expenditure upon all aspects of the wedding, including the bride's trousseau, was controlled by the sumptuary laws. These artificial attempts to restrict personal expenditure had been in existence for at least 200 years, but the one factor common to their operation in all cities was the industry and ingenuity devoted to evading them. The Florentine writer, Francesco Sachetti, in one of his witty novellas described the exasperated reaction of the unfortunate officials whose task it was to prowl the streets, apprehending anybody who seemed to be breaking the law by dressing too luxuriously. It was an impossible task, as one such official said feelingly, 'If I ask a woman why she is wearing a headband – which is forbidden – she tells me it is a garland. I stop another woman saying, "You mustn't wear buttons," and she tells me that they are not buttons, but toggles. I ask another why she is wearing ermine. "It isn't ermine," she says, "it's a suckling." And what, I ask, is a suckling. "A kind of animal," she replies. It's hopeless!' All classes were united in evading the sumptuary laws, whether it was the market women wearing the buttons forbidden to her class, or the parents of Lorenzo de' Medici who, usually so meticulous in observing the state's laws, blithely disregarded them when it came to celebrating their son's wedding.

The girl's trousseau was therefore limited only by the depth of her father's pocket and the major item in that trousseau was the bridal chest, or 'cassone'. Beginning as a plain, though solid, wooden coffer, by the fifteenth century it had become a major work of art. In some parts of Italy the fashion was to carve the

Adimari cassone: detail

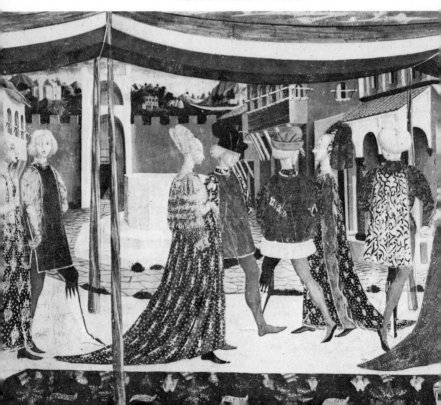

chest: in others – notably Florence – it was painted, a custom which has given posterity a number of vivid pictures of contemporary life. The Adimari cassone not only shows the wedding ceremony but also a rare picture of Florence in the early Renaissance. In the background is the black and white Baptistry that preceded the great cathedral. The wedding party is in black and gold, the rest in more colourful costume, in a procession proceeding from the Baptistry – where a small orchestra is entertaining them – to the bride's house on the other side of the street. Even the poorest girl would hope to have her cassone

Battista Sforza, wife of Federigo da Montefeltro

which, apart from the bed, would form the major article of furniture in the sparsely furnished bedroom.

Though she was denied all political rights and was, according to both civil and canon law, reckoned as being subject to her husband, the Italian woman of this period was by no means her husband's chattel and the overall impression conveyed of married couples at all levels of society is of two people working steadily in partnership towards a common end. Federigo da Montefeltro, that tough, unsentimental soldier, deeply mourned the passing of his wife, Battista Sforza. He was twenty-five years her senior, and she died when she was barely twenty-five years old, yet during their twelve-year marriage they had managed to bridge the gap of years. 'She was the beloved consort of my fortunes and domestic cares, the delight equally of my public and private hours ... ' Battista Sforza admittedly occupied a somewhat unusual position, being obliged to act virtually as regent during the many months that her husband was campaigning away from home, but even at lower levels of society there emerges this clear picture of a wife as her husband's helpmate and, for all practical purposes, his equal. Most of the first-hand evidence relating to marital relationships is derived from letters passing between the wife and her husband who is, usually, a merchant or diplomat away on business. Affection is again and again warmly evident. Niccolò Machiavelli does not seem the most likely person to inspire tender feelings in a young woman, but the letter which his wife wrote to him while he was absent on state business in Rome shows that appearances can mislead. She had heard reports that plague was abroad in the city and was worried about him. 'Imagine if I can be happy when I can rest neither day nor night. The baby is well and resembles you. He is as white as snow, but his head is like a little bit of black velvet and he is as hairy as you are. And his resemblance to you makes me think him beautiful.'

The ideal example of the virtuous and loyal wife was Elisabetta Gonzaga, Duchess of Urbino. The fact that her husband was impotent was grounds enough for declaring the marriage null but steadfastly she remained faithful to him, refusing even to consider a divorce. Castiglione describes how, during one of the debates over which she presided, her guest Cesare Gonzaga somewhat tactlessly began to hold forth on the subject of chastity. He was expatiating on the duchess's own painful situation, congratulating her with elephantine clumsiness, when she interrupted with a forcefulness totally at variance with one of her gentle nature: 'Speak of something else and no more of this, for you have enough to say on other matters.' Even as the romantic love affair can end in the loveless marriage, so the arranged political marriage could become the romantic love affair.

Whether the woman was the wife of a peasant, a merchant, or a prince, she was expected to be able to turn her hand to housewifely tasks. The redoubtable Caterina Sforza, beauty and virago though she was, yet found time to run her home and was particularly proud of her range of recipes. Parisina, Marchioness of Ferrara, made a habit of visiting the local second-hand market to buy old linen. The wife of Marco Cornaro, Doge of Venice, personally patched and re-lined his garments. Beatrice d'Este wrote to her sister Isabella saying that she had planted a whole field of garlic for the seasoning of Isabella's favourite dishes when she could at last favour Beatrice with a visit. Thrift, economy, making-do was the norm even among the wealthy. In the palace of Lodovico Sforza, one of the most prodigal of princes, 'everything is weighed, the hay, the butter, the cheese'. A young Sienese girl, married to a wealthy merchant, wrote to her father chiding herself, 'I have been extravagant and ordered four legs, five pieces of bacon and a little suet. I have bought a pig which leaves me less money, for if one buys cheap it is worth nothing.'

The home to which the young bride was brought might be a labourer's cottage, a merchant's solid house, or a duke's palace but in each case the common characteristic, to modern eyes, would be its sparse furnishings. The Davanzati Palace in Florence, currently set out in sixteenth-century furnishings, is splendidly painted – but curiously comfortless, the rooms with their high walls looking like cells. In this particular palace, the use of glass for windows both provides evidence of the family's wealth and of the relative stability of society. But that stability is still only relative, as witness the massive, iron-studded shutters of those windows.

Piano nobile, Davanzati Palace

The ancient Roman architectural form of the open porch was widespread. Known as the loggia, it was one of the attractive features of every house that could afford the space for it. Usually it was built on the side of the house, less often it was built on top and so formed the upper floor. The roof was held up by pillars, round which vines trained, the beautiful plant being both useful and decorative. Here, in summer, the family entertained its friends to a meal. Here, too, were the great banquets of the nobility with the crowd waiting outside, waiting expectantly for largesse in the form of cheap wine or helpings from the courses. A very large proportion of the vast wedding banquets would have found its way into hungry stomachs through this custom.

As with present day Italy, most families had only two main meals a day, the midday meal (pranzo) and the evening meal (cena). The popularity of The Last Supper as an artists' subject is probably explained by one of the enduring habits of the peninsula, that of regarding the evening meal as a form of entertainment, a habit inherited from classical Rome and bequeathed to modern Italy. Pranzo during the Renaissance was a modest meal, taken as early as 10 am and consisting for the most part of fruit, bread, watered wine and sausage. The cena was begun before darkness fell and was an altogether more elaborate affair. The traditional Italian dish of pasta formed the main course, for only the wealthy could afford meat more than once a week. In all but the poorest houses there would be plenty of salads and cheeses, with fruit and sweet cakes and jellies to end the meal. Wine was served as a matter of course, even to children. Few houses had their private water supply and, except in Rome after the Sistine restoration of the aqueducts in the 1470s, water was always rather suspect. Even a poor man would have his little patch of vines and the wine he made, though harsh to the palate, was justifiably regarded as being a far healthier drink than that obtained from the public wells.

People spent their money on food and clothes, furniture and moveable decorations being considered relatively unimportant. In the earlier period, walls were bare or distempered – it was, indeed, on the high, bare, new walls of the newly rich bourgeoisie that the visual Renaissance may be said to have begun. Initially, the simple craftsman who was painting or distempering might be requested, or might even take into his head, to make a simple design in order to relieve the blank area. The design was to grow into the mural, becoming ever more complex in detail but not changing its function, the decoration of an otherwise bleak room. If one looks behind Gozzoli's mural in the Medici chapel, or Mantegna's in the Gonzaga bridal chamber, or Fra Angelico's in the chapel of Nicholas V in the Vatican one sees simply a plain, bare, rather unattractive cell.

The main hall was furnished with a dining table, a chair for the master of the house and perhaps another for his wife, and benches for everyone else. The bedroom was even more bare, but what it lacked in furnishing was compensated by the splendour of the bed itself. This was the most important item of furniture, and frequently it figured in the marriage contract: usually, it was so big that it would not go through the door and so had to be assembled in the room. It was furnished with a canopy and curtains which could be drawn to make a little, private room –

Bedroom, Davanzati Palace

one of the few places where there was any privacy in the house, although even this could be limited by the fact that some favourite servant's truckle bed might be housed underneath.

The hiring of servants reflected the growing wealth of society. In the late fourteenth century, a leading citizen of Pisa who had designs on the dogeship and was able to spend 30,000 florins to bring it about, had one servant only – a young girl. A little later the Rinuccini family in Florence (which consisted in effect of six families for there were six married sons) made do with five servants. During the fifteenth and sixteenth centuries the number increased astonishingly. Caterina Cornaro, the so-called 'Queen of Cyprus' kept fifty servants. The servants working on the estate of some great lord tended to regard themselves as part of the family, payment in cash being relatively unimportant. Servants for the newly emerging merchant classes contracted themselves for a year. Legally, they were extremely well protected. In Lucca, it was insisted that all female servants should either be married or widowed. In the fourteenth century, a Lucchese who caused his female servant to fall pregnant ran the risk of being hanged, but though this drastic penalty had been modified by the mid-fifteenth century public opinion still insisted that he be heavily fined. The advice given by a moralist to the employers of servants was strikingly at variance with that which Machiavelli, half a century later, was to give to princes. Love, not fear, was the way to handle servants. 'Be gentle and kindly to your servants, give them clothes and so forth ... Strive to be loved, rather than feared. They may perhaps be beaten sometimes, but not for every trifle.'

In the wealthier families, side by side with the servants was that 'enemy of society', the slave. Slavery, which had almost disappeared from Italy, returned on the wave of prosperity. The slave market in Venice alone processed some 20,000 men, women and children each year and every major port had a similar slave trade. So plentiful was the supply that, by the middle of the fifteenth century, even small merchants could buy a human animal to help out in the home, while the nobility came more and more to rely upon them in place of relatively expensive and certainly more arrogant servants. Prices varied immensely. Francesco Datini, the wealthy wool merchant from Prato, near Florence paid 60 florins for a 10-year-old girl, compared with 30 florins for a horse and 60 for his daughter's wedding dress. In general, the lady of the house might expect to pay out six florins for a hard-working but ill-favoured woman to help in the home, while the pretty young girl who would probably grace her husband's bed would cost up to 100 florins. The purchaser had the choice of half a dozen races, white as well as black, Christian as well as pagan or Moslem. 'Tartars are hardiest and best for work. Russians are built on finer lines but, in my opinion, Tartars are best. Circassians are a superior breed wherefore everybody wants one,' a Roman lady noted.

Like servants, slaves were on the whole well treated. In some cities, Florence among them, the children of slaves automatically became free. Romans were among those who declined such an expensive sop to conscience, but the average slave working in a Roman noble's household was probably far better off than a free but poor peasant tilling his few acres of land in the Campagna.

Yet even with this proviso, the reappearance of the slave system was an anomaly in society, one of the vivid contrasts that characterises the period.

7
The social matrix

Crime, poverty and punishment

An enduring impression of the Renaissance in Italy, and one
heightened by the lurid colours used by nineteenth-century
historians, is that of violence. Benvenuto Cellini's dagger sticking
in the vertebrae of his dying victim; Giuliano de' Medici hacked
down in the cathedral at the moment of the raising of the Host;
Niccolò d'Este's beheading of his wife and son; Cesare Borgia's
mass execution in Sinigaglia ... the list is endless; counterpoint,

Mass execution, Pisa: from 'Le Chronache' by Giovanni Sercambi

it seems to the same people's effortless achievement in the arts. Jacob Burckhardt makes the point explicit: it was the Italian's 'imagination' that allowed him to be now angel, now demon, he claims. 'It gives to his virtues and vices a peculiar colour, and under its influence his unbridled egoism shows itself in most terrible shape.'[25] In pursuance of that thesis Burckhardt assembles a Grand Guignol collection of horrors, in the course of it making a remark that must occur to his readers. Given this widespread contempt of law, 'We can only wonder that the state and society were not utterly dissolved.'

Was violence in Italy between the years 1350–1550 different in degree or kind from violence in other places and at other times? Curiously, despite the wealth of gory anecdotes, despite their endless dissection of the machinery of society and blueprints for 'the perfect man', contemporaries made little comment on the causes and possible cures for the violence endemic in their society. There was no lack of generalisations, from the usual assumption that violence was either the punishment of God or the work of the Devil, to Machiavelli's bleak assumption: 'We are an irreligious people, and the cause of corruption in others.' But there was little speculation as to the nature of violence and whether Italians were more or less prone to it than others.

As it happens, posterity is provided with a useful clue to the Italian attitude to violence and crime during the sack of Rome of 1527. Three separate races – German, Spanish and Italian loosely commanded by a Frenchman – were responsible for the sack. During the assault on the city, they acted as a single group but during the weeks that followed, their national characteristics came to the fore. This became very evident during their quest for booty when it was usually necessary to torture the victims to force them to disclose the hiding places of their treasures. The Germans were less successful at this than their Latin colleagues, tending to lose their patience and kill their victims before learning their secrets. All observers agreed that 'In the destruction of Rome the Germans showed themselves to be bad enough, the Italians were worse but worst of all were the Spaniards'. The characteristic German crime was drunkenness, followed by berserk rage and slaughter; the Spanish crime was rape, followed by mutilation; the Italian crime was theft followed by escape. B was noticeable that while the Spanish and Germans looted only articles made of valuable materials or stuffs, Italians added to their booty by taking works of art made of common materials, aware of the possibility of selling them – usually to other Italians.

The sack, and subsequent occupation, of Rome lasted for some three months – from the May to the July of 1527 – at the end of which time the Italian contingent had cannily melted into the background with their loot, leaving the Spaniards and Germans to cope as best they could. Using those three months as a rough and ready instrument of measurement, posterity can come to the broad conclusion that Italian crime was characterised by intelligence, patience and a cold balancing of facts.

However, that is Italian crime in an international context. What was the pattern within their own communities? The Burckhardtian method of presenting a picture by the simple accumulation of anecdotal material, though creating a rich source of social history, is of little use here. Indeed, it results in a distortion: of necessity the only crimes noted by this process are those committed by the rich and powerful or, if by the poor and ordinary, only if they are bizarre enough to attract attention. It is only in our own time, with the statistician coming to the aid of the historian, that a balanced picture is becoming evident. And it is perhaps drably appropriate that where the confident nineteenth century was content to concentrate its researches into the arts and mechanical sciences, the twentieth century is taking particular interest in the mass movements of people and in the springs of violence itself.[26] Quarrying in such unlikely sources as tax records, as well as records of the criminal courts, the new race of statistical historians or historical statisticians seek to show not only what crimes a man committed but also why, what exactly were the social pressures or opportunities that led him to the action. Werner Gundersheimer, working on the unpublished Libro de Giustiziati which lists the executions in Ferrara from 1440 to 1500, shows that the most likely source of violence is within the circle of the ducal court where roughly equal people are struggling for power. The most prevalent crime amongst the people as a whole is theft – but this in turn creates violence, for a common punishment for theft is death: the criminal therefore has a strong reason to kill any witnesses. Apart from the years when

crimes against the state (ie. against the duke) swell the death list
Gundersheimer finds that the average number of executions in
Ferrara is three per year. Ferrara, like most other cities, had few
options but the death penalty as punishment. A rich man could
usually expect to get away with a fine for a serious but
non-political crime; a political prisoner could expect to survive in
gaol for as long as his life had political value; but the state had
neither the resources nor the desire to maintain an ordinary
criminal in prison for a lengthy period. Apart from theft and
homicide, counterfeiting, rape, sodomy and arson all carried the
death penalty. Arson seems to have been a curiously prevalent
crime, in other cities as well as Ferrara. In general foreigners, ie
non-citizens resident within a city, were treated more harshly
than citizens.

In Florence, David Herlihy, using the invaluable catasto
records, examines that most mysterious of phenomena – 'the
mob'. This is a useful portmanteau term, employed whenever the
historian has to describe mass movements that have no obvious
social shape or objective. Herlihy links the pattern of urban
violence partly to the youthfulness of the male population of the
city, partly to the fact that they remained unmarried for some
two decades after puberty. He finds additional evidence in a late
sixteenth-century commentator, Giovanni Botero who, in his
tract *Della ragione di stato* published in 1589, identifies three
major classes in the cities – the rich, the middle class and the
poor. The middle classes had more to lose as a result of violence
Botero observed, and therefore acted as a damper. As a corollary
smaller, poorer cities which had smaller or almost non-existent
middle classes, were more prone to violence than larger cities, a
situation exactly opposite to twentieth-century experience.

The records of the Florentine criminal courts which Gene
Brucker examines have been used in the past mainly to demonstrate political activities and theories. Brucker employs them 'as a
source for perceiving the life style of the Florentine poor'.[27] They
show a restless, rootless people, a confused mass moving in and
out of the city, or backwards and forwards across it in search of
employment and sustenance. Here, at last, is the exact opposite
of the glittering Burckhardtian view. This dull mass of indis-
tinguishable people, precariously living from hand to mouth

chronologically belongs to 'the Renaissance'. It is they who underpin it with their taxes and their work as anonymous masons or carpenters or weavers, but they are light years removed from it in style.

The ordinary person, that 'man-in-the-street' who is at the centre of any sociological study of the twentieth century, is virtually ignored as an actor in the Renaissance drama by the earlier historians. In part, it was simply because their eyes were dazzled by the glamour of the large set pieces and figures: as more and more information about Lorenzo de' Medici or Cesare Borgia emerged, it was only too easy to ignore the anonymous men and women in the background who contributed to their greatness or notoriety.

The indifference regarding the lives of the poor and ordinary arose, too, from the problem of identifying them. Anecdotes about them abound, particularly in the work of the older chroniclers, and such people as the Florentine writer of novelle, Francesco Sachetti. Petrarch, too, had a lively and compassionate eye for the individual. But they achieve immortality by accident – a turn of phrase, a good practical joke, a bizarre circumstance that, for a moment, lifts them out of the crowd. The great ones of the land have their biographers: their portraits are to be seen in numberless paintings; their jewels and costumes exist still. The ordinary man is recorded by contemporaries simply as part of the great man's general background – part of his army, or his court. Posterity can discern him only through the shape of society around him, as it were, from the records of those who, for purposes of state, note his existence whether as criminal or soldier, tax-payer, rioter or pauper.

The evidence uncovered shows that the ordinary people benefited little from the glamorous new society. On the contrary, their condition was probably worsened for it was they who, in large part, paid for it willy nilly. The fourteenth century ushered in a sharp rise in indirect taxation – the 'gabelle' – which bore proportionately far heavier upon the poor than upon the rich. From about 1200 onwards, public financing had been done mostly through direct taxation, in particular the curious financial system known as the 'prestanze' or enforced loans. These were exactions which, though imposed obligatorily, yet bore interest – ranging in some cities up to 20 per cent. As such, they were by no means unwelcome to the richer citizens and tended to pass the poorer citizens by.

The prestanze, however, created an expanding public debt which had to be repaid. From the fourteenth century onwards the cost of military defence, whether in the form of hiring mercenaries or established standing armies, soared dizzily. The bureaucracy expanded, each humanist brought on to the pay-roll increasing pressure just that little more upon the treasury. The state, whether in the person of a prince or a commune, needed more and more money. Behind the glamour and glitter of military conquest was the humdrum need for taxes – that state's quickest way to replenish its coffers. The major justification for the condottiere marching out at the head of his expensively maintained army was the tax-gatherer waiting for his harvest. As often as not, the rallying cry of revolutionaries was 'Down with taxes' as well as the cry for 'Liberty'. Although apologists for the conquering city-state might advance the cause of 'liberty', or the need to protect its own frontiers as the reason for its aggression against its neighbours, the citizens of the newly conquered territory knew better as their taxes were diverted – and usually increased – in favour of their conqueror. Few dominant cities could supply their own need: in the dukedom of Milan the titular capital city generated less than 25 per cent of the state fiscal income.

It was the ordinary man who provided this wealth. During the fourteenth century direct taxation – that is, taxation levied for the most part upon the rich – fell, while gabelle – indirect taxes levied upon the necessities of life – rose dramatically. In Florence, taxes on food as a whole increased tenfold during the latter half of the fourteenth century compared to what they were a century earlier: the housewife could expect to pay 15 soldi, instead of three, for a measure of oil while salt prices were multiplied an astounding twenty times.

At the same time, there was a gradual but definite decline in real wages. Professional moralists like St Antonio of Florence or St Bernardino of Siena might deplore, loudly, the hardness of employers as they trimmed and trimmed their wage budgets. Humanists, with their eyes fixed upon their lofty goals, more concerned with the theory of liberty in ancient Rome than the reality of commercial justice in modern Italy, ignored the trend, or encouraged it. Matteo Palmieri, the great Florentine proponent of civic virtues, went on record as saying that it was sufficient to pay the plebs only enough to keep them alive. And if they died, or left their native city in despair – why, so much the better as a winnowing out of chaff. One is reminded vividly of that other great period in western European history – early nineteenth-century England during the formative years of the Industrial Revolution – when the virtues of self-help were vigorously proclaimed and the weakest who fell out of the race were assumed to have done so out of sheer malice or indolence. The same kind of complaints levied against Victorian factory owners by their workforce can be heard four centuries earlier. In Venice, the shipbuilders complained that their employers were forming cartels to keep down wages: in Genoa, wool merchants were accused of that favourite trick of the unscrupulous employer, paying in 'truck' or goods at a value fixed by the employers, instead of cash.

Even as the Victorian employer salved his conscience by going to church, and allowing his wife and daughters to take soup to the deserving poor, so the Renaissance merchant salved his conscience by contributing to charity. It would be a fascinating, if probably hopeless, task to attempt to calculate how much of the national income was recycled through charity. Some wealthy merchants, like Francesco Datini of Prato, waited till the end of their lives before trying to settle their debt by establishing a personal foundation. Datini's *Casa de Ceppo dei poveri* was so well founded that it still flourishes in the twentieth century. Other rich men preferred to support existing charities, some of which became extremely influential. In Venice the so-called Scuole Grande were so important as to become virtually an arm of the state. Established during the thirteenth century, essentially as penitential organisations, by the fourteenth century they combined charitable with religious activities. The five (later six) Scuole Grande became immensely wealthy: between 1516 and 1564 the Scuola di San Rocco was able to spend 55,000 ducats to build its great hall and engage Tintoretto to decorate it.

Poverty was a working class lot: crime tended to be more

Hospital scene by Domenico da Bartoli

democratic. 'In sharp contrast with the pattern in our cities today, every social class in Renaissance Florence (and not only the poor) was well represented in the criminal courts. This was the result, in part, of a much broader network of prohibitions and controls, and also of a strong, though diminishing penchant for violence, which could motivate the rich and prominent as well as the poor and lowly.'[28]

The statistical analysis of Renaissance society throws light on that sexual crime which endlessly engages the attention of moralists, both contemporary and posterior and which, castigated in writing or from the pulpit, or enshrined in countless

anecdotes seems an inescapable part of the historical phenomenon. Unlike much of Renaissance mythology, there are good
grounds for its predominance. As the catasto returns for Florence
shows, this was essentially a young man's society – an unmarried
young man's society. Half the population was below the age of
twenty-two, and where a woman would reasonably expect to be
married by her mid-teens, her husband was likely to be approaching his forties. Despite the appearance of laxity given by such
writers as Boccaccio, unmarried young women were closely
guarded. Significantly, rape is one of the commoner crimes: for
the less violently inclined, prostitution and homosexuality were
the only available channels for sexual satisfaction. In his
examination of the Florentine criminal records, David Herlihy
found that gambling and prostitution were the major industries
of the underworld. Italian society treated prostitution with much
the same ambivalence as does modern British society. Technically, it was legal. In Florence, the commune itself ran a public
brothel: in Milan taxes levied on prostitutes were allocated to the
upkeep of the city walls. But from time to time society thought it
necessary to harass the prostitute as a tribute to virtue: in
Florence she was obliged to wear distinctive hat and gloves: in
Milan, she was forbidden to wear her hair in the 'coazz', the
Milanese fashion of binding the tresses with ribbons and loading
them with ornaments.

The international nature of Italian society is curiously brought
out by the lists in which prostitutes figure. In 1526 the papal
treasury, in pursuance of that ambivalent attitude to the
profession, listed all prostitutes plying their trade in Rome,
arranging them by nationality. Of the 1,411 listed, 536 were
foreign, 875 were Italian. The major groups among the foreign
were Spaniards (104), French (59), and German (52) and the list
included girls from England, Poland, Flanders, Portugal, Hungary, Greece, Turkey and Albania. There were also 30 Jews and 7
'Negre'. The treasury list unwittingly vindicates the honour of
Roman womanhood. It was commonly assumed, by such
observers as the Venetian ambassador Mocenigo, that the
majority of personable Roman women who could do so, sold
themselves because there was no other means of making a livelihood. The Roman chronicler, Infessura, seems to substantiate

this charge with his statement that, in 1496, there were 6,800 'meretrice' working as prostitutes in the city. In the tax list, however, Roman-born girls were a minority of the whole (198), only a few more than those from Tuscany (187) and Lombardy (109).

In general, the larger blocks probably reflect the advent of a pope from that particular country or Italian locality. It was in

Courtesans by Carpaccio

Rome that the trade or profession of courtesan, as distinct from prostitute, had its earliest flowering. A city dominated by a celibate priesthood, and where there were large numbers of temporarily celibate, and usually cultured men such as the ambassadors of the various powers, inevitably provided a kind of hothouse for the species. In the higher levels of society, the courtesan more closely resembled the Greek hetaira – the 'companion' – than the harlot of a later society and achieved her skill only after an exacting course of study. She was expected to be able to play all musical instruments, and to sing with competence. Many courtesans had very considerable literary skills. One of them, Tullia d'Aragona, earned considerable fame as the author of a treatise on platonic love. Some of them could not only paint, but also discourse intelligently on art – Veronica Franca was able to do this with no less a person than Tintoretto. Aretino claimed that he knew one girl who could recite all the works of Petrarch and Boccaccio by heart, and was able to declaim hundreds of lines of Ovid, Virgil and Horace in the original.

The courts over which these elegantly polished creatures presided were the forerunners of the salon, places where, as the French observer Commines put it delicately, the fee for conversation was exactly the same as for the 'négotiation entière'. The careers of the leading members of this class reflect in no small part the emancipation of women in society. An outstanding example is, again, Tullia d'Aragona. Her father, the Cardinal of Aragon, was the son of King Ferrante of Naples: her mother was a famous demi-mondaine, Giulia Campana, born in Ferrara. Tullia herself was born in the Campo Marzo in Rome. She knew luxury as a child, for her father doted both upon her and her mother, but with his death she had to seek a means of livelihood. If she had been born a boy, she would probably have been legitimised by a complaisant pope and so enabled to enter the Church as a career. As it was, she had no alternative but to follow her mother's profession. How much she succeeded in that is well illustrated by a laudatory description of her on her visit to Ferrara. 'There has just arrived here a very pretty lady, so fascinating in manner that we cannot help finding in her something divine. She sings all sorts of airs and motets at sight.

Her conversation had matchless charm and there is nothing you cannot talk to her about. There is no one here even to hold a candle to her – not even the Marchioness of Pescara.' The Marchioness of Pescara was Vittoria Colonna, one of the leading bluestockings of her day, personal – but platonic – friend of Michelangelo, a great beauty and acknowledged leader of society. Comparing a courtesan with an aristocrat of this intellectual calibre, is an indication of the height to which she could climb.

The world of the courtesan is the elegant side, the cultured side, of Renaissance sexuality. The hidden, seamier side appears sporadically in the records of criminal courts, a side where urban procurers prey upon poor, illiterate country girls: where young girls are bought and sold as part of a countrywide white slave traffic. Punishment for such offenders was harsh: Gene Brucker cites the case of a Florentine procurer, Niccolò di Ginuta, who was hanged after evidence was produced of his impressively wide-ranging activities. But he was probably the tip of an iceberg.

The sense of moral outrage, the belief that wealth and culture were loosening the bonds of morality that kept society together, is nowhere more bitterly expressed than in the sermon of San Bernardino. He was talking about Florence and though, as a Sienese, he would have no particular love for Siena's traditional enemy, neither was he a bigot. Nevertheless, the picture he painted of the Tuscan republic at the moment when it was entering upon its most brilliant period is appalling. 'Florence was never so beautiful and adorned, she never sailed so far upon the seas, she was never more powerful nor noble, but her people are the most wretched upon earth, owing to sodomy and women's extravagance. Go to the Ponte Vecchio there by the Arno: put your ear to the ground and listen. You will hear a great lament, voices rising to heaven crying, Vengeance! Vengeance of God! What are these cries? They are the voices of innocent babes thrown into your Arno and your privies, or buried alive in your gardens to avoid the world's shame: the cries of babies killed in their mothers' bellies by the drugs of barbers, apothecaries and doctors. The cries of souls who might have been born but were not, on account of the accursed vice of sodomy.' Bernardino's evidence is particularly impressive for he was no grim fanatic, but

a balanced, civilised and well informed person. He singles
Florence out for his attack, but there is little doubt that the vices
he attacked – homosexuality and infanticide – were as widespread elsewhere.

Religion and morality

Religion is the traditional bulwark against immorality, but in
trying to assess the role of the Christian Church in Italy, posterity
again encounters a paradox at the heart of affairs. Or rather, not
one paradox, but a collection each linked to the rest. The Church
provides one of the most obvious channels whereby Renaissance
values were transmitted to the future, whether in visual form
through the innumerable sacred buildings and objects, or
intellectually through the work of writers. But at the vital point
where 'the Church' in the person of the parish priest came in
contact with the laity, there was an abysmal ignorance. 'With the
rarest exceptions, parish clergy were ill-educated and ignorant,
quite uninterested in the ideas and practices we summarise in the
word Renaissance.'[29] And ignorant, too, of their own religious
inheritance: in some parts of the country, 'Christians' made the
sign of the cross without knowing what it meant.

The corporate religious impulse which, among the laity,
created those confraternities which had so profound an effect
upon the social life of their day, among the professedly religious
only too often produced deep scandal. Priuli's description of the
monasteries of Venice as brothels might seem to be the simple
product of anti-clericalism were it not for the evidence of
Ambrogio Traversari. A member of the Order of Camaldoli, he
visited a large number of monasteries in an official capacity, and
his reports leave little doubt that in probably the majority of
monasteries in this order alone almost every rule of conduct was
habitually ignored. And finally, to compound the problem, is the
lack of documentation. This seems like the ultimate paradox for
an organisation whose survival depended upon the transmission
of documentary evidence, which was itself the object and subject
of endless debate and whose centre and headquarters possessed
the world's greatest library and archive system. The Vatican was
not Italy: the Papacy was not the parish church, and that

fragmentation of Italy which provided so powerful an impulse for the Renaissance as a whole, had a lamentable effect upon the preservation of church records.[30] 'The almost total neglect in Italy of such parish records as do survive makes it hard to generalise securely.'[31]

Whatever the motivation, religion was woven into the very stuff of life – indeed, not so much woven in it as infusing it as ineradicably as any dye. The violent anti-clericalism that surfaced again and again over the years was merely the reverse of that faith, and frequently a product of it. Dante spent a large part of his life belabouring the arch-cleric, Boniface VIII, but Dante's entire personal life was inflexibly religious. Petrarch's attack upon the Avignonese papacy was barely this side of decent but his personal life, again, was not simply 'religious' but virtually meaningless if divorced from it.

The Italian drew in with his mother's milk the need to draw a distinction between man and office, between the Holy Father whose troops might at that moment be battering at the walls of his city, and the Holy Father in whose hands were the keys of heaven and hell. To the outsider, the whole country seems to be simply a lay order, differing only in degree not in kind from the formal hierarchy whose profession was religion. At the turn of the fourteenth and fifteenth centuries the whole country was caught up in one vast penitential movement, the Bianchi. Quite spontaneously, tens of thousands of people donned a simple white uniform or habit, seeking out enemies, making pilgrimages to 'enemy' cities to exchange the kiss of peace. The confraternities devoted to good works each had a religious basis. They were a species of social club, and the more wealthy played important roles as patrons of art. But most were under the tutelage of a particular saint, chosen because he or she reflected the major objective of the confraternity, and took an active part in the great religious festivals.

The Italians' preoccupation with religion ensured that they controlled the supra-national organisation which, despite its problems, still exerted enormous powers throughout Europe. There were almost as many bishoprics for Italy as there were for the whole of northern Europe. Major cities such as Venice, Milan or Florence and even relatively minor cities such as Ferrara or

Mantua each had its cardinal, whereas the 'oltremontanes' counted themselves lucky to have one or two for the whole country. The pantheon of saints, each conferring very useful prestige upon his or her homeland, was overwhelmingly Italian. And the only real debate about the patria of the next pope was about the exact part of Italy from which he would come.

The sturdy nature of Italian Christianity easily withstood the impact of humanist questioning. On the surface, it may well have seemed that the ancient faith was rapidly being eroded when scholars with their affectation of classicism dubbed the saints 'gods', referred to Christ as Apollo, and seemed anxious to prove a correspondence at all levels between paganism and Christianity. But this was a mere playing with words and toying with concepts. At a more serious level was the debate as to whether humanist learning in itself was corrupting, tending to draw the mind away from the one true study. Fra Giovanni Dominici was one of those who emphatically believed that it did and said so loudly and frequently for he was a famous preacher much sought after by city officials. A man becomes what he knows, he said firmly: if a young mind has been fed with nothing but images of Venus and Mars, given no other drink but that of the works of Plato and Aristotle instead of the Fathers, then there will be no room in that mind for the true images of Christianity. Another friar, Giovanni da Prato, was even more forthright: he not only rejected the classics but he 'detested and spat upon them'. Not all religious men were automatically anti-clerics. Bernardino of Siena illustrated his lively vernacular sermons – intended as much for illiterate peasants as for sophisticated urbanites – with liberal quotations from the classics. He took the commonsense view of assessing the value of a writer from his moral, rather than his chronological, standing, recommending Cicero but not Ovid, Dante but emphatically not Boccaccio 'who produced books he had better not have written . . . and perhaps regretted them in his old age'. Ranged upon the other side were men such as Lorenzo Valla who, not content with demolishing the papal claims to inherit the Roman Empire embodied in the forged Donation of Constantine, mocked asceticism and attacked monasticism. Poggio Bracciolini took the attack upon religious orders even further with his trenchant *Dialogue on hypocrisy*. 'I don't know what they [the friars] do except to sing like crickets – and they are far too well paid for such an activity. They carry on as though they were performing the labours of Hercules. But it scarcely bears thinking what they would do if they actually had to work for a living, ploughing the fields in wind and rain.'

Such controversies – carried on with all the vicious use of personal insult of which the humanists were eminently capable – were conducted in the rarified upper levels of society and by specialists even at that level. For most people there was little change. Sophisticates at the court of some great prince might enjoy the revivals of Terence or Plautus, performed against backdrops employing the exciting new technique of perspective. The majority still turned to the Church as their major source of entertainment; in particular, to the representation of the Mysteries whose staging would be undertaken by one or other of the guilds or quarters of the city. Their presentation might be more sophisticated – in Florence Brunelleschi designed a marvellous machine for the Feast of the Annunciation which enabled Gabriel to fly down to earth – but the subject matter remained traditional with personified Virtues vanquishing personified Vices. These Mysteries were presented in one or other of the major squares which, for the purpose, had been turned virtually into one huge theatre with elaborate scaffolding. The so-called Processions, in particular that of Corpus Christi, could virtually take the whole city as its stage. Pius II lovingly detailed the Corpus Christi Procession in Viterbo which he himself had organised. The façade of the entire street from the citadel to the cathedral was virtually rebuilt, all roofs being lowered to the same level and all fronts moved back to a common frontage. Each cardinal was allocated a section of the route which he decorated to the extent of his purse, which was considerable, and his taste, which varied greatly. Each then provided a species of tableau vivant which came into operation as the procession passed through his sector. 'The cardinals of Coutances and Lebret, after the custom of their country, had covered the walls with tapestries (which they called arras) and constructed altars rich with gold and silver. After came the houses decorated by the Referendarii. Under an altar raised aloft they put a youth impersonating the Saviour, who sweated blood and filled a cup from the healing stream from a wound in his side. And they had boys winged like angels who sang epic verses or elegiacs by learned scholars ... The cardinal of San Sisto had a representation of the Last Supper ... the cardinal of Porto exhibited a huge dragon and many malignant spirits ... the cardinal of Santa Susanna had a fountain of white wine decorated with flowers ...' For page on page Pius described in minute detail elaborate shows which must have taken months to prepare, cost several kings' ransoms in the aggregate and were swept into oblivion on the following day.

Attitudes towards the Jews varied from what could be called a contemptuous tolerance through to occasional local expulsions. In Rome, they were obliged to submit to a ritual spurning on the occasion of each papal coronation: the elders of the community stood humbly on the papal processional route holding the Books of the Law to receive recognition from the new pope. 'We acknowledge the Law but condemn the principals of Judaism for the Law has been fulfilled through Christ.' But they were treated well enough until the reign of the Carafa pope, Paul IV, in the 1550s. They were then confined to the Ghetto – following the lead of Venice a century earlier – and the populace, taking their cue, indulged in such fancies as obliging Jews to run in the Carnival races after first being forced to eat a heavy meal. Throughout Italy, as throughout Europe, the association with usury ensured that they were simultaneously feared and hated. In Milan, Filippo Visconti, not the most obviously religious of men, decided that Jewish usury was contrary to divine law and expelled them in 1443. Contrary to popular opinion, the average Jewish money-lender operated on a very small scale: certainly the great banks of the period were run by Christians, engaged in their uneasy tightrope walk between business needs and religious condemnation. In a society that was relying increasingly on specie, or coined money, even poor people had to be provided with some means of obtaining it in an emergency and in 1454 the Franciscan Order established the Monti di Pietà (Banks of Pity) which, in various forms, have survived ever since. The Franciscans, strongly anti-Jewish, argued that Christians should borrow only from Christians and the Lateran Council approved the establishment of what were, in effect, pawn-broking houses.

Characteristically, this social innovation was carried through by Franciscans for friars were intimately involved in the life of the people. It was precisely this close involvement that produced the hatred which again and again broke over their heads, the kind of hatred so violently expressed by Poggio Bracciolini and which provided the stimulus for endless salacious stories. Friars tended to have more than their fair share of fanatics and zealots in their ranks: the man who sincerely objected to the corruption of society was far more likely to don the ragged brown habit of a Franciscan, and go barefoot into the street, than to enter some well-founded monastery where the canonical hours were irritating interruptions in the good life. That man, too, was likely to go to extremes in reproving the follies and vices of the citizens. The activities of few merchants could bear too close and prolonged a scrutiny, and a citizen who might be happy to assent to general religious propositions in church was disinclined to be upbraided for stretching his cloth, watering his wine, or clipping his coins, by some pale friar in the market place. Their endless begging, too, irritated even the most charitably inclined and their skill in wheedling money out of foolish women, together with their propensity for working their way into the domestic scene, aroused the suspicions alike of the miserly and the uxurious.

But a popular friar could exert immense influence. The stock in trade of all friars was simple enough: a rough wooden pulpit to set up in the market-place, a portable screen to separate, ceremonially, men and women was enough. The more histrionically minded could add various props: a feather from the wing of the archangel Gabriel, a phial of the Virgin's milk, a piece of the True Cross, and, as garnish, add a dash of anti-Semitism to their sermons. These were the ones who gave their profession its bad name and earned the hatred of the educated. But the probability is they were in the minority.

Far more characteristic, save for the fact that he was canonised, was the career of Bernardino of Siena. A member of the aristocratic Albizesschi family, he was at first attracted to the monastic life but believing that such a life was the abandoning of responsibility he took the Franciscan habit in 1402 at the age of twenty-two. For forty years he travelled the length and breadth

St Bernadino preaching by Pietro di Sano

of Italy preaching, preaching, preaching. A little, spare man, his cheeks hollow with privation, bald and with only a single tooth in his head, barefoot in the coldest weather, his dominant characteristic was gaiety. Unlike his intellectual peers who believed that the more recondite and abstruse their arguments the more they displayed learning, he deliberately set out to make himself intelligible to the illiterate and the stupid, illustrating his theses with homely allusions drawn from the life around him. Posterity has a double record of Bernardino's effervescent style and practical approach. The painting of Sano di Pietro shows him mounted in his simple wooden pulpit in the great Piazza del Campo in Siena where he gave so many of his sermons. Beside him are the city officials, proud to be associated with so distinguished a son of Siena: before him men and women of all classes kneel to receive his blessing. Somewhere in that crowd will be a humble wool carder, Benedetto di Maestro Bartolommeo who though poor, had an unusual skill – not only the ability to write, but to take down verbatim the speaker's words, following him faithfully in soaring flights or humorous interjections, or recording the interruptions unavoidably experienced in a busy town square. Bernardino combined a profound religious sense with the liveliest curiosity about mundane affairs; many of his sermons are, in fact, essays in sociology. Compassion came more quickly to his lips than condemnation, but he had no hesitation in excoriating either the tyrannical master, the dishonest servant, or the religious establishment itself if need be. He was accused, and cleared, of heresy: offered, and declined, three bishoprics, and canonised within six years of his death – testimony to the universal love in which he was held.

If Bernardino was the illuminated side of the religious intellect, Girolamo Savonarola was its dark side; though contemplating that tragic career is to realise that only a slight shift in emphasis at a critical point would have produced another saint for the Italian pantheon. Born in Ferrara in 1452, he came to Florence in 1489. The Medici were in exile, the threat of the first foreign invasion hung over all Italy and the Florentines, despite themselves, were again seeking a leader. Savonarola had already gained prestige by cleansing the monastery of San Marco of the corruption which seemed to be an inescapable element of the enclosed orders, and

Girolamo Savonarola by Fra Bartolommeo

when he stepped upon the politico-religious stage it was as a champion of morality – and of republicanism. He was prepossessing in neither appearance nor speech. The vivid portrait of him, painted by Fra Bartolommeo whom he had converted, shows a forceful but ugly face with great beaked nose and burning eyes. Contemporary reports of his sermons show that they were regarded as being only average, in both content and delivery. Italians, however, were accustomed to great orators delivering impassioned sermons with mechanical perfection: they stirred the listener while they were being delivered and then were forgotten. No man could doubt Savonarola's sincerity, the absolute conviction with which he warned of the coming wrath of God hovering over Italy. His prophecies and visions earned him a fame which went far beyond Florence; his attacks upon the Borgia pope were retailed with delight.

Pope Alexander marked him down for attention at a more convenient occasion, but for the moment he was secure among the tough citizens of Florence. He scourged them for their immorality and they flocked to his sermons by the thousand. He ordered them to cleanse their bodies and homes of the devil's frivolities, and they burnt their precious ornaments in the Piazza della Signoria. Scents, mirrors, false hair, musical instruments, carnival masks were thrown on the pile – but so too were books containing not only suspect pagan authors but such eminently respectable Christians as Petrarch. The great pile represented not only a fascinating cross section of contemporary art but also a substantial cash value, and a Venetian merchant, who happened to be present, offered 22,000 florins cash for the objects. The Florentines replied by throwing his own portrait on the pile before setting light to it.

It was at this period of social upheaval that Florence adopted the Venetian constitution, setting up a Great Council modelled on that of Venice. Savonarola approved it, subsequently announcing that Christ alone was King of Florence. But the reforming zeal in the theocratic kingdom became fanaticism, not the least unpleasant aspect of which was the bands of 'holy' children who roamed the city, seeking out further ornaments and fripperies of the devil. The inevitable reaction set in: just a year after the triumphant auto-da-fé of 1497, his power crumbled. The people abandoned him to the powerful enemies who had been waiting for this moment: he confessed that he had been deluded and his visions false. He was first hanged, then his body burned in the same square where he believed that he had witnessed the triumph of Christ over the world.

The activities of both San Bernardino and Savonarola

appealed, in their different ways, to the same theatrical element that was so characteristic of the people and of the time. It is to be doubted, though, if those activities had any long-lasting results. There was a leaven at work in society, attempting to restate traditional Christian virtues in modern terms, but that leaven was working outside the formal body of the Church. It was seen in its most characteristic form in the schools which Guarino da Verona and Vittorino da Feltre were running in Ferrara and Mantua respectively. The schools had as their objective the training of the future rulers of society and both men were determined that their young charges should be as familiar with ethics as with Greek. Vittorino da Feltre was particularly insistent that he was training a man for citizenship, not simply for scholarship, laying great emphasis on what he called 'the heart' and what the Victorians would have called character-training – self-restraint, self-reliance, modesty, courage and compassion. These were the qualities upon which a man or woman should base his or her life. And how effective was both that code and his teaching can be gauged by the fact that one of his pupils was Federigo da Montefeltro, Duke of Urbino. Indirectly, Vittorino would have influenced the greatest book of the day on etiquette in its broadest sense, the *Courtier* of Baldassare Castiglione.

The seeds of the book were sown in the four years from 1504 to 1508 when Castiglione was resident in Urbino but it was not published until nearly twenty years afterwards, and then only because it had been pirated in a garbled edition and Castiglione was forced to bring his long, lovingly polished editing to a close and publish in order to protect his name. Very obviously, the book filled a void for it was immediately and astonishingly successful, taking the author's name to every corner of Europe where polite society was admired. Posterity is faced with something of a problem in semantics in assessing the book for since Castiglione's day the image of the courtier has suffered a decline, becoming either the image of a fop or of an intriguing social climber. Even the Italian feminine of the word – la cortigiana or courtesan – has simply become a synonym for a high-class harlot. But, for Castiglione, the courtier was the cream of civilised society. He did not have to be nobly born: admittedly, he usually was for only those born into the upper classes had the

Baldassare Castiglione by Raphael

leisure or opportunity to practise the arts. Lorenzo de' Medici put the case with unusual brutality, 'Only men of noble birth can obtain perfection. The poor, who work with their hands and have no time to cultivate their minds, are incapable of it.' Castiglione's recognition that 'courtesy' was a quality of mind and not of class went far to explain the wide influence of the book. The courtier must be able to acquit himself in all manly exercises – wrestling, running, riding – but should be equally at home with literature, able to speak several languages, play musical instruments, write elegant verse. Everything should be done with a casual air so that his conversation, though sensible, is sprightly. He was even enjoined to study the form and nature of jokes; and following Castiglione's earnest courtiers as they plod humourlessly along in the wake of a joke is to gain a sudden glimpse of the changes that time can create in human society. In love, the courtier was to be discreet and honourable: in war courageous but magnanimous. Above all, he was to be a man of his word, loyal to his prince – but loyal too to those dependent upon him.

Castiglione's courtier, therefore, differs at every possible point from Machiavelli's prince, although here not only time but race can interpose a distorting medium. In reviewing a new edition of *The Prince* and speculating upon the difference between Italian and English morality, Lord Macaulay drew a percipient parallel based upon the differing national viewpoints of the characters of Othello and Iago. An English audience, while deploring Othello's act, yet regards him with sympathy, he points out, whereas an Italian audience, while also deploring Iago's act, tends to regard Othello as a fool. It is with this caveat in mind that a non-Italian must approach both Machiavelli and his most famous work.

Viewed from almost any angle, Machiavelli's life can hardly be seen as other than a failure. As a career diplomat, rising to be Secretary to the Republic, he never wielded any real authority. Even during his most famous exploit of all, when he attended Cesare Borgia during the latter's whirlwind conquests, he was present either as subordinate to another official or simply as observer. As a convinced republican he was obliged to spend his later years currying favour with the now openly despotic Medici, and even so spent long spells unemployed and penurious. His personal appearance and habits were totally at variance with the personality that comes across in his political writings: there he is ice-cold, logical, in total command. In real life he was shabby, lecherous and adulterous. Something of that dual character comes across in his portraits: their expression is almost hangdog,

Niccolò Macchiavelli by Tito di Santi

almost furtive yet with an inner, self-mocking integrity. To his friends – and they were many – he presented a delightful character: gay, courageous, witty, immensely learned but wearing his learning lightly. He was, despite all superficial evidence to the contrary, essentially an idealist – and a republican. It was this idealism which, paradoxically, led him to regard, if only briefly, the terrible Cesare Borgia as a possible saviour of Italy; an Italian champion resolute enough to oppose the new waves of barbarians from the north and so give Italians a chance to work out their own destiny. How, then, did a man like this come to write a work like *The Prince*?

There have been few writers so misjudged as this republican who produced the classic textbook on the practice of tyranny. It is as though a doctor, having diagnosed a disease, were to be accused of inventing it. Machiavelli was well aware of the construction likely to be placed on his work and went out of his way to stress that this was a picture of things as they were: therefore, given that the prince was necessary in civil life (and it was becoming increasingly evident that he was), then it was best that he should learn how to conduct himself in the most perilous craft in the world. He should preferably be a good man 'but the manner in which men live now is so different from the manner in which they should live that he who deviates from the common course of practice and endeavours to act as duty dictates necessarily ensures his own destruction'. It seems a jaundiced view of the world but, curiously, Machiavelli's fellow citizen, the Medici Pope Clement VII, unwittingly used almost identical words when, after the sack of Rome in 1527, the Venetian ambassador Contarini was urging him to adopt a spiritual rather than a worldly role: 'I see perfectly that the way you point out ought to be the right way ... but I tell you that in this world the idea does not correspond with the reality, and he who acts from amiable motives is a simpleton.' All Niccolò Machiavelli did was to give lapidary form to the practice of self-interest.

8

The Renaissance manifest

The 'rebirth' of art

The visitor to the Sistine Chapel normally enters it from an unobtrusive little door beside the altar. The first impression of the Chapel is of a high, dark, narrow, crowded room. The impression gained of the crowd itself is of a pinkish blur, for most people are facing in the general direction of the altar and looking upward, either towards Michelangelo's Last Judgement above the altar or, with head at a steeper angle, at his ceiling. The visitor joins the throng and, after a greater or lesser period dependent upon the flexibility of his or her neck muscles, lowers the gaze. It is usually only at this stage that the ordinary visitor becomes aware that the blur of colour high up on the walls consists of ten supreme works of art, from the hands of as many different artists. The illustrated guide books continue the same emphasis, providing endless photographic details of Michelangelo's work, dismissing that of his colleagues with a handful of general reproductions. The Sistine Chapel, in short, is an ideal example of the problem presented by Italian Renaissance art: the sheer quantity of superb material stuns the mind, reducing to an inferior level work which, in any other place, would be singled out for unique attention.

The Sistine Chapel and its parent building of St Peter's pose, unavoidably, that nagging problem regarding the dating and origin of the cultural phenomenon. The student of the sciences, of warfare, of law, even indeed of literature can work around that problem, blurring its outlines. The student of art and architecture sees it stated unequivocally in every Italian art

St Peter receiving keys by Perugino, in the Sistine Chapel

gallery, every ancient Italian street: once there was this kind of art, suddenly there is that. Ernst Gombrich sums up that transition by comparing a French manuscript illumination of the Entombment of Christ, painted between 1250 and 1300, and Giotto's painting of the same subject, executed about 1306. In the one, all is pattern and form – handsome but unrelated to the human condition: in the other, the human emotion of grief affects the very angels. If art is the outward expression of society, then what is demonstrated here is a civilisation changing in mid-stride. The change, in fact, affects and is affected by only a small – a minute – section of that civilisation. But it is a symbol of profounder movement, the surface motion of very deep waters.

It was in trying to account for such a phenomenon as Giotto that Giorgio Vasari coined that literally immortal word, 'rinascita'. And here it is essential to place Vasari himself in context for it is from his book, *Lives of the most excellent Italian architects, painters and sculptors*, that posterity derives so much of its

Entombment by Giotto

knowledge of the Italian Renaissance in art. In the opinion of
Peter and Linda Murray, it is 'perhaps the most important book
on the history of art ever written, both as a source book and as an
example for all the later Italian historiographers'.[32] Born in
Arezzo in 1511, Vasari worked as a painter of no little merit both
in Florence and Rome. It was during a dinner party in Rome in
1546, in the grand new palace of Cardinal Farnese, that he was
urged by his illustrious host and fellow guests to collect and

publish details of the lives of Italian artists. The first edition appeared four years later and a second, larger edition was published in 1568. It is this edition which, translated again and again into most European languages, has profoundly coloured the European view of the cultural renaissance.

Yet, to a certain extent, Vasari is himself 'posterity' for by the time he came to write his book the movement had taken its final form. The first impetus, indeed, had spent itself and it was during the time he was working on his book that the style now known as 'High Renaissance' emerged. Vasari was closer to the springs than we are, but still outside them. What, exactly, did he mean by rinascita? What, exactly, was being 'reborn'? The classic, ie. 'ancient', Roman world is the standard answer. Struggling to define what had been taking place in Italy over two centuries before him, Vasari remarks, 'In order that my readers may better comprehend what it is that I call "old" and what "antique", I add that the antiques are works before the time of Constantine, and the old are such as were executed from the days of Silvester (c. AD 300) onward, by a certain residue of Greeks, whose profession was rather that of dyeing than painting.' By Greeks he meant Byzantines and heartily attacked their work. Virtue lay only in the Roman past and Renaissance Italy, as heir to Rome, was supposed to have found its soul by recreating that past.

Vasari's emphasis on the revival of antiquity led to a distortion of history which has somewhat affected posterity's view of the Renaissance. In architecture and sculpture there was emphatically a rinascita, a return to the values of the classic Greek and Roman worlds. But painting – which, of all arts, is perhaps pre-eminently *the* Renaissance art – owed little to antiquity. The Greeks and Romans knew nothing of the optical laws that governed perspective (see page 246). In particular, their eyes were fixed upon the world of man, the world of nature being used as back-cloth or frame. The Renaissance artist looked directly into the world and, at first falteringly, treated it as an entity in its own right. The fourteenth century Florentine artist, Cennino Cennini, touched clumsily upon that approach which would be so triumphantly used by his successors. 'If you wish to draw mountains well, so that they appear natural, procure some large stones, rocky and not polished, and draw from these.' The idea of a handful of stones standing in for the Alps or Appennines seems wholly ludicrous, but Cennini's insistence that they should be 'rocky and not polished' was a pointer to the new road the artist was taking, the road to reality in nature.

All this tended to be obscured by that emphasis on 'rebirth'. Petrarch, the greatest classical scholar of his day, took that concept to its logical end when he created his poem *Africa*; writing an epic, in Latin, about a Roman hero, inviting comparison with Virgil on Virgil's own ground. Petrarch failed for it is rarely, if ever, possible to copy absolutely faithfully.[33] Petrarch's technical failure was also an artistic failure. In most cases the artists who thought they were re-creating ancient Rome were, in fact, creating what they thought ancient Rome to be like. Their technical failure became an artistic triumph, a fusion that created an entirely new style which was the outward form of the period.

Renaissance art not only provides a window into the world of the Renaissance, but also a means of tracking posterity's changing reaction to that world. Vasari's description of the murals in Assisi is a matter-of-fact reproduction in words. 'Poverty is walking on bare feet on thorns and has a dog that is barking behind her, and near her a boy is throwing stones at her, and another who is busy pushing some thorns with a stick against her legs.' Walter Pater's hot-house prose poem on the Mona Lisa, though in part discharging a similar task to Vasari's and anticipating the function of a modern art photograph, also reflects the nineteenth century's intuitive, romantic approach to Renaissance art. Currently, the use of computers to establish the provenance of artists and the detailed analysis of their contracts reflects the twentieth century's preference for factual knowledge, its belief that a whole picture can best emerge by a careful assembling of parts.

Although we now know much more about the 'how', we are as far as ever from knowing the 'why', a limitation we share with contemporaries of the phenomenon. Writing in the 1430s, Lorenzo Valla stated the problem for himself, for his contemporaries and for posterity. 'I do not know why the arts most closely approximating the liberal arts – painting, sculpture in bronze and stone and architecture – had been in so long and deep decline and almost died out with literature itself, nor why they

Poverty by Giotto

have come to be aroused and come to life in this age, nor why there is so rich a harvest both of good artists and good writers.' There is a certain satisfaction in knowing that even those who contributed to the phenomenon were uncertain of its cause.

Contemporaries might be uncertain as to why this great change occurred, but there was a universal chorus of agreement as to who started the change, and that was Giotto di Bondone. The current preference for evolutionary theory, its justifiable suspicion that society is not transformed at a touch by great men stepping out of the shadows, has an ally in Dante Alighieri. Discoursing on the transitory nature of fame, Dante remarked, 'Once Cimabue held the field in painting: now Giotto has the cry and thus the other's fame is obscured.' One of the almost mandatory anecdotes, recorded by the sculptor Ghiberti, has Cimabue discovering Giotto and bringing the simple shepherd boy to Florence to teach him the trade of artist. But whatever the demands of historical justice, contemporary or near contemporary writers insisted on giving Giotto the palm for 'restoring art to the better path adhered to in modern times'; as Vasari puts it. Giotto's popularity brought him not only fame but a fortune. In this latter he was very much a Florentine, hiring out a loom which gave him a substantial annual profit, loaning at interest, engaging notaries to look after his many business affairs. Yet he too was subject to the vagaries of fashion. Certainly when Vasari came to write his biography some 200 years after Giotto's death in 1337, it was to record again and again that this or that work of the Master had totally disappeared, or been destroyed, or covered by whitewash. The Black Death of 1348 undoubtedly contributed to the discontinuity but, whatever the cause, Giotto's work was a prefiguring, rather than a firm opening statement of the movement which came to flowering in Florence in the early fifteenth century.

Until the end of the fourteenth century Italy shared with the rest of Europe that same art form which, for the sake of convenience, has been labelled the 'International Style'. It was, essentially, the product of men who shared the same cultural heritage, moving with facility between court and court throughout western Europe and it suffered a sea-change when the concept of regionalism, if not precisely of nationalism, developed out of what had been the concept of Christendom. In the words of Ernst Gombrich, 'Thanks to the growth of cities, the International Style was perhaps the last international style Europe has seen.' In Italy, the powerful influence of civic patriotism moulded the developing new style as it moulded all other aspects of social life.

The trend first became apparent in Florence. The city retained her dominance in art for barely a life-span, but until the 1470s Florence was a kind of dynamo providing energy and illumination for the entire peninsula. Her artists went abroad to other cities, rarely briinging anything back as they returned to refresh themselves at source. In 1435 Leon Battista Alberti returned from exile to marvel at the changes that had been wrought in his home and recorded how it came about. The dedication in his *Treatise on Painting* is a tribute both to those who were making the change and the spell which Florence cast over her children. He describes movingly how, after the exile 'in which the Alberti family had grown old' he came back to his city 'beloved above all for its beauty' and singled out a small band of artists for especial praise – 'you, Filippo (Brunelleschi): our dear friend Donatello the sculptor and Nencio (Ghiberti) and Masaccio' all producing work worthy to be compared with any of the masters of antiquity. Alberti's dedication shows, too, one of the factors that led to change: the close relationship of those who wrought it, even bitter enemies unavoidably learning from each other, each stimulating the other, cross-fertilising, creating on a miniature, civic scale that larger process that was taking place with Italy itself as the stage.

The process began about the turn of the century when, in 1401, the Florentine Signoria turned its attention to the refurb-ishing of the ceremonial centre of Florence – the group consisting of the cathedral, the campanile begun by Giotto in 1334 and completed to his design in 1359, and the octagonal Baptistry. The little black and white building held a very special place in Florentine affections. It was commonly supposed to have been a temple built by Julius Caesar himself (the Florentines falling into the common error of mistaking a Romanesque for a Roman work) and when, in 1401, it was decided to offer a thanksgiving for the city's escape from plague, the Baptistry was chosen to benefit. The wealthy Guild of Cloth Merchants (Calimala), which was responsible for the cathedral group, announced that they would finance the design and casting of a pair of bronze doors for the Baptistry and threw the design open to competition.

Out of the many entrants, seven were chosen to live at public expense while each executed a quatrefoil panel on the same subject – the sacrifice of Isaac. Two of the entrants, the 23-year-old Brunelleschi and the 20-year-old Lorenzo Ghiberti, produced a work which caused very considerable difficulty for the judges. Both the panels exist today, one *in situ* in the door, the other in the Bargello Museum. Comparing the two, posterity finds it impossible to say which is the 'better' piece. Both artists had boldly parted from tradition to show Isaac as a naked youth: Ghiberti's piece was perhaps the more technically advanced for it was cast in one piece, whereas Brunelleschi assembled his in sections and, conversely, was the more daringly original of the two. The syndics of Calimala were quite at a loss to choose and

Sacrifice of Isaac by Brunelleschi

came to a compromise, suggesting that the artists should share
the work. Brunelleschi declined and took himself off to Rome
while Ghiberti began work upon the doors which Michelangelo
was to call the Door of Paradise. Twenty-two years were to pass
before they were completed, whereupon Ghiberti almost
immediately began work upon a second pair whose production
took almost as long as the first. During the forty odd years he
spent on these bronze miracles it is possible to see, in his
contracts, the changing status of the artist. In the first contracts,

Sacrifice of Isaac by Ghiberti

he is treated essentially as an artisan, expected to put in a full day's work 'like any journeyman' and recording in a special time-keeping book every break in the working day. In the later contracts he was treated far more as a free agent, permitted to undertake other commissions. Ghiberti, too, made explicit that changing status by boldly including his own portrait in the doors – a little, balding man peering knowingly out of the bronze like a creature from another dimension of time.

Meanwhile, in Rome with his friend Donatello, Brunelleschi

Lorenzo Ghiberti, self-portrait

was finding out just how the ancients had built their enormous structures. The pragmatic Romans assumed he was digging for treasure, unable to imagine why any sane person should expend so much energy to uncover remains of their once great city. But

Brunelleschi was engaged in an entirely new approach to the past – examining the originals, rather than copies of copies. One of his discoveries – or, possibly – inventions, was the ulivella. Intrigued and puzzled by the existence of regular-shaped holes in the huge stone blocks of the buildings, he assumed that they had been made there to allow the block to be gripped by some machine or device, and designed a kind of grappling iron to fit. Whether or not the Romans had actually used such a device, it was extremely useful – a neat demonstration of the practical benefits to be gained from the past, either through true re-discovery or through interpretation.

Brunelleschi returned to Florence at about the time that the syndics of Calimala were puzzling over the problem of completing the Cathedral. Arnolfo di Cambio had begun it over a century before, in 1296, and it had been completed, all save the dome, by 1369. For over half a century the great hole in the roof had been covered by a temporary structure while the debate went on regarding the means of bridging this immense space. Many considered it impossible but in 1417 the Wool Guild called a special meeting to debate the problem. Brunelleschi attended that meeting.

The sequence of events, between that meeting of the Wool Guild and Brunelleschi's triumphant completion of the dome nearly twenty years later, is rich in anecdotal material, much of it apocryphal. Brunelleschi, a diminutive, cantankerous, opinionated man who excelled in half a dozen disciplines, was a gift to chroniclers and gossips. How he was thrown out of one meeting and was mocked in public for his mad architectural ideas: how he triumphed over his rival Ghiberti, played practical jokes on fellow workers, showed up the pompous and the ignorant all added to that store of 'burla' in which Florentines delighted, whether they were true or not. Even at a more serious level there is the same element of mythologising. The received canon has long been that Brunelleschi went to Rome, studied how the Romans built their vast structures and triumphantly applied their technique to the completion of Florence's cathedral. But the cathedral was a Gothic, not a Roman building, and though Brunelleschi's studies in Rome formed a valuable part of his technical training, it was only a part. Like his invention – or

Brunelleschi: portrait by Vasari

re-invention – of the ulivella, he added his own gifts, thus making a fusion. It was a process that was repeated again and again during the fifteenth century, elements of antiquity and modernity combining to make a totally new compound.

In addition to the technical problems, however, there was one social hazard the architect had to overcome. Work was proceeding at a feverish pace when Brunelleschi was arrested on a technicality. The arrest was the work of his enemies – for one of the less attractive results of the emergence of the artist as an identifiable, and ambitious, personality was the bitter rivalry between fellow practitioners, rivalries that could drag on for years transcending even the grave as one strove to injure the reputation of another. Brunelleschi going to extreme lengths to humiliate Ghiberti; Torrigiano marking Michelangelo for life during the course of a quarrel on relative merits; Michelangelo coldly dismissing the work of Leonardo de Vinci; Cellini attacking everybody – this was the reverse of the coin. Brunelleschi's enemies were, in the main, architects who were able to charge him with transgressing a basic guild regulation. He had served his apprenticeship as a goldsmith, had never been a member of the mason's guild and therefore had no right either to undertake the work of a mason or, even worse, direct masons. His enemies were powerful; but he was backed by an even more powerful body, the Calimala, the richest guild in Florence whose syndics now watched unbelievingly as their cherished project was brought to a halt. Exerting their formidable influence, Brunelleschi was freed within hours and his attackers were themselves put in prison. It was more than a personal triumph for him: it was an establishment of the principle that the artist was a free man, subject to no one guild.

The dome was completed on 31 August 1436. Sixteen years had been required to built this, the first Renaissance dome in Italy, the largest unsupported dome in Europe, bigger than the Pantheon which had been Brunelleschi's model, bigger even than the great dome which Michelangelo was to raise a century hence over St Peter's in Rome. It became the symbol of Florence, whose citizens were fond of referring to it as though it were the product of some great natural force 'a structure so large that it stood higher than the hills and was wide enough to cover with its shadow all the people of Tuscany', as Alberti put it. Even in the twentieth century, Florentines express home-sickness by saying that they long 'for the dome'.

The dome is Brunelleschi's most obvious contribution to his native city, and to the new world. And after the dome, the chapels and palaces he built for his wealthy fellow citizens stand testimony to his genius for they were to serve as models for half the civilised world for the next five hundred years and more. One other invention of his is even more widespread in the modern world, if less obvious, and that was the invention of perspective. 'This is a Latin word meaning looking through something (*durchsehung*)', Dürer noted, enthusiastically adopting the technique. 'An Italian word' might have been a better phrase for the invention owed nothing to any classical forerunners but was a gift of Renaissance Italy, through yet another Florentine, to the world. Alberti described its effect to a generation for whom it was still an almost magical technique: 'I describe a rectangle of whatever size I wish, which I imagine to be an open window

Brunelleschi's dome, Florence

Perspective I: Trinity by Masaccio

Perspective II: Salome's offering by Donatello

through which I view whatever is to be depicted there.' Like the difference between Giotto's mourning spectators and its formal precursor, perspective literally gave a new vista to society. Its most dramatic form in this early period was that employed by the young Masaccio in the Church of the Carmine in Florence. Born in 1401, Masaccio was dead by 1428, but in that brief span of time he took up where Giotto had left off nearly eighty years before, and adding to it the mysterious, potent ingredient of perspective which he probably learnt from Brunelleschi. His massive, real figures stand out in a real universe, imposing themselves upon the observer. As a young man Michelangelo used to stand, transfixed, before these calm and solid evocations, copying them to fix them in his mind so that eventually some essence of the experimental period of the Renaissance found its way into the Sistine Chapel, that shrine of the High Renaissance.

The artist in society

Until the fifteenth century the term 'artist' had no particular significance, being virtually interchangeable with 'artisan' or 'craftsman'. The term commonly used for guilds – 'arti' – was indicative of this wide, generalised concept: there was an arte for the shoemaker, no more and no less valid than the arte for the goldsmith, which was itself merely a subdivision of the immensely powerful Silk Guild (Arte della Sete). The guilds

Bas-relief showing arts of Florence by Nanni di Banco

extended their control, as a matter of course, over the decorative as well as over the useful arts. Sculptors and architects were enrolled, logically enough, with the masons, and painters formed a subdivision of the apothecaries on the general principle that they had to have some acquaintance with chemistry to prepare their colours. The emergence of the artist from the guild is usually seen as a gaining of freedom, a throwing aside of restrictions placed by lesser men. Certainly Brunelleschi's quarrel with the masons could be interpreted in this light. Yet equally certainly, there is no evidence that membership of a guild trammelled the skills of a Donatello or a Ghiberti or any of the acknowledged geniuses who happened to be plying their trade in the earlier, rather than the later, period.

Far from resenting the obligation to join associations, painters and sculptors formed their own groups or 'compagnie', created both within and across the boundaries of the larger guilds. The reasons were both social and technical. Socially, they could help each other; the fortunate supporting the less fortunate in lean times, the group as a whole sharing both profits and losses – in particular the bad debts which were a feature of a booming but still unstable economy. Technically, an increasing amount of work was done in co-operation, either on a species of conveyor belt system (two or three men might be engaged at successive stages in the shaping of a pillar from rough hewing to final carving) or working side by side. The growing popularity of the process known as 'buon fresco' demanded such an approach to work. It had been introduced in the thirteenth century, and time itself had shown that it was the most permanent of all forms of mural for the colouring became an intrinsic part of the plaster itself. The wall was first roughly plastered: over this the cartoon was traced and over this outline was laid a layer of fine, smooth plaster – the 'intonaco'. The cartoon was either re-drawn over this, or the artist (carrying a picture of the cartoon in his head) swiftly painted it from memory on the still wet plaster. Only so much plaster was laid as could be covered in one day's work and, provided there was room, any number of men could work side by side from the top of the wall downwards. It was a system which placed a premium on the skill of the individual at absorbing the style of the master – the man who had created the cartoon – so that no matter how large the mural, the treatment was homogeneous. The system was somewhat analogous to the twentieth-century film director who, working through the distinctive talents of his cast, yet places his imprint upon the finished whole.

In addition to these large set tasks, the 'bottega' would produce a variety of smaller articles for sale, either on speculation or on commission, and ranging from painted scabbards and armorial bearings to holy pictures and statues. Demand for religious art was constant and widespread, providing the bread and butter for hundreds of small 'botteghe'. The demand could come from a peasant who had scraped together a few lire and wanted his own personal reminder of the promises and threats of the after-life: from a parish priest who might have a relatively large sum at his disposal and who would be prepared to commission a mural or even an altar-piece, or from a merchant who had made his fortune and was now somewhat anxiously desirous of propitiating fate. Few of these clients regarded the religious productions of the botteghe as being anything but talismans, their beauty of execution being decidedly secondary to the cost of their ingredients. The potential client had little interest in the identity of the craftsman producing his order, but if expensive colours were to be used – gold, silver or blue made from the semi-precious lapis-lazuli – then the fact was clearly specified in the contract, along with the date of delivery of the finished piece. Commissioned work was almost invariably done on these written contracts which, in addition, usually specified how many figures were to appear in the finished painting, doing what and bearing what attributes. Religious paintings touched on the delicate ground of religious orthodoxy and the wise craftsman ensured that his client stated exactly what he wanted. Few would go to the lengths of the French painter, Enguerrand de Quarton, who, instructed to depict God the Father and God the Son so that his finished work agreed with the dogma of consubstantiality ('there shall be no difference between the Father and the Son' his contract stated) produced two figures who could have been twin brothers. But fewer still would branch out on their own and attempt to give a new interpretation to the age-old mysteries. Even the colour of the Virgin's costume was invariably shown as blue, custom transcending itself to become piety.

A fairly typical patron was Francesco Datini, the wool merchant of the little town of Prato who, beginning with nothing, ended as an immensely rich man. After he had made his fortune both social and religious pressure prevailed upon him to decorate his house with religious paintings. He was a superstitious, rather than a religious man, indifferent to any form of aesthetics and he went about the business of commissioning holy pictures with the same dour eye for a bargain which had made his fortune in wool. In 1373 he was ordering from a bottega in Florence 'A panel of Our Lady on a background of fine gold, and a pedestal with ornaments and leaves, handsome and the wood well carved, making a fine show with some figures by the best painter, with many figures. Let there be in the centre Our Lord on the Cross, or Our Lady – whomsoever you find – I care not, so that the figures be handsome and large, and the best and finest you can purvey and the cost no more than $5\frac{1}{2}$ or $6\frac{1}{2}$ florins.' The fresco of Datini, which Filippo Lippi painted some fifty years after his death on the house he had given to the poor, is an involuntarily sardonic comment on the supposedly religious impulse that motivates such work. His plump figures loaded with rings, his corpulent body swathed in expensive scarlet, Datini patronisingly puts his arms around a group of four Pratese town officials who are drawn to half the scale of himself.

Members of a bottega usually contracted for three years, renewing or disbanding their company but always either re-forming it, or joining another. The practice began to die out at the beginning of the fifteenth century under new pressures – in particular, the dominance acquired by a number of great painters who could afford to regard members of the bottega virtually as their employees, and by the emergence of the grand patrons like the Medici in Florence, the Gonzaga in Mantua and the Sforza in Milan. The vast majority of the workers in these art shops are virtually anonymous, apart from their Christian names or nicknames appearing on their contracts. They were conscientious and skilled rather than brilliant but they formed the tilth from which the genius of the fifteenth century could blossom.

A people so passionately addicted to the provision of

handbooks for social affairs, whether it was the conduct of war, politics, family life or etiquette, were not going to overlook the conduct of art. The *Libro dell' Arte*, written in the 1390s by the Florentine, Cennino Cennini, was the work of a practical man – the working artist. In his introduction he gives a touching mixture of religious faith and professional pride: honour must first be paid to God and his saints, in particular Saint Luke, first of all Christian artists and patron of artists. But after them it is proper to acknowledge such great forerunners as Giotto and Taddeo Gaddi and Agnolo Gaddi, Cennini's own master. The writer then gives a survey of the working life and problems of an artist. It is necessary to serve at least a seven-year apprenticeship and the boy should begin by learning how to draw. Cennini provides some very useful practical hints here – hints which also become invaluable source material for the art historian, for he explains not only how to prepare surfaces for drawing, but also how to prepare the necessary instruments and materials. He goes on to describe the grinding and preparation of materials for colours, how to work with them, in particular the difficult but rewarding new medium of oil paints. Through his book, posterity receives a glimpse into pre-Vesalian anatomy: women are ill-proportioned by nature; the lower animals have no fixed form because they lack reason; men have one rib less than women.

Cennini touches on that most volatile and unpredictable of creatures, the patron, pointing out to his reader that, in the last analysis, he who pays the piper calls the tune. The love-hate relationship between artist and patron occurs in every society where the artist has to earn his living through his art, and the patron is desirous of prestige. It becomes particularly evident in Italy from the fourteenth century onwards, partly through the sheer quantity of artistic material produced, partly through the growing recognition that appreciation and possession of that material was an index of social status. The artist had only a limited number of options for the earning of money. He could sell his wares through his shop like any other shopkeeper. The advantage of this system lay in the independence it gave him, its disadvantage was the unpredictability of return and the unavoidable taint of shopkeeping. Michelangelo, for one, was very indignant at the mere suggestion. 'I was never a painter or a sculptor like those who set up shop for that purpose.' The better – or, at least, more fashionable – artists, could hope for more or less permanent employment in the household of some great man or at the court of a prince, like Mantegna in Mantua or Leonardo at the Sforza court in Milan. It gave the artist considerable prestige and domestic security (though not necessarily cash for princes were notorious for their reluctance to disgorge money). But even the greatest artists at court ran the risk of becoming a courtier, of frittering his time away on frivolities. Cosimo Tura, who was paid a salary by Borso d'Este, contributed very substantially to Ferrara's reputation as a centre of art, but he also painted furniture and designed bedroom equipment. In Milan, Leonardo seems to have spent a very large part of his time designing gewgaws for table decorations, or elaborate toys and displays for ceremonial occasions.

In addition to the close watch on the subject matter kept by ecclesiastical authorities, the unfortunate artist now only too often had to endure the interference of the client or patron who, stuffed with humanist learning, wanted to dictate minutely the composition of the picture for which they were paying. The letters of Isabella d'Este show the interfering patron at her worst. She wanted to decorate her boudoir with a number of allegories, was somewhat hampered by the fact that she could not paint, and was a sore trial to the artists she brought in to remedy that deficiency. Perugino was one such unfortunate. She commissioned him to paint an allegory, sent him two ribbons showing the height and width she wanted the panel to be, and enclosed a lengthy detailed letter: 'My poetical invention, which I wish you to paint, is a battle of Chastity against Love. Pallas will appear as having vanquished Cupid. She has broken his golden arrows and his silver bow and thrown them at his feet. With one hand she holds the blind boy by the bandage he is wearing and with the other she is about to strike him with her lance. Diana must also have some share in this victory. Some part of Venus's dress – her mitre, her garland or her veil, perhaps, will be slightly torn ... ' On and on went the minute instructions – and this was only one letter out of fifty-three which the unfortunate Perugino received on this single subject. The tougher-minded Bellini refused to be so coerced. She had tried to induce this prickly artist to create another of her allegories, using Pietro Bembo as intermediary. Bembo interviewed Bellini, then wrote diplomatically, 'He is quite prepared to oblige your Excellency ... but does not want to be given a number of arbitary limitations which would thwart his usual conceptions.' Disregarding the warning, Isabella bombarded him with her usual instructions and in the end Bellini, closely examining them, curtly said the task was impossible.

A substantial part of the artist's fee could be in kind, and Vasari's pages are full of anecdotes of the arrogance, coupled with meanness, of the patron who still regarded the artist as just another workman employed to cover so many square yards with paint. Domenico Ghirlandaio and his brother, David, employed to decorate a monastery, were fed on scraps. David eventually exploded, poured a bowl of soup over the contemptuous monk waiting on them, belaboured him with an enormous stale loaf and when the abbot remonstrated 'replied in a fury, declaring that the talents of Domenico were worth more than all the hogs of abbots of his sort that had ever inhabited a monastery'. The gentler Paolo Uccello, also employed to decorate a monastery, ran away. When asked why, he complained that the abbot fed him on nothing but cheese, 'What with his cheese soups and cheese pies, I'm turning into cheese myself. I daren't go near a carpenter for fear he melts me down into glue!' The battle of all battles between artist and patron took place long after the emancipation of the artists when Michelangelo and his patron, Julius II, were locked again and again in stormy argument.

It is against this background of decidedly non-altruistic patronage that the contribution of the Medici has to be measured. Initially, their involvement was that of any wealthy and powerful family of necessity drawn into public affairs: old Giovanni had sat on the committee debating the merits of Brunelleschi's and Ghiberti's *Isaac*, and in due course his son, Cosimo, had sat on the committee convened to consider the completing of the cathedral. Cosimo was the first of the Medici to undertake patronage on a large scale, beginning the contribution of that enormous sum of 600,000 florins which his grandson, Lorenzo, calculated that the family had directly contributed to the arts and public services. Cosimo's preference lay in architecture: it was he who gave Brunelleschi his first major commission – the Foundling Hospital – and at one stage had actually considered employing the same architect to build his new palace but on seeing the splendid design that Brunelleschi produced he decided, cannily, that his fellow citizens might resent one of their number living in such royal style, and commissioned the more restrained Michelozzo. It was characteristic, too, that of all the artists with whom he might have built up a personal relationship, it was Donatello, the sculptor. Donatello produced for his patron the statue of David which set all Florence talking, the first free-standing bronze statue since the days of Rome. He produced, also, the *Judith slaying Holofernes* which for years graced the Medici courtyard but then, when the family was first expelled from the city, it was removed by the Signoria to a public place and an inscription placed upon it warning other tyrants what fate to expect in a free city. Cosimo established something of a precedent in his relationship with Donatello, delicately treading the tightrope between friend and employer, between patron and artist. Once, somewhat troubled by Donatello's almost perversely scruffy appearance, he gave the sculptor a splendid new coat. Donatello wore it briefly out of respect to his friend, but then abandoned it and Cosimo never again pressed that particular point.

By the time that Lorenzo inherited the leadership of the family even the deep coffers of the Medici were showing signs of depletion. Certainly he was never as wealthy as his grandfather and was directly responsible for far fewer commissions: nevertheless, he probably contributed more through discerning and encouraging latent talents. Writing nearly a century after Lorenzo's death, Vasari turned this essentially spontaneous patronage into a full-scale academic curriculum, creating the myth of the Garden of San Marco 'near the Piazza San Marco in Florence, full of fine and ancient sculptures: the loggia, the paths and the surrounding rooms had the finest ancient marble figures, paintings and other such things ... All these objects were as a school or academy to the young painters and sculptors.' Certainly no contemporary of Lorenzo's mentioned this avant garde school and neither is it possible to identify its supposed location in the modern city. Lorenzo's contribution was probably far more fruitful, far more valuable than the creation of yet another formal academy: what he did create was an ambience which could not fail to affect those who came within its influence and who, in turn, contributed to its unique admixture.

The frescoes which Ghirlandaio painted in the Sassetti Chapel in Santa Trinità between 1482 and 1485 give some indication of the intellectual and social pattern of the Medici court – and at the same time illustrate the contemporary indifference to historical anachronism. The subject concerns the prophecies of Christ's birth and the locale is supposed to be Augustan Rome; but it is an Augustan Rome which bears a remarkably close resemblance to fifteenth-century Florence and the people who stand around discussing, or awaiting, the awesome news are unequivocally citizens of Florence. Lorenzo is there, and his mother, the stately Lucrezia Tornabuoni, and his children. The men and women of the great leading families of the city – Albizzi and Tornabuoni and Sassetti – are clearly portrayed, but alongside these powerful people are the thinkers. Angelo Poliziano, poet and historian, who owed his education to the generosity of the Medici and was now entrusted with the education of Lorenzo's three boys: he appears twice, once shepherding his young charges and once in sober conversation with his peers. Those in that group include Marsilio Ficino, the philosopher whose fusion of Platonism and Christianity provided one of the potent stimuli of the Renaissance: Christoforo Landino, one of the greatest of all commentators on Dante, and Gentile de Becchi, once Lorenzo's own tutor. In a little space by himself the Greek scholar Giovanni Argiropulo looks broodingly into the distance while in a little group, patiently awaiting the news of the birth of the Christ child, is Ghirlandaio himself, looking out a little self-consciously and surrounded by members of his family.

The Sassetti frescoes are not unique. Again and again on the walls of churches or private chapels, or in the newly developed easel pictures artists, and philosophers can be seen mingling with the great. But Ghirlandaio brings out in a remarkable way the element of social ease between the groups. And he illustrates, too, that ambivalent attitude to the past. On the one hand, the interest in the 're-birth' of classical antiquity gained in strength. The same Ghirlandaio who turned Augustan Rome into fifteenth-century

Florentine ladies: detail from mural by Ghirlandaio

Florence could actually invent a prophecy to strengthen the classical content of one of his religious paintings. In his *Adoration of the Shepherds* the uncompromisingly classical sarcophagus used as a cot for the Child bears the legend, 'I, Fulvius the Augur of Pompeius, slain by the sword near Jerusalem, prophesy that the Godhead will use this sarcophagus where I lie.' Yet side by side with this obsession was a readiness to employ anachronism. Ancient Hebrews, Egyptians or Romans appeared in costume that would not have seemed out of place in contemporary Florence or Venice or Rome: Apollo was usually depicted as a young dandy; Jesus Christ in the robes of a fifteenth-century scholar. In Verrocchio's *Tobias and the Angel*, neither would have attracted particular attention – save for the angel's wings – if they had been walking down the Via Tornabuoni. Behind them, too, the harsh Judean landscape has become the soft landscape of Tuscany. Castagno's *Last Supper* takes the theme to an extreme. These are not working-class Jews sharing a frugal meal in a humble eastern inn, but upper-class Romans of a scholarly turn of mind, debating some interesting philosophical point while waiting for their banquet to appear. Posterity, however, has reason to be grateful for this approach for, in trying to portray ancient Jerusalem or classical Rome, the artists portrayed their own world.

9

The golden age

Milan of the Sforzas

'It is indisputable that since the time of the Roman Empire ... Italy had never known such prosperity or such a desirable condition as that which it enjoyed in the year of Our Lord 1490 and the years immediately before and after. For, all at peace and quietness, cultivated no less in the mountainous and sterile places than in the fertile regions and plains, knowing no other rule than that of its own people, Italy was not only rich in population, merchandise and wealth but she was adorned to the highest degree by the magnificence of many princes, by the splendour of innumerable noble and beautiful cities, by the throne and majesty of religion ... ' With that splendid opening, Francesco Guicciardini began his *History*, that first attempt by an Italian to tell the history of Italians, and not simply recount the glories of Romans or Venetians or Florentines or Sienese. He was writing in the 1530s, a little over a generation after that tranquil golden age. Hindsight, no less for him than for much later posterity, gives the impression of an ineluctable tragedy, beginning with the French invasion of 1494 and ending with the great set piece on the banks of the Tiber shortly after dawn on Monday 7 May 1527. Hindsight was not wholly wrong for there was a logical sequence, of a sort, the same kind of logical sequence that develops after a tiger has been let into a crowded room. And the man who let in that tiger was Ludovico Maria Sforza.

On 26 December 1476, Galeazzo Maria Sforza, Duke of Milan, fell under the daggers of three youthful idealists. The dead man's widow, in conjunction with her theological advisers, later came to the conclusion that so vile a man must now undoubtedly be in hell and petitioned the pope to intercede for him personally. Despite the contrast between the characters of the assassinated man and those of his assassins, the citizens of Milan rose not to claim their 'freedom' but to hunt down those who had given it to them. They were executed with the necessary refinements, and the Milanese returned to the business of everyday life.

There was, however, a constitutional problem for the heir to

Galeazzo Maria Sforza: portrait by Antonio del Pollaiolo

the dukedom, Gian Galeazzo Sforza, was only seven years old. His mother acted as regent until 1480 when she was succeeded by his uncle Ludovico, a plump, suave, swarthy man of twenty-nine. Ludovico was to reign, first as regent, then as usurper and finally as duke in his own right, for over twenty years. During this period he gained an international reputation for political astuteness, and his court became a brilliant centre of Renaissance culture. Neither the reputation for politics nor for culture were deeply rooted. When he died in a prison cell in France in 1508 Milan was a French city, Italy was being prepared as an arena for the battles of France and Spain, and Milanese culture was in eclipse.

Born in 1451, the sixth and youngest son of the great condottiere-duke, Francesco Sforza, Ludovico was the archetypal Renaissance prince. He was an exemplar not only because of his personality, but for the web of plots and counter-plots with which he surrounded himself. 'Born for the ruin of Italy' was the judgement of his near-contemporary, Paolo Giovio, an opinion echoed and elaborated again and again until it seems that the entire responsibility for the Italian tragedy was placed upon his plump shoulders. Pre-eminently, Ludovico is a candidate for Burckhardtian honours, and Burckhardt's pen portrait perpetuates the unfavourable opinions. 'The Moor[34] is the most perfect type of the despot of that age and, as a kind of natural product, almost disarms our moral judgement. Notwithstanding the profound immorality of the means he employed he used them with perfect ingenuousness: no one would have been more astonished than he to learn that, for the choice of means as well as ends, a human being is morally responsible.'[35] But Ludovico was simply acting according to the prevailing moral code and, after his initial error, was as much victim as aggressor – and honest enough to recognise his mistakes. After the invasion, and all that came from it, he opened his heart to the Venetian ambassador, Marco Foscari: 'I confess that I have done great wrong to Italy, but I had to act because of the position I was in. I did it most reluctantly.'

'The position I was in' – this was itself exemplary, something he shared with the majority of Italian sovereigns – the endless preoccupation about legitimacy. He was not only an illegal ruler, but a member of a dynasty of dubious legality, which had succeeded another dynasty that had purchased its legality with hard cash. The Visconti dukedom, purchased by Gian Galeazzo Visconti in 1394, came to an end with the death of the last legitimate heir in 1447. Francesco Sforza, the last duke's condottiere, married his employer's illegitimate daughter, establishing a tenuous link. But there was, in effect, a joker in the pack. Gian Galeazzo Visconti's only daughter had married a French duke, Louis of Orleans and their marriage contract had stipulated that, should the male Visconti line ever die out, the State of Milan would become the inheritance of Louis of Orleans – and

Ludovico Sforza (il Moro) by the Maestro della Pala Sforzesca

his heirs. In the early years of his usurpation, Ludovico was too preoccupied with establishing a dominance over his nephew, the legitimate duke, to worry over much about that theoretical French claim. But it existed, and its final enforcement was to destroy him.

Ludovico was an energetic and enlightened ruler, certainly serving Milan far better than the sickly, frivolous young Gian Galeazzo Sforza would ever have done. The culture of Sforza Milan, in its purely social aspect, was probably in advance even of that of Florence. Machiavelli, indeed, believed that the Florentines got their taste for corrupting luxury on witnessing the prodigal display made by Galeazzo Sforza and his wife Bona when they visited Florence in 1471. Ludovico was a genuinely

Gian Galeazzo Sforza, Duke of Milan

cultured man, addicted like all Sforzas to vulgar display but also sensitive to the humanist currents of the day, encouraging the new learning in its practical as well as decorative aspects, attracting the leading artists of the day with expansive promises, among them Leonardo da Vinci and the architect Bramante, both on the threshold of their careers. Leonardo came to Milan, improbably enough, as a lute player, bringing with him that strange instrument shaped from a horse's skull decorated with silver. In his letter of self-recommendation he mentions his painting skills virtually as an afterthought: it is his prowess as an engineer, in particular a military engineer, that he stressed. 'I have plans for bridges, very light and strong ... I have plans for destroying every fortress or other stronghold ... I have also plans for making cannon ... covered chariots, catapults ... ' His letter was designed to appeal to what all Italy knew to be Ludovico's dominant characteristic, ambition, and the knowledge that sooner or later he would come into military conflict with his rivals. In the event, Ludovico never used these martial arts of Leonardo's. Probably the most valuable practical works he did for his master was designing locks for the complex new system of waterways that Ludovico wanted for Milan. Like the Este, he was interested in agriculture and its vital accessory, irrigation, and one of the end-products was an extension and improvement of the canal system that was of such priceless value to Milan's booming trade.

Milan was immensely wealthy. Many years later, when the dukedom had finally passed into the hands of the Spanish, the Italian Giovanni Botero, author of the *Ragione di Stato* stated that, 'The duties from the merchandise of Milan are worth more to the Catholic King than the mines of Zacatecas and Jalisco.' It was the merchants of Milan, pursuing their trade of middleman, who had first made that wealth and then, in effect, created the dukedom by preferring the rule of a single, strong dynasty to endless republican upheavals. The population of metropolitan Milan at the turn of the sixteenth century was around 100,000, while for the dukedom as a whole it was about a million. The ducal income was in the region of 700,000 ducats – about half that of the king of England. Looking back over the final years of Sforza Milan the French observer, Commines, was of the opinion that if Ludovico had reduced his tax demands to 600,000 ducats he might well have survived. But that Ludovico could not do. Milan's consistent policy, for well over a century, had been one of aggression, of expansion. At the end of the fourteenth and beginning of the fifteenth century, the Florentines, for one, were convinced that the duke of Milan was aiming for a crown – the crown of Italy itself.

For the Florentines, and for that part of posterity seduced by the golden tongues of Florentine propagandists, Milan was a tyranny – that is, a human community whose entire resources were at the arbitrary disposal of its head. But how great was the duke's control over the million or so people who, on paper, put him among the sovereigns not simply of Italy but of Europe? Historiographically, Milan has an abundance of contemporary anecdotal and biographical material, liberally provided by humanist writers and, since the nineteenth century, numberless devoted monographs have shed brilliant light on this or that aspect of its long history. However, there is nothing equivalent to the Florentine catasto to give a neutral, bird's eye, authentic view of society, and the mass of civic archives have yet to be calendered on a comprehensive basis similar to the computer studies of the catasto. In a brief but invaluable paper, *Ludovico Sforza and his vassals*, Bueno de Mesquita examined selections from the archives of the 'vassal' cities, giving some idea of the true composition of the state behind the monolithic appearance.

The state of Milan developed by an amoebic process, spreading, expanding, absorbing. But the territories she absorbed – in particular the great families who ruled in those territories – retained their essential identity. Neither Visconti nor Sforza could have hoped to suppress families who were very nearly as powerful, and frequently far older, than themselves. Sometimes the families dealt with each other as though they were still independent, with only a cursory nod towards their supposed lord in Milan. For its part, Milan's role varies from that of elder brother, to father and occasionally, but only very occasionally, to stern autocrat. Sometimes Ludovico, or his officials, was obliged to lean heavily upon a transgressor, sometimes to act almost cajolingly, depending on the status of the particular family. The selection of documents throws fascinating light on the thankless task of local officials who have to apply the law as laid down by those safely distant in the capital. In one instance, Milan told the Commissioner of Piacenza that he must apply the law to all, great and small alike. The official replied feelingly that that was all very well, but what happens when the transgressor 'was the lord Sforza of great condition and uncle of your Excellency' – in other words, when it is another branch of the ducal family which had been stirring up trouble. There was evidently a considerable amount of embarrassed head-scratching in Milan before someone came up with the suggestion of setting a thief to catch a thief – appointing the Lord Sforza as Governor of Piacenza with specific instructions to settle the trouble caused, in large part, by his own men.

It is significant that the petitions from the provinces were rarely addressed to the rightful duke, but to Ludovico who also, as often as not, replied in his own persona. This was the core of the Milanese problem: the legitimate duke was an incompetent nonentity; the effective leader was a usurper. Outwardly, Il Moro seemed totally secure, one of the leading statesmen of Italy negotiating as an equal with other heads of state. Internally, he never succeeded in grappling with the problems of the territorial barons who simply deserted him during the testing time. Meanwhile, the personal tangles at the heart of his court simultaneously multiplied, and began the chain of events that would lead to his destruction and the embroilment of all Italy when, in 1488, the legitimate duke, Gian Galeazzo, married Isabella of Aragon daughter of King Alfonso of Naples.

There is an irony in the fact that Naples, which had largely been a spectator rather than an actor in the Italian Renaissance, should have been a major cause in bringing its intensive creative period to an end. For if the Renaissance owed its birth to the interaction of a multiplicity of distinct communities 'the life of the Italian people, as a story cast around self-determining city states, came to an end in 1494.'[36] And it was the dizzying pattern of Neapolitan politics that led, via Ludovico Sforza, to that first French invasion of 1494.

The history of the kingdom of Naples was an epitome of the history of Italy – fragmented, incoherent, anarchic. It was a cultural palimpsest, Byzantine, Saracen, Norman, German,

Angevin and Spanish rulers in their turn placing their imprint upon the kingdom before going their way. In theory, Naples was a fief of the Papacy: in practice, the King of Naples conducted himself as an absolute monarch – when he could control his own barons, which was not often. Politically, the kingdom tended to swing from the most oppressive, most viciously cruel tyranny to a virtual anarchy where the territorial barons scrambled for power. Unlike the other major Italian powers – even the

The Neapolitan Renaissance symbolised: the triumphal arch of Alfonso I (died 1458)

supposedly supranational Papacy whose monarch was usually an Italian – the King of Naples was invariably of foreign origin, claimants from Sicily, Spain, France and even Hungary scrambling on and off the throne.

The last major change of dynasty had taken place in 1442 when Alfonso V of Aragon ousted the Angevin claimant and, styling himself Alfonso I of Naples, began a rule that was to last sixteen years. During his reign it seemed as though the new culture might indeed root itself in southern soil. It was he who built that beautiful triumphal arch in the vast Gothic castle which so neatly stands as a symbol of the Renaissance penetration in Naples. He was a genuinely cultured man – Il Magnanimo the humanists called him in gratitude for his generous support and, in return, they weaved the usual flattering humanist myths around him. He was supposed never to have travelled without a copy of Caesar or Livy; he regarded the birthplace of all Roman writers as sacred ground; he was supposed to have been cured of an illness simply through hearing a few pages of Quintius Curtius read aloud. Certainly that connoisseur Cosimo de' Medici recognised a fellow mind and cannily claimed his friendship by sending him a codex of Livy.

Alfonso's generosity attracted the usual swarm of hungry humanists but few were of any great or permanent stature. Outstanding among them was that Lorenzo Valla who was later to prove such a thorn in the side of the Papacy. Here, clearly enough, was a demonstration of the fact that the new learning could have practical value for Valla's devastating exposé of the forged Donation of Constantine was obviously a useful weapon for any king whose crown was in the gift of the pope.

With Alfonso's death in 1458 affairs in Naples took a darker turn. His bastard son and successor Ferdinand I (commonly called Ferrante) shared something of his father's culture: he had, after all, had some brilliant scholars as tutors, among them Valla himself, and Panormita, whose book *De dictis et de factis Alphonsi regis* enshrined the legend of Alfonso the Magnanimous. Another tutor was the same Alfonso Borgia, a sober-sided lawyer who, as Pope Calixtus III, was to launch the Borgia clan in history.

But there was a streak of something near madness in

errante, a dedicated cruelty with which he clamped his rule
upon the kingdom. It was rumoured indeed that his unknown
mother must have been a Moor, so refined and imaginative were
the means with which he pursued his lust for blood and torture.
His son, Alfonso, was, if anything, worse, gaining the sobriquet
of – simply – il feroce giovane.

Unlike his father and grandfather Alfonso was indifferent to
the new culture, contemptuous of books, pursuing a military
career. But both father and son, whatever their moral or cultural
shortcomings, were highly skilled survivors in the lethal game of
Neapolitan politics. In particular, they skilfully exploited the
matrimonial web which linked the ruling families of Italy
together. Alfonso was married to Ippolita Sforza of the Milanese
dynasty, his sister Eleonora became the wife of Ercole I of Ferrara
and, in due course, mother of Isabella and Beatrice d'Este) and
even his bastard daughter Sanchia became a useful link when she
was married off to Joffre, the bastard son of Pope Alexander VI.
It was his legitimate daughter Isabella who was married to Gian
Galeazzo Sforza, legitimate duke of Milan, in 1488. And, to
entangle finally the Milanese affairs, in 1491 Ludovico Sforza,
regent of Milan, married Beatrice d'Este, cousin of Isabella of
Aragon.

Accounts of Beatrice's character vary considerably. Some
contemporaries describe her as an arrogant girl, joyfully seizing
on the opportunity of crowing over her one-time playmate
Isabella, the true duchess of Milan. But others see Beatrice as a
loving if impetuous personality, struggling to establish herself
with a husband who had put off marriage to continue to enjoy his
mistresses and who still maintained a relationship with him.
Whatever the cause of the domestic friction, the result was the
same, with the usurping ruler and his wife established in the great
Castello in Milan while the legitimate duke and duchess withdrew to the beautiful, but subordinate, city of Pavia some fifteen
miles away. It was from there that Isabella bombarded her
grandfather and father with protests and lamentations and
complaints. Bernardino Corio, the contemporary Milanese
writer, inserted one of her letters in his History and though he
probably polished it, it does convey a lively picture of the
impossible situation in which all found themselves. 'Everything is

in his power,' Isabella complained, 'while we are left withou
friends or money and are reduced to live as private persons. No
Gian Galeazzo but Ludovico is recognised as lord of th
kingdom. His wife has lately born him a son, whom everyon
prophesies will succeed to the dukedom and royal honours wer
paid to him at his birth while we and our children are treated wit
contempt ... If you have fatherly compassion come to our hel
and deliver your daughter and son-in-law from the fear o
slavery, restoring them once more to their rightful kingdom ...'

Beatrice d' Este, wife of Ludovico Sforza by Piero della Francesca

Il Moro's character, his insatiable ambition combined with total deviousness makes it easy to cast him in the role of villain, the man who brought ruin on his country for the most limited and short-sighted of objectives – to protect himself from the vengeance of his in-laws. But he was only part of a whole, controlling part of a tangle of threads from all over Italy and France that happened to pass through Milan. Refugees from the degenerate courts of Naples and Rome were making their way over the Alps to the court of young King Charles VIII of France, working on his muddled mind to enter Italy, reform the Church now being blasphemed by the Borgia pope, take over the Crown of Naples which was his by right of descent from the Angevin rulers – and incidentally, having done all these things, restore them to positions of power and comfort. An alliance between Ludovico, Venice and Alexander Borgia had petered out, leaving each pursuing his own objective. Lorenzo de' Medici, the statesman who above all others had striven to establish a balance of power in Italy, had died. Dead, too, was old King Alfonso of Naples, an appalling man but a canny ruler and in his place now reigned his grandson Alfonso, father to the dispossessed Duchess of Milan, deadly enemy of Ludovico, an impetuous and therefore a dangerous man. There seemed no reason why Ludovico Sforza should not also send his emissaries beyond the Alps, cajoling, encouraging, promising. Charles listened avidly. He was a grotesque looking youth, his heavy jaw permanently hanging because of the adenoids from which he suffered, and of limited intelligence but convinced that through Italy lay the path to the glory for which so many French nobles hungered, to the puzzlement of their Italian counterparts. Charles would probably have entered Italy in any case, but the Milanese invitation promised him an easy entry, almost literally throwing open the gates. He would go on a crusade, he announced – and in the process acquire the crown of Naples that had been taken from his ancestor's head by the usurping Spaniards.

That first French invasion of 1494 – 'first year of the miserable years' as Francesco Guicciardini later called it – was almost a comic opera. Alexander Borgia, with one of his flashes of sardonic wit, remarked that the French conquered Italy with wooden spurs (as for a tournament) and a stick of chalk (for the quarter-master to mark out billets). They swept down the peninsula, through Florence, through Rome and so to Naples. There they were defeated – not by the King of Naples who had promptly fled while the Neapolitans, with practised ease welcomed the restoration of the Angevins – but by the southern diseases that had laid low even greater armies than theirs. They trailed back north, to find that the Italians had closed ranks behind them so that they had to fight their way through. The expedition ended ingloriously enough, but it had demonstrated yet again that Italians were the worst enemies of Italians, that he who could exploit that fact could be their master. In 1499 a French army again crossed the Alps, but this was a tougher army led by a far more formidable man than the unfortunate Charles. He, with typical clumsiness had struck his head on a low lintel and died in agony, stretched out in a latrine, and his cousin succeeded him on the throne of France, taking the title of Louis XII.

Louis had the same major objective as Charles – the acquisition of the kingdom of Naples. But he brought with him a second title deed – that of the dukedom of Milan, playing, in effect, that joker in the pack which had been lying dormant for nearly a century: Louis XII was the direct descendant of the same duke of Orleans to whose heirs Milan had been promised in the event of a failure in the Visconti main line. Ludovico Sforza, son of the only condottiere who had won a state by force of arms, fled without striking a blow in his defence. Commines, Louis' counsellor, perspicuously summed up the character of the fox of Milan: 'This Ludovico was a wise man, but very timorous and humble when he was in awe and false when it was to his advantage.' He had tried the falseness with success again and again, doubling back and forwards on his tracks. However, as Commines saw, in adversity he fell to pieces. He returned to a brief triumph, but finally fell into Louis's hands and was taken across the Alps, still a relatively youthful man of forty-nine, into life-long captivity. The brilliant court of Milan did not outlast its creator. Its fate, indeed, seemed to be curiously echoed by the fate of the works of its star, Leonardo da Vinci – the colossal equestrian statue that never progressed beyond a model and was destroyed by French bowmen; the model for the ideal township

Sketches for an equestrian monument by Leonardo da Vinci

that never got off the drawing board; the marvellous military
equipment and vehicles that never progressed beyond drawing
or toys – above all that supreme work of art, *The Last Supper*, in
refectory of Sta Maria delle Grazie that was already deteriorating
while its creator was packing his bags.

Rome, the golden city

In 1473, Pope Sixtus IV decreed the construction on the Vatican
Hill of a large, rather gaunt building which would serve, among
other purposes, as a safe place for conclaves and which
eventually took his name as the Sistine Chapel. Over the years, a
number of superb paintings appeared on its walls, but the ceiling
remained the simple affair of gold stars on a blue ground as
painted by the architect, Pier Matteo d'Amelia, until 1508. That
was the year in which a reluctant Michelangelo, at the behest of
Pope Julius II, began to transform the ceiling into his own vision
of the Creation, finishing his work eventually in 1512. Twenty
four years later, in 1536, he began painting the *Last Judgement*
on the west wall, completing it in 1541.

The startling contrast between ceiling and mural can be put
down, in part, to the difference between a vigorous confident
young man in his thirties and an ailing, ageing, disillusioned man
in his sixties. But an artist reflects his environment as well as
himself and the contrast is also a high watermark, or frontier
between two states of mind that were themselves the result of
sudden social change. The luminous glory of the ceiling is the
product of the years when Rome was a treasure house of talent,
the confidence of its rulers and shapers reflected in those
stupendous figures where mankind is raised to its zenith, scarcely
to be distinguished from the divine. *The Last Judgement* was
painted after the traumas of the sack of Rome and the first
rumbling of the Reformation. The overall colour scheme is
composed of sombre browns and blues and greens. The domin
ant figure is not the creating Deity, but the cursing Christ
flanked by his avenging saints, more interested in condemning
the damned than welcoming the saved, and mankind itself is
represented as being harassed by devils, or dragged rotting from
graves by indifferent angels. *The Last Judgement* symbolises in

Damned soul recognising its fate. Detail from the 'Last Judgement' by Michelangelo, Sistine Chapel

paint, by a Florentine, what the Dutchman Erasmus expressed in words when lamenting the fate of the City. 'What stranger from the far ends of earth were not received by her as an honoured guest. To how many was she not dearer, sweeter and more precious than their own native land? Was there any, who lived in Rome, who did not leave her walls unwillingly? Who indeed, is there who does not share our grief, for we have seen Rome taken by a more cruel foe than the Gauls of old and exposed to barbarities unknown in the days of the Scythians, and Huns and Goths and Vandals.'

The decades immediately preceding the sack of Rome saw the city approaching the apogee of its splendour. It seemed scarcely possible that this golden city was a decrepit provincial town just a lifetime earlier. The procession of popes over those seventy years or so had ranged from the virtuous to the vile, from the scholarly Nicholas V to the morally degenerate Alexander VI. Each had added something, adapting, expanding the plans of his predecessor. Their cardinals poured in their wealth, each building his own superb palace, scouring Italy for artists to embellish it, creating in each a court of its own. No longer did the popes have to go on dangerous and uncomfortable tours: the world now came to Rome.

The golden city of the golden age received its final polish during the pontificate of the Medici pope, Leo X, second son of Lorenzo the Magnificent, who came to the throne in 1513 on the death of Julius II. A roly-poly, affable hedonist of thirty-eight who was credited with the words, 'God has given us the Papacy – let us enjoy it', he could not but appear a dilettante compared with his volcanic predecessor. Leo was at his best in social situations – regally dominating a procession, taking part in hunting expeditions (to the dismay of conservatives who did not know how to kiss the papal foot when it was encased in riding boots), presiding at banquets, swapping spontaneous hexameters with professional poets, judging art objects. But there was also the Florentine instinct for culture, coupled with the Medici talent for administration which made him far more than a lightweight. He inherited the dismaying task of continuing the building of St Peter's, tackling it with skill and dedication even though his decision to fund the building by indulgences was to prove disastrous. His relationship with Luther, up to the final inescapable break, was tolerant, intelligent. In the intricate world of Italian politics, rendered now even more complex and lethal with the advent of Spain and France upon the peninsular stage, he wove a devious path, playing one against the other, always keeping his options open.

In Rome, his patronage was generous and astute. It was he who was responsible for the virtual refounding of the Sapienza, appointing professors in faculties across the whole range of current learning, from philosophy to astronomy. His personal preference was for classical Latin, in particular for poetry, and some scores of young poets were heavily subsidised from the papal-Medici purse. He encouraged the theatre, establishing something of a precedent here, for before him only Alexander Borgia had dabbled in a field which was still looked at askance by the old fashioned as of dubious morality.

Leo X by Raphael

Leo X (as Leo I meeting Attila)

It was in the field of art, though, that he excelled, in particular his patronage of Raphael Sanzio: the portrait of Leo that best presents his personality is that by Raphael showing the pope toying with the eyeglass his shortsightedness forced him to adopt, while on the table before him lies an exquisitely illuminated manuscript and behind him are his secretary on the right and on the left his cousin Giulio, soon to become Clement VII. Raphael had come to Rome during the pontificate of Julius II, effortlessly gaining not only fame and fortune but good will from all ranks of men. Leo had, in effect, inherited both Raphael and Michelangelo from his predecessor but the younger man was infinitely easier to deal with and gradually he moved to the front in Rome while Michelangelo went back to Florence, to work on the Medici tombs there among much else. In his *Stanze* in the new halls of the Vatican, Raphael contributed to that personality cult which was a feature of the Leonine reign, in a series of murals immortalising the actions of Leo's great namesakes in history – Leo I, who had halted Attila; Leo III who had crowned

Charlemagne; Leo IV, who had built the Leonine city – giving to each the plump features of the Florentine pope. But Raphael assumed responsibility, too, for the building of St Peter's, accepting the commission with an engaging admixture of pride and humility. He also undertook for Leo the first scientific survey of the ruins of Rome. In his brief of authorisation the pope observed, 'Great quantities of stone and marble are frequently discovered with inscriptions or curious monumental devices which are deserving of preservation for the promotion of literature and the cultivation of the Latin tongue. But these are frequently cut or broken, for the sake of using them as materials in new building.' In Leo's reign, at last, the long and dismal onslaught by Romans on Rome began to be slowed. The Ferrarese scholar, Celio Calcagnini, was particularly impressed by Raphael's work: 'This is nothing short of a plan of the city of Rome which he is producing in its ancient aspect and pro- portions. By digging out the foundations of ancient monuments and restoring them to the description of classical authors, he has filled Pope Leo and all Rome with such admiration that they regard him as a god sent down from heaven to restore the Eternal City to its former majesty.'

Then, in mid-stride, it all ended with the sudden death of Leo at the age of forty-six in 1521. The golden bubble collapsed in on itself, for it had been built on credit – the credit extended by the bankers of Florence and Genoa and Venice to a young pope who, reasonably, had another thirty years of life expectancy in which to pay back the debts. Papal finances for Leo's reign are unclear, with few hard figures to substantiate the account of an endlessly flowing cornucopia which most contemporary writers present. The Venetian ambassador in Rome at the time of Leo's death reported to his Senate that the late pope had spent about 5 million ducats during his eight-year pontificate. The papal income being around 400,000 ducats the inference is that Leo died at least $1\frac{1}{2}$ million ducats in debt. Or, to be exact, Leo died leaving his successor a debt of $1\frac{1}{2}$ million ducats. And the man who was to bear the full weight of that burden was his devoted cousin, Giulio.

Giulio de' Medici was the illegitimate son of Lorenzo de' Medici's beloved brother Giuliano. After Giuliano had been hacked down in the cathedral of Florence during the Pazzi conspiracy, Lorenzo sought out his brother's child and brought him up as one of the family. In due course, the boy followed his cousin Giovanni into the Church and when Giovanni climbed the ultimate height, to emerge as Pope Leo X, Giulio benefited. It was not pure nepotism on Leo's part: Cardinal Giulio de' Medici was an admirable lieutenant – conscientious, loyal, discreet, devout. But those who elected him as pope in 1523 overlooked one fatal flaw in his character: it was precisely those virtues that had made him a good lieutenant that made him, as Pope Clement VII, the most disastrous of pontiffs to sit upon the throne of St Peter for many years. When it was all over, his fellow Florentine Francesco Vettori, surveying the débâcle, came to the opinion that, 'If one considers the lives of previous popes, one may truly say that, for more than a hundred years, no better man than Clement VII sat upon the throne. Nevertheless, it was in his day that the disaster took place while these others, who were filled with all vices, lived and died in felicity. Neither should we seek to question whom the Lord our God will punish – or not punish – in what manner and in what time it pleases him.'

Whether or not Divine punishment was eventually visited upon Pope Clement, his Roman subjects paid, rapidly and terribly, for his defects of character. As cardinal and Vice Chancellor he merely had to analyse, assess, and advise: as pope he, and he alone, had to act. And making a decision to act was the one thing Pope Clement could not do. Francesco Guicciardini came to Rome to act as counsellor to the man he had greatly admired as a cardinal and was appalled by the way in which Clement met the mounting menaces from the outer world. 'It is bad to make a bad decision, but worse to make none at all,' was the gist of Guicciardini's advice – excellent advice which had not the slightest effect. The peace of Italy would have been threatened with such a man at the centre of affairs even in what passed for normal times, but the train of events that had begun in the last decade of the fifteenth century was coming to a head in the third decade of the sixteenth. For the first time in centuries there was again a truly great Emperor in Europe: Charles V, born in 1500, heir by genetic chance to Spain, Burgundy, the Netherlands, Austria – and Naples; claimant, by imperial right, to Milan. In France, the dashing young François I who believed in any case that he had been robbed of the imperial crown, was intent on securing his Milanese and Neapolitan rights. In England, Henry VIII was demanding that the pope should give him his divorce from the powerful young emperor's aunt. In Florence, republicanism was rearing its head, the Medici family was hard put to keep its hold upon the city . . .

Here, perhaps, was the heart and core of the tragedy: at a time when, above all else, the occupant of the papal throne should have been an international statesman, his horizon was bounded by his native city. In the Middle Ages the Papacy, for all its grievous faults, had thought in terms of eternity and universality. In the early Renaissance, the vision of the popes narrowed to Italy. In those dangerous days, from the time of Leo onwards, it had narrowed down finally to one Tuscan city. Spanish and

Charles V by Titian

French armies moved onto Italian soil to fight out their differences, presenting their dusty claims to this or that piece of Italy, demanding that the Holy Father should declare for one or the other. For four years Clement ran with the hare and hunted with the hounds with increasing desperation, changing sides at times at an hour's notice. 'I will come into Italy and revenge myself on the fool of a pope,' the normally restrained Charles V burst out after one particularly maladroit – and treacherous – change.

When the disaster came it was an accident, the sack and massacre that no one intended. The 'imperial' army of some 22,000 Spaniards, Italians, and Germans that assembled in Lombardy in the winter of 1526–7 was, theoretically, under the command of a French renegade, the Duke of Bourbon. In fact, no man controlled them. They had defeated the French in one great

Sack of Rome: death of the imperial general, Bourbon. In the distance, the Castel Sant' Angelo

battle and now looked for payment. It came in small amounts from Spain, or was wrested from the wretched Milanese, now finally Imperial-Spanish citizens. The men grew hungrier and ever more savage, looking now towards Rome whose Holy Father had been incautiously allied with the French at the moment of the French defeat. They demanded ransoms. Go-betweens from Spain began the long tortuous negotiations while the army began to drift southward. Now Clement would agree, now go back on his agreement. Now he would accept the reality of events and offer a reasonable sum, then he would halve it, cancel it, begin negotiations elsewhere. The southward drift of the starving, virtually leaderless army turned into a determined march which brought them outside the walls of Rome on Sunday 6 May. One final demand for ransom was ignored, the military defenders of Rome believing its fourteen miles of decaying city walls, garrisoned by part-time soldiers and 5,000 professionals, could withstand the ragamuffin army, for the city was well supplied with artillery.

Late on that mild spring night, the great bell of the Capitol began clanging its harsh warning, calling the citizens to arms as it had done so often in the past. At midnight, the clanging of the bell was answered by the roar of drums from the army camped now on the Janiculum hill, traditional springboard for attack upon the city. At dawn a heavy mist was seen to rise from the Tiber, a mist which drifted up the Janiculum, hiding attackers from defenders and masking the great guns of the Castel Sant' Angelo and the other strong points.

By 1 pm the city was in the hands of the mercenaries.

Notes and sources

Notes and modern works cited. A bibliographical description will be found in the bibliography on pages 296–301.

1 Hale. *Renaissance Europe*, p. 8
2 Tillyard. *The English Renaissance*, p. 10
3 Symonds. *Renaissance in Italy*, p. 3
4 Laven. *Renaissance Italy*, p. 253
5 Michelet. *Histoire de France*, VII, 7f.
6 Ferguson. *Renaissance in history*, p. 179
7 Symonds. *op. cit.*, p. 9
8 Voltaire. Quoted by Ferguson, *op. cit.*, p. 94
9 Cronin. *The flowering of the Renaissance*, p. 176
10 Hay. *Italian Renaissance*, p. 165
11 Waley. *Italian city republics*, p. xi
12 Lopez. *Medieval trade in the Mediterranean world*, p. 9
13 Martines. *Violence and civic disorder*, p. 143
14 Symonds. *op. cit.*, p. 217
15 In Ferrara she is still remembered with affection. The little nun who showed her tomb to the author in 1978 spoke warmly of her. 'She was a good woman, a good woman. We pray for her every day. It was her brother . . . he was bad. Bad. And mad.'
16 Lanciani. *The destruction of Ancient Rome*, p. 196. It had been packed with statuary, awaiting the torch and 'was wholly made up of statues of the Vestales maximae. The statues and fragments had been closely packed together, leaving as few interstices as possible . . . there were eight nearly perfect statues and we were agreeably surprised to find among the broken ones the lower part of the lovely seated Vesta with footstool which, alas, is now hardly recognisable.'
17 Lane. *Venice and history*, p. 285
18 Contarini's book *De magistratibus et republica Venetorum*, which enshrined if it did not create the myth, was translated into English in 1599 by Lewes Lewkenor – in time to influence Parliamentarians during the Civil War and even, in due course, the framers of the Constitution of Carolina, and of Pennsylvania. The translation used in the present chapter is Lewkenor's.
19 'But you've been cuckolded by the Turk,' was the remark of du Bellay, French ambassador to Rome, on news of a resounding naval defeat for Venice. The ceremony of the Wedding, long discontinued, was revived in the 1970s, the ring being cast by the Abbot of San Giorgio Maggiore. The present writer asked the abbot how he felt about being, in effect, heir to the Doges: 'I feel ridiculous. But it pleases the tourists.'
20 Lowry. *The world of Aldus Manutius*, p. 8

21 Gundersheimer. *Ferrara*, p. 8

22 Symonds. *op. cit.*, vol. I, p. 92

23 Gundersheimer. *op. cit.*, p. 6

24 Burckhardt. *Civilization of the Renaissance*, p. 46

25 *ibid.*, p. 436

26 An outstanding example of the new approach is the symposium, held by the UCLA in 1969 on the theme 'Violence and civil disorder in Italian cities 1200–1500' on which this present section is based.

27 Martines. *op. cit.*, p. 163

28 *ibid.*, p. 165

29 Hay. *The Church in Italy in the fifteenth century*, p. 98

30 In his survey of Italian fifteenth century Christianity in *The Church in Italy in the fifteenth century*, Denys Hay cites an Italian scholar who reported that fifteenth and sixteenth century records in more than half the episcopal archives he contacted had been dispersed or destroyed.

31 *ibid.*

32 Murray. *A dictionary of art and artists*, p. 460

33 We have seen a lively demonstration of this in our own time with the forgeries of Van Meegeren. He had excellent motives to perfect his art for his Nazi clients would have been well able to visit their displeasure upon him. His forgeries took in a very large number of people. As John Cornford has pointed out, however, a generation later, the women in Van Meegeren's Vermeers have a disconcerting resemblance to film stars.

34 Ludovico's nickname, 'Il Moro', was derived from his baptismal name, Maurus, but can be translated as Moor or mulberry. Ludovico adopted both as symbols, the Moor being the skilled, resourceful native of Africa whom he admired and mulberry being supposedly the wisest tree, being the last to put out leaves after the winter and the first to bear fruit. Sometimes both devices are used together as, in that supremely hypocritical painting in which Ludovico, half Moor, half mulberry tree shelters his helpless young nephew. Ladies of the court tended to dress in mulberry shades in not-very-subtle compliment.

35 Burckhardt. *op. cit.*, p. 41

36 Martines. *Power and imagination*, p. 387

Appendix I:
A note on Italian currencies

The variety of currencies used in Italy during the period covered by this book faithfully reflected the peninsula's fragmented history.

In the tenth century, Charlemagne's currency reform had substituted a silver-based currency in place of the Roman gold *soldo*. A pound (libbra) of silver was divided, physically, into 240 denari: twelve of these made a soldo and twenty soldi a lira.

A currency based upon small pieces of silver was adequate for local transactions of relatively small value. But with the growth of international trade and an expanding luxury market, the sheer physical problem of moving around great quantities of silver bullion became ever more apparent. It was the mercantile cities who made the inevitable shift to gold. Florence began the process by introducing the gold *fiorino* of 3·5 grammes, deemed to be equal to one pound of silver. Genoa also introduced a gold coin named after the city, the genovino, Milan followed with the ambrogino, named after the city's patron saint, and finally, in 1284, Venice re-introduced the ducat, which Roger of Sicily had first minted in silver in 1140.

Although all these gold coins were of equal value, the florin became the most widely used. A popular Florentine propaganda story tells how a Florentine ambassador at the court of the duke of Milan during a period of political tension, was invited by the duke to visit his treasury. The Florentine politely admired the piles of gold coins, agreed that they demonstrated the great wealth and power of the duke, then neatly turned the veiled threat by picking up one of the coins to display the lily of Florence upon it. 'I see that this shows our emblem. If you have so many, how much more must we have – who make them?'

The popularity of the florin may have been a result of the beauty of its design or, more likely, because it inspired confidence. The Florentine mint rigorously controlled the standard of coining: a merchant receiving a gold florin could be confident that its face value and actual value were the same. 'The grease of St John Goldenbeard', so-called because of the picture of St John the Baptist on the coins' verso, was a universal solvent, accepted by friends and enemies alike of Florence.

The only real rival of the florin was the Venetian ducat of the same weight. In 1399 papal officials in Rome began to issue a gold coin, called the ducato di camerale or fiorino camerale, which was slightly lighter than the others. All sovereign Italian cities continued to mint their own coins, the fractional differences between them contributing to the money-changers' profits.

Notoriously, it is difficult to give modern equivalents of currency values. Until relatively recently a very crude, rule-of-thumb method, would give the gold ducat or florin the equivalent value of £1 sterling but the runaway inflation of the 1970s, together with the dizzily escalating value of gold, makes this now quite meaningless. There is, too, an inherent problem arising out of the changes in the value of the currency itself between approximately 1350–1550. In addition to the ordinary changes that must occur over two centuries are the effects created by expansion of international trade and, above all, by the flow of gold and silver into Europe from the New World. There are also the intangible but very real changes created by new modes of thought – by 'job creation' in short. Coluccio Salutati, the first humanist Chancellor of Florence, was paid 100 florins a year in the closing years of the fourteenth century: how much of this was in recognition of his value as propagandist? In Padua in the 1470s a skilled compositor in the new-born printing trade could earn around four ducats a month – the same rate of pay as for an illuminator. The cost of living must obviously vary greatly from place to place and time to time. But the invaluable catasto returns in Florence show that in the 1430s one could live on fourteen florins a year.

Appendix II: Genealogies

FLORENCE

THE MEDICI
Rulers from 1429 *to* 1537

Guccio de' Medici, Gonfaloniere, 1299
(Tomb in court of Riccardi Palace)

Salvestro de' Medici
Gonfaloniere 1378

Vieri de' Medici
c. 1391

Giovanni, son of Bicci (Averardo)
Lived 1360–*c.* 1429 (old portrait in Uffizi)

} Ancestors

Cosimo ('Pater Patriae')
Ruled 1429–64
m. Contessina dei Bardi
Exiled 1433–4

Lorenzo
Ancestor of later
Medici rulers

Piero ('the Gouty')
1464–9
m. Lucrezia Tornabuoni

Giovanni
d. 1463

Lorenzo ('the Magnificent')
1469–92
m. Clarica Orsini

Guiliano
Killed by Pazzi conspirators
1478

Piero ('the Unfortunate')
1492–94
Expelled 1494
Drowned in Liris 1503

Giovanni
(Pope Leo X
1513–21)

Giuliano
Duke of Nemours

Guilio
(illeg.)
(Pope Clement VII
1523–34)

Lorenzo
'Duke of Urbino' 1516
d. 1519

Ippolito
(illeg.)

FERRARA

THE ESTE DYNASTY

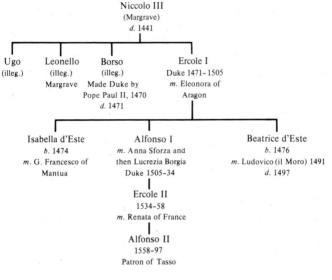

Niccolo III
(Margrave)
d. 1441

| Ugo (illeg.) | Leonello (illeg.) Margrave | Borso (illeg.) Made Duke by Pope Paul II, 1470 *d.* 1471 | Ercole I Duke 1471–1505 *m.* Eleonora of Aragon |

Isabella d'Este
b. 1474
m. G. Francesco of Mantua

Alfonso I
m. Anna Sforza and then Lucrezia Borgia
Duke 1505–34

Beatrice d'Este
b. 1476
m. Ludovico (il Moro) 1491
d. 1497

Ercole II
1534–58
m. Renata of France

Alfonso II
1558–97
Patron of Tasso

NAPLES

THE ARAGONESE DYNASTY

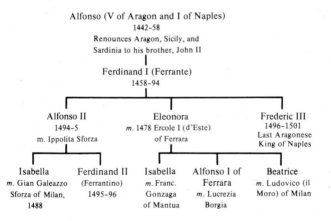

Alfonso (V of Aragon and I of Naples)
1442–58
Renounces Aragon, Sicily, and
Sardinia to his brother, John II

Ferdinand I (Ferrante)
1458–94

Alfonso II
1494–5
m. Ippolita Sforza

Eleonora
m. 1478 Ercole I (d'Este) of Ferrara

Frederic III
1496–1501
Last Aragonese
King of Naples

Isabella
m. Gian Galeazzo Sforza of Milan, 1488

Ferdinand II
(Ferrantino)
1495–96

Isabella
m. Franc. Gonzaga of Mantua

Alfonso I of Ferrara
m. Lucrezia Borgia

Beatrice
m. Ludovico (il Moro) of Milan

MANTUA

GONZAGA DYNASTY

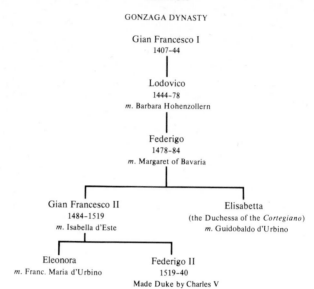

Gian Francesco I
1407–44

Lodovico
1444–78
m. Barbara Hohenzollern

Federigo
1478–84
m. Margaret of Bavaria

Gian Francesco II
1484–1519
m. Isabella d'Este

Elisabetta
(the Duchessa of the *Cortegiano*)
m. Guidobaldo d'Urbino

Eleonora
m. Franc. Maria d'Urbino

Federigo II
1519–40
Made Duke by Charles V
in 1530

MILAN

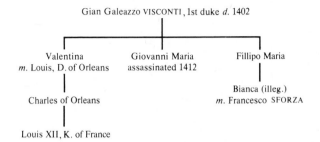

VISCONTI

Gian Galeazzo VISCONTI, 1st duke *d.* 1402

| Valentina | Giovanni Maria | Fillipo Maria |
| *m.* Louis, D. of Orleans | assassinated 1412 | |

Charles of Orleans

Bianca (illeg.)
m. Francesco SFORZA

Louis XII, K. of France

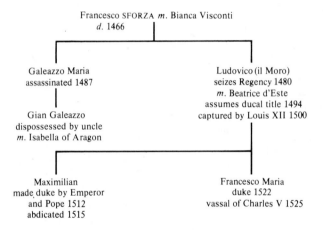

SFORZA

Francesco SFORZA *m.* Bianca Visconti
d. 1466

Galeazzo Maria
assassinated 1487

Ludovico (il Moro)
seizes Regency 1480
m. Beatrice d'Este
assumes ducal title 1494
captured by Louis XII 1500

Gian Galeazzo
dispossessed by uncle
m. Isabella of Aragon

Maximilian
made duke by Emperor
and Pope 1512
abdicated 1515

Francesco Maria
duke 1522
vassal of Charles V 1525

Appendix III:
Popes and Venetian Doges of the Renaissance

THE PAPACY
1316–1523

		Accession
(1314–16 *no Pope*)		
John XXII	⎤	1316
Benedict XII		1334
Clement VI		1342
Innocent VI	⎬ 1309–77, 'Babylonian Exile' at Avignon	1352
Urban V		1362
Gregory XI	⎦	1370
Urban VI	⎤	1378
Boniface IX		1389
Innocent VII		1404
Gregory XII	⎬ 1378–1417, Great Schism.¹	1406
Alexander V		1409
John XXIII		1410
Martin V	⎦	1417
Eugenius IV		1431
(Antipope, Felice V)		
Nicholas V		1447
Calixtus III (Borgia)		1455
Pius II (Piccolomini)		1458
Paul II		1464
Sixtus IV (Della Rovere)		1471
Innocent VIII (Cibo)		1484
Alexander VI (Borgia)		1492
Pius III (Piccolomini)		1503
Julius II (Della Rovere)		1503
Leo X (Medici)		1513

	Accession
Adrian VI	1521
Clement VII (Medici)	1523

¹The Schismatic Popes were 'Clement VII,' 1378–94, and 'Benedict XIII,' 1394–1417.

VENETIAN DOGES
1311–1539

Giorgio ('Zorzi') Marino, 1311–12
Giov. Soranza, 1312–28
Francesco Dandolo, 1328–39
Bart. Gradenigo, 1339–42
Andrea Dandolo, 1343–54
Marino Faliero, 1354–55
Giov. Gradenigo, 1355–56
Giov. Dolfino, 1356–61
Lorenzo Celsi, 1361–65
Marco Cornaro, 1365–68
Andrea Contarini, 1368–82
Michele Morosini, 1382
   (Dies of the plague.)
Ant. Venier, 1382–1400
Michele Steno, 1400–13

Tommaso Mocenigo, 1414–23

Francesco Foscari, 1423–57

Pasquale Malipiero, 1457–62

Cristoforo Moro, 1462–71

Niccolò Tron, 1471–73

Niccolò Marcello, 1473–74

Pietro Mocenigo, 1474–76

Andrea Vendramin, 1476–78

Giov. Mocenigo, 1478–85

Mario Barbarigo, 1485–86

Agostino Barbarigo, 1486–1501

Leonardo Loredano, 1501–21

Ant. Grimani, 1521–23

Andrea Gritti, 1523–39

Appendix IV:
Chronological outline

Non-Italian events in italics

1304	Petrarch born
1321	Dante dies
1334	Giotto begins Florentine campanile
	1336 Palace of the Popes, Avignon, begun
1337	Giotto dies
	1339–1453 Hundred Years' War
1347	Rienzo Tribune of Rome
1348	Black Death
1370	Leonardo Bruni born
1375	Coluccio Salutati Chancellor of Florence
1377	Brunelleschi born
1377	First (abortive) return of Papacy to Rome
1380	Poggio Bracciolini born
1386	Donatello born
1390	John Hawkwood Florentine Captain-General
1394	Gian Galeazzo Visconti first Duke of Milan
1396	Manuel Chrysoloras established in Florence
1400	Masaccio born
1404	Leon Battista Alberti born
	1415 Battle of Agincourt
1420	Martin V returns to Rome
1427	'Catasto' returns, Florence
1431	Mantegna born
1433–34	Cosimo de' Medici exiled
1435	Alberti's Treatise on Painting
1436	Dome of Florence cathedral completed
1439	Cosimo de' Medici dies
1444	Federigo Montefeltre Duke of Urbino

1444   Biondo's 'Roma instaurata'
1450   Urbino palace modernised
1452   Leonardo da Vinci born

        1453   Fall of Constantinople
1469   Machiavelli born
1469–92 Lorenzo de' Medici leads Florence
1470   Venetian defeat at Negroponte
1474   Alberti's treatise 'I libri della famiglia'
1475   Michelangelo born
1480   Ludovico Sforza Regent of Milan
1483   Sistine chapel consecrated
1483   Guicciardini born
1487   Titian born
1492   Death of Lorenzo de' Medici

        1492   Columbus' First Voyage
1494   French invasion

        1500   Birth of future Charles V
1500   Capture and banishment of Ludovico Sforza

        1501   Portuguese caravels return from India
1504–8 Castiglione at Urbino
1505   Demolition of old St Peter's begins
1509   Venetian defeat at Agnadello

        1509–47   Henry VIII, King of England
1519   Charles V Holy Roman Emperor
1511   Vasari born
1525   Battle of Pavia
1527   Sack of Rome
1532   Machiavelli's *The Prince* published

Bibliography

Abbreviations:
  ASI   Archivo storico italiano
  FSI   Fonti per la storia d'Italia
  RIS   Rerum italicarum scriptores: NS – New Series

Alberti, Leon Battista. *I libri della famiglia*: trans. as *The Family in Renaissance Florence* by Renée Neu Watkins, 1969. A highly readable translation which lightens and humanises Alberti's elaborate prose.

Anglo, Sydney. *Machiavelli: a dissection*, 1969. An assessment of Machiavelli through his literary work: notable for its demolition of *The Prince* as a major work.

Aretino, Pietro. *Selected letters*: trans. by George Bull, 1976. The translation beautifully reflects Aretino's racy, colloquial style; contains 95 of the letters, mostly from the first two Books.

Baron, Hans. *The crisis of the early Italian Renaissance: civic humanism and republican liberty in an age of classicism and tyranny*, 1966. Study of the Milanese–Florentine confrontation of the 1390s, and of the political and cultural factors affected by it.

Baxandall, Michael. *Painting and experience in Fifteenth Century Italy*, 1972.

Bisticci, Vespasiano da. *Lives of Illustrious Men of the Fifteenth Century*: trans. by William George and Emily Waters, 1926.

Bruckner, Gene A. *The Florentine popolo minuto and its political role*, in: Martines, *Violence.*

Bruni, Leonardo. *Istoria fiorentina*: tradotto in volgare da Donato Acciajuoli. Read in conjunction with its predecessors, Dati's *Istoria* and the 'Minerbetti' chronicle (q.v.) gives an excellent bird's-eye view of the changing pattern of historiography over the climacteric period.

Bryce, James. *The Holy Roman Empire*, 1887. Despite its age, still the standard work on the subject. See also: Heer, below.

Bueno di Mesquita, D. M. *Giangaleazzo Visconti, duke of Milan*, 1941. Minutely documented account of the rise of the first Italian politician to transform a 'despotism' into a dukedom. *Lodovico Sforza and his vassals* in Jacob, E. F., below.

Burckhardt, J. *Civilization of the Italian Renaissance in Italy*: trans. by S. G. C. Middlemore, 1929.

Burke, Peter. *Tradition and innovation in Renaissance Italy*, 1974. Notable for its use of computer-type studies to arrive at assessments of Renaissance artists. *The Renaissance*, 1964.

Butterfield, H. *The statecraft of Machiavelli*, 1940.

Cartwright, Julia. *Isabella d'Este Marchioness of Mantua 1474–1539*, 2 vols, 1903. *Baldassare Castiglione: his life and letters 1478–1529*, 2 vols, 1908. Both biographies make generous use of the letters of the subjects, the work on Isabella d'Este being particularly valuable in this context.

Castiglione, Baldassare. *The Book of the Courtier*: trans. by Sir Thomas Hoby, 1561. 1900. Hoby's translation has been used in the present book because the quotations better convey the sense of elapsed time, than those from a modern translation. There is, however, an excellent contemporary translation, with introduction, by George Bull (Penguin, 1967).

Chojmacki, Stanley. *In search of the Venetian patriciate*, in Hale: *Renaissance Venice*.

Cognasso, Francesco. *L'unificazione della Lombardia sotto Milano*, 1955. Clearly shows the evolution of a federation, rather than the creation of a tyranny.

Contarini, Gasparo. *De magistratibus et Republica Venetorum*, trans. as *The Commonwealth and government of Venice* by Lewes Lewkenor, 1599.

Corio, Bernardino. *Storia di Milano*, 1856.

Cronin, Vincent. *The Florentine Renaissance*, 1967. *The Flowering of the Renaissance*, 1969. Although the discussion of the Renaissance is formally from the viewpoints of Florence, Rome and Venice alone, they give an excellent general picture. Particularly valuable for their use of minor contemporary writers, usually overshadowed by the glamorous.

Dati, Goro. *Istoria di Firenze*, 1735. Preoccupied with the Florentine crisis of the 1390s. In evolutionary terms, Dati is midway between 'Minerbetti' and Bruni (q.v.).

Emerton, Ephraim. *Humanism and tyranny: studies in the Italian trecento*, 1925.

Ferguson, Walter K. *Renaissance studies*, 1963. *The Renaissance in history: five centuries of interpretation*, 1948. Ferguson is an academic who has not forgotten the excitement of discovery, and the belief that history is as much art as science. His generous rehabilitation of Burckhardt restores the concept of 'the Renaissance' as an identifiable unit.

Ficino, Marsilio. *The letters*: trans. by members of the Language

Department of the School of Economic Science, London; preface by P. O. Kristeller, 1975.

Gardner, Edmund G. *Saint Catherine of Siena*, 1907. Dated, but very useful study of the interrelating political, religious and cultural strands of the late fourteenth century, with copious quotations from contemporary and near-contemporary sources.

Goldthwaite, Richard A. *Private wealth in Renaissance Florence*, 1968.

Gombrich, E. H. *The story of art*, 1952.

Gregorovius, Ferdinand. *History of the city of Rome in the Middle Ages*, vols VI–VIII, 1900. Still presents the only comprehensive picture of the city – cultural, political, social – from the fall of the Empire to the sack of Rome of 1527: trans. by Annie Hamilton.

Grosskurth, Phyllis. *John Addington Symonds*, 1964. Makes full use of Symonds' own unpublished memoirs to fill in gaps discreetly left by earlier biographers.

Guicciardini, Francesco. *The history of Italy*: trans. by Austin Park Goddard, 1763.

Guicciardini, Luigi. *Il sacco di Roma*, 1758. Eyewitness account of the sack of 1527.

Gundersheimer, Werner L. *Ferrara: the style of a Renaissance despotism*, 1973. *Crime and punishment in Ferrara*, in Martines: *Violence*.

Hale, J. R. *Florence and the Medici: the pattern of control*, 1977. Analyses the techniques whereby the Medici acquired, and exercised power in a 'democracy'. *Renaissance Europe 1480–1520*, 1971. (Ed.) *Renaissance Venice*, 1973. Essays, by various hands, presenting a cross-section of current Italian, American and English academic studies of Venetian Renaissance history.

Hay, Denys. *The church in Italy in the fifteenth century*, 1977. Study of the social role and the transmission of cultural values through the Church. *The Italian Renaissance in its historical background*, 1961. Short (203 pp.) but indispensable introduction to modern academic views of the Renaissance phenomenon, conducted from the point of view that 'the Renaissance is the last epoch when one man can hope to have a direct view of most of the sources'.

Heer, Friedrich. *The Holy Roman Empire*: trans. by Janet Sonderheimer, 1967. Where Bryce (q.v.) provides the philosophy of the Empire, Heer attempts a cultural history from its origins to its dissolution.

Herlihy, David. *Some psychological and social roots of violence in the Tuscan cities*, in Martines: *Violence*.

Jacob, E. F. (Ed.). *Italian Renaissance Studies*, 1960.

Lanciani, Rodolfo. *The destruction of Rome*, 1899.

Lane, Frederic C. *Venice and history*: collected papers, 1966. Emphasis is on the commerce – and particularly, the shipping – and the banking system of the Republic.

Lopez, Roberto Sabatino and I. W. Raymond. *Medieval Trade in the Mediterranean World: illustrative documents translated with introduction and notes*, 1961. Rich collection of original documents, from the tenth century onwards, with a very considerable number drawn from Italian sources.

Lowry, Martin. *The world of Aldus Manutius: business and scholarship in Renaissance Venice*, 1979. Departs from the usual approach of treating Aldus in exclusively bibliographical terms to give a finely detailed picture of the birth of publishing.

Macaulay, Thomas Babington. *Machiavelli*, in his *Critical and historical essays*, 1865.

Machiavelli, Niccolò. *The Prince*: trans. by L. Ricci, 1903. *The Discourses*: trans. by Leslie J. Walker; edited by Bernard Crick, 1976.

Mallet, Michael. *The Borgias*, 1969. De-mythologises the family, treating its members as ordinary, successful, if thoroughly unscrupulous Renaissance politicians. *Venice and its condottieri*, in Hale: *Venice*.

Martinelli, Giuseppe (Ed.). *The world of Renaissance Florence*, 1968. Essays by various hands; superbly illustrated.

Martines, Lauro. *Power and imagination: city-states in Renaissance Italy*, 1979. Takes the story of the Renaissance back into the eleventh century, and forward into the late sixteenth. (Ed.) *Violence and civic disorder in Italian cities 1200–1500*, 1972. Essays, by various hands, on the causes of civic violence.

Mattingley, G. *Renaissance diplomacy*, 1955.

Michelet, J. *History of France*, 1855.

'Minerbetti'. *Cronica volgare di Anonimo Fiorentino . . . gia attribuita a Piero di Giovanni Minerbetti*, in RIS NS XXVII, 2. Traditional-style chronicle, immediately preceding that of Goro Dati's (q.v.).

Mitchell, R. J. *The laurels and the tiara: Pope Pius II*, 1962.

Murray, Peter and Linda. *A dictionary of art and artists*, 1976.

Mussi, Giovanni de'. *Chronicon Placentinum*, in RIS XVI. Contains the famous attack on the doctrine of the 'temporal dominion' of the Papacy.

Nohl, J. *The Black Death*: trans. by C. H. Clark, 1926. Covers Europe generally, but with copious material from Italian sources, including Boccaccio's descriptive introduction to the *Decameron*.

Oman, Charles. *A history of the art of war in the Middle Ages*, 1924.

Origo, Iris. *The merchant of Prato*, 1957. Detailed, meticulous, but lively use of the immense Datini archives to give a rounded picture of an early Renaissance merchant, Francesco di Marco Datini. *The world of San Bernardino*, 1964.

Panofsky, Erwin. *Renaissance and renaissances in western art*, 1960.

Pastor, Ludwig. *The history of the popes from the close of the Middle Ages*: ed. Frederick Ignatius Antrobus, Vols 5–7, 1899. Although even Pastor found some of the Vatican archives closed to him this remains, and probably will remain for the foreseeable future, the only comprehensive work on the post medieval papacy.

Pecchai, Pio. *Roma nel Cinquecento* (Vol. XIII of *Storia di Roma*), 1948. Emphasis is on the social life of the city with the papacy as background.

Petrarch, Francesco. *Lettere* ... volgarizzate da G. Fracassetti, 5 vols, 1863–7.

Pius II (Aeneas Sylvius Piccolomini). *The Commentaries*: abridgement trans. by Florence A. Gragg, 1960.

Platina, B. *The lives of the Popes*: trans. by W. Benham, n.d.

Priuli, G. *I Diarii*, in RIS NS XXIV 2.

Pullan, Brian. *Rich and poor in Renaissance Venice*, 1971. Detailed (689 pp.) study of the origins and operation of the Venetian charities, the Scuole Grande. *A history of early Renaissance Italy*, 1973.

Queller, Donald E. *The development of ambassadorial relazioni*, in Hale: *Venice*.

Ricci, Corrado. *Pintoricchio*: trans. by Florence Simmonds, 1902.

Richards, G. R. B. *Florentine merchants in the age of the Medici*, 1932.

Ricotti, Ercole. *Storia della Compagnie di Ventura in Italia*, 1893. Despite its age, still remains the only comprehensive account of the rise and fall of the mercenary companies.

Ridolfi, Roberto. *The Life of Francesco Guicciardini*: trans. by Cecil Grayson, 1976. Invaluable for its use of Guicciardini's unpublished papers to throw light on events in the Vatican leading up to the sack of Rome. *The Life of Niccolò Machiavelli*: trans. by Cecil Grayson, 1963.

Symonds, John Addington. *Renaissance in Italy*, 7 vols, 1875–86.

Tillyard, E. M. *The English Renaissance: fact or fiction?* 1952.

Treccani degli Alfieri, Fondazione. *Storia di Milano*, Vols VI–VII, 1955–6.

Vasari, G. *Le vite de piu eccelenti pittori, scultori ed architettori*, 1878.

Vettori, Francesco. *Sommario della Storia d'Italia dal 1511 al 1527*, in Archivio Storico Italiano, App. VI, 1848.

Waley, Daniel. *The Italian city republics*, 1969. Concentrates on the evolution of the city-state from the commune between late eleventh to early fourteenth century.

Watkins, Renée Neu. See Alberti.

Weiss, Roberto. *Un umanista veneziano: Papa Paolo II*, 1958. Corrects Platina's biased portrait.

Wilkins, E. H. *Life of Petrarch*, 1961. *Petrarch's eight years in Milan*, 1959. Excellent study of the means whereby an early humanist earned a living while maintaining a quasi independence from his patrons.

Woodward, W. H. *Vittorino da Feltre and other humanist educators*, 1897.

Photographic Acknowledgments

J. Allan Cash 2, 14, 34; Biblioteca Riccardiaria 12; Foto Roniaglia 11; Fotografia Scientifica 17–18; Frick Collection 43; Italian State Tourist Office 47; Mansell Collection 1, 4–6, 8–10, 13, 15–16, 19–33, 36–9, 41–2, 44–6, 48–55, 57–60, 62–89; National Gallery of Art, Washington 56; Mario Perotti 3; Siena Archives 7.

Index